Stop Walking on
Eggshells

When someone you love has Borderline Personality Disorder

PAUL T. MASON, M.S.

RANDI KREGER

MJF BOOKS
NEW YORK

Published by MJF Books
Fine Communications
322 Eighth Avenue
New York, NY 10001

Stop Walking on Eggshells
LC Control Number: 2009932340
ISBN-13: 978-1-60671-001-2
ISBN-10: 1-60671-001-X

Could you be some redemption
Could you be some relief
Could you be a safe haven
Do you promise to believe
When I tell you these stories
Every pain and hard won glory
Bear witness to a life
Lived with good intentions so far
So believe me, heal me
Believe me, it's all true.

—Carrie Newcomer, "Bearing Witness"
from *My Father's Only Son*

Fasten your seat belts, it's going to be a bumpy night.
—Bette Davis, *All About Eve*

*No matter how confused, self-doubting or ambivalent we
are about what's happening in our interactions with other
people, we can never entirely silence the inner voice that
always tells us the truth. We may not like the sound of
the truth, and we often let it murmur just outside our
consciousness, not stopping long enough to listen. But when
we pay attention to it, it leads us toward wisdom, health
and clarity. That voice is the guardian of our integrity.*

—Susan Forward, Ph.D.

This book is for the children, young and old, whose lives have been affected by BPD. And to our teachers: the hundreds of people who told us their stories, shared their tears, and offered us their insight. You made this book possible.

Contents

Foreword

People with Borderline Personality Disorder (BPD) challenge those close to them with their often bewildering mood shifts and unpredictable behavior. For those people who have relationships with persons with BPD, whether they be relatives, friends, spouses, parents, or children, this book should prove a godsend. It delineates the ways in which borderline individuals' (BPs) behavior and communications frustrate and perplex those around them but goes further in articulating specific strategies that those close to the person with Borderline Personality Disorder (non-BPs, as they are termed in this book) can effectively cope with these kinds of behaviors. The authors, Paul Mason, M.S., and Randi Kreger, are able to manage the delicate task of appreciating the dilemmas that non-BPs face each day, while at the same time not simply blaming the person with BPD in a simplistic fashion. They suggest ways in which friends and relatives can attempt to bring the BP to treatment with the recognition that this may not always be possible, and they also outline a variety of treatment approaches that have proved helpful to people with BPD from pharmacological therapy to cognitive behavioral therapy, such as Marsha Linehan's Dialectical Behavioral Therapy (Linehan 1993).

The authors also touch on some of the putative root causes of BPD, from temperamental sensitivities in regulation of emotions or control of impulses (probably grounded in the biology of the brain) to early environmental factors. As we recognize some of the biologic foundations of this disorder, which are discussed in my recent book *The New View of Self* (Siever and Frucht 1997), as well as appreciate the often abusive experiences that people with this disorder have undergone in their childhood, we begin to appreciate that BPD represents a series of maladaptive traits that stem from survival strategies developed early on in the life of the BP that, at the time, seemed the only viable method to get their needs met. For example, an infant or young child who is very emotionally sensitive to the comings and goings of their mother and other caretakers may respond to separations from their mother, for instance, by crying, particularly if they are prone to express their emotions rather than inhibit them. The parent may react to crying spells by trying to indulge the child or alternatively ignoring them, actually increasing the likelihood of these behaviors recurring. The child may learn that these emotion storms or temper tantrums are the only way they know to get attention when they feel frustrated or upset and these patterns continue into adulthood. Parents who aren't unusually adept at handling these affective storms may fall into the trap of either excessive indulgence or, at other times, ignoring the child. Parents who tend to be depressed may neglect the child, while those who are impulsive and aggressive may even be abusive. These traumas tend to worsen these behavior patterns. The BP thus is prone to the appearance of abandonment and may use "desperate means" to arouse that feeling (Gunderson 1984).

Thus, when we see the adult BP, we see an individual who has learned a variety of "techniques" to manage their own self-esteem and emotional swings by trying to control the behaviors of those they depend on and wanting to stay near them. They have difficulty seeing how their controlling behaviors are destructive to their relationships because they know no other alternative. The crucial point that the authors emphasize again and again, particularly in the later stages of the book, is the need for the BP to take responsibility for their behavior and for the non-BP to also take responsibility for their role in the relationship. Whatever has transpired before for both parties, it is only by taking on responsibility for these behaviors as an adult that the possibility of true change can occur. Mason and Kreger are to be applauded for their efforts in making the frustrating and perplexing behavior of the BP more understandable and for providing extraordinarily useful tools for non-BPs to use in dealing with the paradoxes and dilemmas these relationships present.

—Larry J. Siever, M.D.

Acknowledgments

First and foremost, I would like to thank the two men in my life who made this book possible: my husband, Robert Burko, and my good friend and literary agent, Scott Edelstein.

Robert made countless emotional and financial concessions during the three long years of research and writing. Without his quiet faith, generous nature, and profound love, this book would have been a dream deferred.

Scott was more than my agent: he was my mentor, my coach, my emergency hot line, my chief cheerleader, my number-one believer. When I doubted this book would ever get published, he assured me that it would. When I felt like quitting because the sacrifices were too great, he reminded me of the people whose lives I had changed. His sense of humor and unwavering support sustained me and helped me believe in myself.

I was accompanied on this three-year journey by an incredible group of people whom I have met only electronically. They literally saved people's lives by creating a caring Internet community that freed them from their isolation and gave them hope. Without their hard work and devotion to this cause, there would be no Internet-based support groups, no BPD Central World Wide Web site, and no "Walking on Eggshells" booklet. Special thanks to A. J. Mahari, Alyssa (Alyfac), David Anders, Harwijn B., Anita F., Martin Cleaver, Edith Cracchiolo, Sharon Harshman, Patty Johnson, Lee Meinhardt, Daniel Norton, Rachel Russo, Kieu Vu, Kristin Wallio, and Mark Weinstock.

The non-BP mailing list, one of the Internet support groups, debuted in January, 1996. When the twelve list members shared their experiences of living with someone with BPD traits, they found they were not alone. Since then, the group has grown to three hundred and spawned two other groups: one for parents of BPD children and one for adult children of borderline parents. While each member of these lists is special, I must single out clinician Elyce M. Benham, M.S., who has been our "ship's counselor" since the beginning. Her gentle humor, compassion, and professional insights have brought hope to many grieving and confused list members.

The non-BP list has also been blessed with a handful of members who are recovering from BPD. Even though they had reason to feel unwelcome at times, they cared enough to stay and educate us about the true cost of living within the grips of this disorder. When needed, they reminded us diplomatically that both borderlines and non-BPs must accept responsibility for their part in the relationship. Their courage is an inspiration; their grace and compassion provided light along the path to understanding, forgiveness, and healing.

Dozens of clinicians and BPD advocates from all over the globe contributed their insights to this book. Valerie Porr, M.A., founder of the Treatment and Research Advancements Association for Personality Disorders (TARA-APD), spent countless hours helping me put the pieces of the BPD puzzle together. Mike Chase, F.N.P., analyzed and organized hundreds of Internet postings for the chapter on children with BPD.

Clinicians interviewed for this book include Elyce M. Benham, M.S.; Joseph T. Bergs, M.D.; Mari E. Bernhardt, A.C.S.W.; Lori Beth Bisbey, Ph.D.; Barbara Blanton, M.S.N.; James Claiborn, Ph.D.; Kenneth A. Dachman, Ph.D.; Jane G. Dresser, R.N.; Bruce Fischer, Ph.D.; MaryBelle Fisher, Ph.D.; John M. Grohol, Psy.D.; John Gunderson, M.D.; Paul Hannig, Ph.D.; Perry Hoffman, Ph.D.; Janet R. Johnston, Ph.D.; Ikar J. Kalogjera, M.D.; Otto Kernberg, M.D.; Jerold J. Kreisman, M.D.; Marsha M. Linehan, Ph.D.; Richard A. Moskovitz, M.D.; Thomas Meacham, M.D.; Susan B. Morse, Ph.D.; Cory F. Newman, Ph.D.; Andrew T. Pickens, M.D.; Margaret Pofahl, A.C.S.W.; Joseph Santoro, Ph.D.; Larry J. Siever, M.D.; and Howard I. Weinberg, Ph.D.

Many books not related to BPD were also influential in my thinking. Chief among them was The Dance of Anger (1985) by Harriet Goldhor Lerner, Ph.D. Its fundamental concepts are interwoven into every page of this book. When I first read it many years ago, it changed my life. I feel honored to be able to pass along Lerner's wisdom, and I am indebted to her for her inspiration. Books by Susan Forward, Ph.D. also influenced this work, chiefly Emotional Blackmail (1997) and Toxic Parents (1989). I highly recommend all three books.

Finally, I would like to thank my co-author, Paul Mason, M.S., for being such a delight to work with; my publisher, New Harbinger Publications, for the same reason; my stepdaughter, Tara Gerard, for her working title; my favorite singer/songwriter Carrie Newcomer, for permission to use her remarkably on-target lyrics; my mother, Janet Kreger, for supporting my writing efforts since grade school; and Edith Cracchiolo, my guardian angel throughout this project.

And to you, dear reader: we wrote this book so that your own journey would be easier. Knowing that you would benefit gave meaning to the often painful experiences of the borderlines and non-borderlines interviewed for this book.

—R.K.

Many people have encouraged me and supported me in the writing of this book. I wish to thank them all and am especially grateful to the following people:

Monica, my wife, whose unconditional faith and belief in me throughout the three years of this project was unmatched. Despite the long hours, she was always supportive and encouraging while working full-time as a stay-at-home mom. And thanks to my children, Zachary, Jacob, and Hannah who, in their own ways, consistently remind me of the important things in life.

My parents, Thomas and Jean Mason, whose love, values, and persistence throughout life's struggles have been a cornerstone on which I continue to build.

My colleagues at All Saints Health Care System, Inc. and Psychiatric Services, for providing a challenging and supportive clinical environment in which to practice and try new things. Their willingness to risk and think outside the box has helped shape my career and direction as a mental health professional.

My graduate school mentor, Kathleen Rusch, Ph.D. who nurtured and supported my earliest interests in Borderline Personality Disorder. In the main, without her early support and confidence it is highly likely that my clinical and professional interests would have turned elsewhere.

I would like to similarly acknowledge all the clinicians and advocates who contributed their insights, experiences, and knowledge to this book.

Finally, I would like to thank my co-author, Randi Kreger, and our literary agent, Scott Edelstein, who approached me with the idea to write this book more than three years ago. Without both of their persistence and efforts, I would still be just considering it.

—P.M.

Introduction

Intimate Strangers: How This Book Came to Be

I must be defective.

That was the only explanation I could think of for his behavior. Why did he act so loving one moment and then rip me to shreds the next? Why did he tell me I was talented and wonderful and then scream at me that I was contemptible and the cause of all his problems? If he loved me as much as he said he did, why did I feel so manipulated and powerless? And how could someone so intelligent and educated sometimes act so completely irrational?

On a conscious level, I knew I hadn't done anything to deserve this treatment. But over several years, I came to accept his view of reality—that I was flawed and everything really was my fault. Even after the relationship ended, my feelings of distrust and low self-esteem remained. So I began seeing a therapist.

After several months, she revealed something to me about my former friend that would radically change my life—and those of many others: "The behavior you describe is very characteristic of someone with Borderline Personality Disorder," she said. "I can't make a diagnosis since I've never met him. But from what you've said, he certainly seems to fit the criteria."

Borderline Personality Disorder? I had never heard of it. She recommended that I read *I Hate You—Don't Leave Me* by Jerold Kreisman, M.D. I did—and discovered that my friend's confusing behavior matched seven out of the nine traits for Borderline Personality Disorder (BPD) listed in the clinician's "bible," the *Diagnostic and Statistical Manual (DSM-IV)*. Just five traits are needed for a diagnosis.

I wanted to learn more about how the disorder had affected me. I needed to know how to heal. But I could find just two books about BPD for consumers, and they were more like popular explanations of BPD than practical self-help books for family members.

So I decided to write my own self-help book. Because BPD affects six million people in North America, I figured that at least eighteen million family members, partners, and friends—like me—were blaming themselves for behavior that had little to do with them.

A friend who knew I wanted to write the book with a credentialed mental health professional suggested that I contact a colleague of hers, Paul Mason. A psychotherapist, Paul had worked with borderlines and their families in inpatient and out-patient settings for ten years. A respected journal had published his research on the subtypes of BPD. He had also given several professional and community presentations on the subject.

Like me, Paul strongly believed that friends, partners, and family members of those with BPD desperately needed to know they were not alone. "Family members tell me that they're in an emotional combat zone, and they just don't know how to react anymore," he said.

Paul began researching the book, searching the professional literature for relevant studies. Many articles discussed the difficulties of treating borderline clients, whom some practitioners view as being needy, challenging, and slow to improve—if they get better at all. But although the articles outlined coping techniques for trained professionals who see borderline patients one hour a week, most glossed over the needs of the untrained family members who interact with the person seven days a week.

In the studies that did discuss "the family," the term almost always referred to the family of origin of the person with BPD. The focus was to determine the role the early family environment played in the development of the disorder. In other words, the studies looked at behavior directed toward the person with BPD rather than the behavior of that person toward others.

While Paul buried himself in professional journals, I began interviewing dozens of mental health professionals about what the "non-borderline," or non-BP (the partner, friend, or family member of a person with BPD), can do to take control of their own lives and stop "walking on eggshells," while remaining supportive of the person they care about. Some of these clinicians were well-known BPD researchers. Others were local professionals recommended by friends.

I was in for a surprise. Although BPD by definition negatively affects those in relationships with borderlines (BPs), most mental health professionals I spoke with—with a few notable exceptions—were so overwhelmed by the needs of their borderline patients that their advice for non-BPs was quite limited.

But as I continued interviewing, the body of knowledge grew. Each clinician offered a unique perspective. One psychotherapist, for example, focused on what non-BPs can do in the face of borderline rage. A social worker addressed the question of BPD "manipulation." A psychiatrist discussed the need for family members to take care of themselves and stop expecting the person with BPD to meet all their emotional needs.

Paul and I had uncovered essential information for people who care about someone with BPD. But we didn't have a book yet—not the detailed, supportive guide we wanted to write. Enter the Internet.

My new computer, which I had purchased for my public relations, marketing, and writing business, came with a disk for America Online (AOL). Curious to see the Internet firsthand, I installed the program.

I discovered an entire world that I didn't know existed. Internet newsgroups and message boards on AOL are like colossal recovery support groups in the biggest church basement in the world. The "netizens" I met there—both BPs and non-BPs—weren't waiting for professionals to come up with the answers. They were sharing coping strategies, exchanging technical information, and offering emotional support to intimate strangers who understood exactly what they were going through.

I started by reading the years of accumulated postings of hundreds of BPs and non-BPs on America Online. I sent E-mail messages to the recent posters, asking them to participate in our research. Most did, delighted that someone was finally addressing the need for more consumer information about BPD.

As we conversed back and forth via E-mail, I began identifying the primary concerns of family members, partners, and friends. Then I asked people with BPD for their perspective. For example, when the non-BPs spoke of their helplessness in the face of borderline rage, I asked the BPs to articulate what they were thinking and feeling during a rampage and how others could best respond.

Initially, the people with BPD distrusted me. But over the months, as their confidence in me grew, they revealed their deepest feelings about themselves and described the incredible devastation wrought by the disorder. Many told me horrific stories of sexual abuse, self-mutilation, depression, and suicide attempts. "Being a borderline feels like eternal hell—nothing less," wrote one woman. "Pain, anger, confusion, hurt. Never knowing how I am going to feel from one minute to the next. Sadness because I damage those I love. Once in a great while I'll get too happy, and then feel anxious because of that. Then I cut myself. Then I feel ashamed that I cut myself. I feel like my life is an endless 'Hotel California' and the only way to leave is to check out permanently."

Some of the therapists didn't have much hope that people could actually recover from BPD. But on AOL and the Internet, I met many people who had greatly improved through a combination of therapy and medication. Their joy in feeling normal for the first time in their life sometimes brought me to tears. And, for the first time, I understood how the BP in my own life must have felt. Behavior that had seemed incomprehensible to me now made sense. For the first time, I understood on a gut level that those years of unprovoked emotional assaults weren't really about me. They probably resulted from his own sense of shame and his intense fears of being abandoned. The discovery that he was a victim, too, turned some of my anger into compassion.

The stories from the family members on the Internet were just as horrifying. Partners told me about spouses who told damaging and embarrassing lies about them—or even filed false charges of abuse. Loving, bewildered parents of children diagnosed with BPD traits spent their entire life savings trying to help their children, only to be implicitly or explicitly accused of child abuse.

Adult children of BPs talked about their nightmarish childhoods. One man said, "Even my body functions were criticized. My borderline mother claimed that I didn't eat, walk, talk, think, sit, run, urinate, cry, sneeze, cough, laugh, bleed, or hear correctly." Siblings of borderlines spoke of having to fight for their parents' attention and worrying that their own children might develop the disorder.

With the assistance of volunteers I met on the message boards, I established a World Wide Web site about BPD (http://members.aol.com/BPDCentral) and organized an Internet E-mail support group for non-BPs. Most were flabbergasted to discover that so many other people shared an experience they thought was unique. For example, three members of the non-BP Internet support group (sometimes called a "list") reported that major arguments had taken place at airports. Four members said that the borderline in their life had been furious at them for days because of something they did in the BP's dreams.

Despite these similarities, we found striking differences between the experiences of non-BPs in "chosen" relationships (e.g., friends, lovers) and "unchosen" relationships (e.g., parents, siblings, children). For example, in chosen relationships some of the most common issues are deciding whether to stay in or leave the relationship, trying to protect children from BP behavior, and feeling pain from broken love relationships. When the BP is a blood relative, the non-BPs sense of obligation and guilt may be much more intense, and leaving the relationship may not be an option. In order to better meet their particular needs, the parents of borderline children split off and formed their own group, as did the adult children of borderlines. A college student with BPD also formed an Internet support group for those with the disorder; it quickly became a lifeline for borderlines all over the world who had been isolated in their struggles.

Paul and I began to organize this mass of information very slowly. We developed a system: I would come up with ideas and suggestions based on Internet discussions and give them to Paul, who would revise them, expand on them, and put them into a theoretical framework.

Other times, Paul would develop recommendations based on his research that I would fine-tune and distribute to list members for their "real world" observations. We both marveled at the technology: with just a stroke of a key, the Internet made it possible to obtain feedback from hundreds of people across the globe.

When we were both satisfied with our work, we shared it with Paul's colleagues, other mental health professionals, and well-known BPD researchers who had spent years working with borderline patients and their families. They confirmed that their patients and family members had the same kinds of concerns as our Internet corespondents. To further ensure the accuracy of our data, we asked Edith Cracchiolo, M.A., a professor of psychology at Cerritos College in Norwalk, California, to conduct a survey of the non-BPs in our Internet support group.

Of course, we weren't able to satisfy everyone. When I first considered writing the book, I couldn't figure out why it had never been done before. Several months into the project, the reasons became quite clear. Borderline Personality Disorder is a controversial, complex topic. Just defining it is like trying to catch a fish with your bare hands, blindfolded and in the rain. Theories on what causes BPD are plentiful but inconclusive. Treatment is hotly disputed by reputable researchers.

On top of all this, most insurance plans deny payment for treatment because "BPD is incurable"—even though several studies have shown that this isn't true. Ironically, the same plans will pay when a desperate borderline lands in the emergency room after deeply cutting themselves or swallowing a handful of pills.

Most frustrating of all was the lack of recognition of BPD by the mental health community, and, consequently, the general public. According to the American Psychiatric Association (APA), the incidence of BPD is nearly that of schizophrenia and bipolar disorder combined. Yet most professionals we interviewed acknowledged that their training did not adequately prepare them to diagnose and treat this challenging disorder. Some had heard only one or two lectures on the subject.

And although the APA formally recognized BPD in its *Diagnostic and Statistical Manual* in 1980, too many professionals seemed to use the controversy surrounding the disorder as a reason not to take it seriously. As of this writing, the American Psychiatric Association, the National Alliance for the Mentally Ill, and the National Institute for Mental Health have yet to produce their own brochures explaining BPD. This lack of attention to BPD is baffling and frustrating to us and all our Internet contacts.

Writing this book proved to be as emotionally difficult as it was intellectually challenging. Many people with BPD included veiled or explicit suicide threats in their responses to my questions. Each day, I received at least one desperate letter from someone who had just discovered the existence of BPD from the BPD Central World Wide Web site and wanted guidance about what to do next.

The most anguished letters came from non-borderline partners—usually husbands—concerned about emotional abuse of their children by a partner with BPD. These men felt thwarted by judges and social service systems that considered mothers essential and fathers optional and deemed even severe verbal abuse to be unproven at best, irrelevant at worst.

The result of our three years of effort is the book you now hold in your hands. It is not the last word on the subject. It is only the beginning. We hope that it sparks interest in new research, helps clinicians educate their clients, provides support and comfort to family and friends, and offers hope that people with BPD can get better. Most of all, we hope it will help you—and countless others like you—get off the emotional roller coaster you've been riding since someone with BPD came into your life.

—Randi Kreger

PART 1

UNDERSTANDING BPD BEHAVIOR

1

Walking on Eggshells: Does Someone You Love Have BPD?

After fifteen years of marriage, I still couldn't figure out what I was doing wrong. I did research in libraries, talked to doctors, spoke to counselors, read articles, and chatted with friends. I spent fifteen years wondering, worrying, and believing too much of what she was telling me about myself. I doubted myself and hurt so much without not knowing why—not knowing the truth.

Then one day, I finally found the answers on the World Wide Web. I started crying with relief. Although I can't get my borderline significant other to admit she needs help, at least I finally understand what's going on. It's not my fault. Now I know the truth.

—From the non-BP Internet
support group

Is someone you care about causing you a great deal of pain?

- Do you find yourself concealing what you think or feel because you're afraid of the other person's reaction or because it just doesn't seem worth the horrible fight or hurt feelings that will follow?

- Do you feel that anything you say or do will be twisted and used against you? Are you blamed and criticized for everything wrong in the relationship—even when it makes no logical sense?

- Are you the focus of intense, violent, and irrational rages, alternating with periods when the other person acts perfectly normal and loving? Does no one believe you when you explain that this is going on?

- Do you feel manipulated, controlled, or even lied to sometimes? Do you feel like you're the victim of emotional blackmail?

- Do you feel like the person you care about sees you as either all good or all bad, with nothing in between? Is there sometimes no rational reason for the switch?

- Are you afraid to ask for things in the relationship because you will be told that you're too demanding or that there is something wrong with you? Are you told that your needs are not important?

- Is the person always denigrating or denying your point of view? Do you feel that their expectations of you are constantly changing, so you can never do anything right?

- Are you accused of doing things you never did and saying things you never said? Do you feel misunderstood a great deal of the time, and when you try to explain do you find that the other person doesn't believe you?

- Are you constantly being put down? When you try to leave the relationship does the other person try to prevent you from leaving in a variety of ways (anything from declarations of love and promises to change to implicit or explicit threats)?

- Do you have a hard time planning anything (social engagements, etc.) because of the other person's moodiness, impulsiveness, or unpredictability? Do you make excuses for their behavior or try to convince yourself that everything is okay?

- Right now, are you thinking, "I had no idea that anyone else was going through this?"

If many of these comments sound familiar, we have good news for you. You're not going crazy. Everything is not your fault. And you're not alone. These things may be happening because someone close to you has traits associated with Borderline Personality Disorder (BPD). Following are three true stories of people who discovered that someone they care about had the disorder. As with all the examples in this book, the stories are based on those shared on the Internet support groups, though we have changed many details to conceal their identities.

Jon (non-BP)

Being married to someone with BPD is heaven one minute, hell the next. My wife's moods change by the second. I'm walking on eggshells trying to please her and avoid a fight for speaking too soon, too quickly, in the wrong tone, or with the wrong facial motions.

Even when I do exactly as she asks, she gets mad at me. One day she ordered me to take the kids somewhere because she wanted some time alone. But as we were leaving, she threw the keys at my head and accused me of hating her so much I couldn't stand to be in the house with her. When the kids and I got back from the movie, she acted like nothing had happened. She wondered why I was still upset and told me that I have problems letting go of my anger.

It wasn't always like this. Before we got married, we had a whirlwind, fantasy courtship. She idolized me—said I was perfect for her in so many ways. The sex was incredible. I wrote her love poems and bought her expensive gifts. We got engaged after four months, and a year later we were married and on a ten-thousand-dollar dream honeymoon.

But right after the wedding she began taking meaningless little things and turning them into mountains of criticism, interrogation, and pain. She accused me of wanting other women constantly and would point out imaginary "examples" to substantiate her claims. She became fearful of my friends and began cutting them down. She said bad things about my business, my past, my values, my pride—anything connected to me.

Still, every once in awhile the "old" her comes back—the one who loved me and thought I was the greatest guy in the universe. She's still the smartest, funniest, and sexiest woman I know, and I'm still very much in love. The marriage counselor thinks that my wife might have BPD, but she insists that I'm the one who is screwing up our relationship. She thinks that the counselor is a quack and she won't go back. How can I make her get the help she desperately needs?

Larry (non-BP)

We knew something was wrong with our adopted son, Richard, when he was eighteen-months old. He was cranky, cried a lot, and would scream for three hours straight. At age two, he began having several tantrums a day—some lasting for hours. Our kind, Marcus Welby–type doctor simply said, "Boys will be boys."

When Rich was seven, we found a note in his room saying he was going to kill himself when he turned eight. His elementary school teacher referred us to a local psychiatrist, who told us he needed more structure and consistency. We tried positive reinforcement, tough love, and even diet modification. But nothing worked.

By the time Rich was in junior high, he was lying, stealing, skipping school, and raging out of control. The police became involved when he attempted suicide, started cutting himself, and threatened to kill us. He would dial the child abuse hotline each time we disciplined him by sending him to his room.

Our son manipulated his teachers, his family, and even the police. He could be very sharp and charm the socks off people with his wit, good looks, and sense of humor—his grandmother calls him a born politician. Every counselor was convinced that his behavior was our fault. By the time they saw through his deception, he would refuse to go back. And each new therapist never took the time to read through his chart, which by now was several inches thick.

Finally, after threatening the life of a teacher at school, he wound up in the first of four short-term treatment centers. At various times we were told that he was bipolar, had Attention Deficit Disorder, or suffered from Post-Traumatic Stress Disorder from some unknown trauma. One psychiatrist said he was suffering from "depression with psychotic disorder." Lots of people told us he was just a bad kid.

After four hospitalizations, our insurance company told us they would no longer pay. The hospital said he was too sick to come home. And the local psychiatrists were advising us to go to court and have ourselves declared unfit parents. Somehow, we found a state-subsidized inpatient hospital where he received his first official

BPD diagnosis. They put him on various meds, but said that there was little hope of him getting better.

Rich did manage to graduate from high school and enter college, which ultimately was a disaster. His maturity level now is about age eighteen, although he's twenty-three. Reaching adulthood has helped some, but he still fears abandonment, can't sustain a long-term relationship, and has quit four jobs in two years. His friends come and go because he can be overbearing, obnoxious, manipulative, and opinionated. So he depends on us for money and emotional support. Our relationship with him is strained at best. Yet we're all he has left.

Ken (non-BP)

My mother's love for me was conditional. When I didn't do what I was supposed to—chores or whatever—she would rage and cut me down and say that I was a horrible kid who would never have any friends. But when she needed love, she would become affectionate and hug me and talk about how close we were. There was never any way to predict which mood she would be in.

My mother seemed to resent it if someone else seemed to be taking up too much of my time and energy. She was even jealous of our dog, Snoopy, who I loved more than anyone else. One day I was cuddling with Snoopy and she came along and started screaming that I had no life because all I did was sit around the house and pet the dog. I always thought that I was the one who had done something wrong—or I thought that I was something wrong.

She took it upon herself to improve me by constantly telling me how I needed to change. She saw something wrong with my hair, my friends, my table manners, and my attitude. She seemed to exaggerate and lie to justify her assertions. When my father protested, she dismissed him with a wave of her hand. She always had to be right.

Over the years, I tried to meet her expectations. But when I did, they changed. Despite years of stinging criticism, I never became accustomed to it. I turn cold inside when anyone—especially a woman—starts criticizing me. Today, I have trouble getting close to people. I can't trust anyone completely—not even my wife. When I feel especially close to her, I brace myself for the inevitable rejection that I know will come. If she doesn't do something I can label "rejecting," I will rebuff her in some way—like getting mad at her for something stupid. Intellectually, I know what's happening. But I feel powerless to stop it.

The Extremity and Intensity of BPD Behavior

People with BPD feel the same emotions other people do. They do many of the same things that other people do—or would like to do. The difference is that they feel things more intensely, act in ways that are more extreme, and have difficulty regulating their emotions and behavior. BPD does not cause fundamentally different behavior, but behavior that is very far to one side of the continuum.

People with BPD are not on the border of anything. Researchers coined the term "borderline" in the first half of this century, when they thought that people who exhibited behaviors we now associate with BPD were on the border between neurosis and psychosis. Although this concept was discarded in the 1970s, the name stuck.

Following are thoughts, emotions, and actions common to people with BPD. No one person with BPD will—or even could—have all of these. However, as the number of "yes" answers increases, so may the likelihood that this person may have BPD.

Thoughts That May Indicate BPD

Does this person:

_____Alternate between seeing people as either flawless or evil? Have difficulty remembering the good things about a person they're casting in the role of villain? Find it impossible to recall anything negative about this person when they become the hero?

_____Alternate between seeing others as completely for them or against them?

_____Alternate between seeing situations as either disastrous or ideal?

_____Alternate between seeing themselves as either worthless or flawless?

_____Have a hard time recalling someone's love for them when they're not around?

_____Believe that others are either completely right or totally wrong?

_____Change their opinions depending upon who they're with?

_____Alternate between idealizing people and devaluing them?

_____Remember situations very differently than other people, or find themselves unable to recall them at all?

_____Believe that others are responsible for their actions—or take too much responsibility for the actions of others?

_____Seem unwilling to admit to a mistake—or feel that everything that they do is a mistake?

_____Base their beliefs on feelings rather than facts?

_____Not realize the effects of their behavior on others?

Feelings That May Indicate BPD

Does this person:

_____Feel abandoned at the slightest provocation?

_____Have extreme moodiness that cycles very quickly (in minutes or hours)?

_____Have difficulty managing their emotions?

_____Feel emotions so intensely that it's difficult to put others' needs—even those of their own children—ahead of their own?

_____Feel distrustful and suspicious a great deal of the time?

_____Feel anxious or irritable a great deal of the time?

_____Feel empty or like they have no self a great deal of the time?

_____Feel ignored when they are not the focus of attention?

_____Express anger inappropriately or have difficulty expressing anger at all?

_____Feel that they never can get enough love, affection, or attention?

_____Frequently feel spacey, unreal, or out of it?

Behaviors That May Indicate BPD

Does this person:

_____Have trouble observing others' personal limits?

_____Have trouble defining their own personal limits?

_____Act impulsively in ways that are potentially self-damaging, such as spending too much, engaging in dangerous sex, fighting, gambling, abusing drugs or alcohol, reckless driving, shoplifting, or disordered eating?

_____Mutilate themselves—for example, purposely cutting or burning their skin?

_____Threaten to kill themselves—or make actual suicide attempts?

_____Rush into relationships based on idealized fantasies of what they would like the other person or the relationship to be?

_____Change their expectations in such a way that the other person feels they can never do anything right?

_____Have frightening, unpredictable rages that make no logical sense—or have trouble expressing anger at all?

_____Physically abuse others, such as slapping, kicking, and scratching them?

_____Needlessly create crises or live a chaotic lifestyle?

_____Act inconsistently or unpredictably?

_____Alternately want to be close to others, then distance themselves? (Examples include picking fights when things are going well or alternately ending relationships and then trying to get back together.)

_____Cut people out of their life over issues that seem trivial or overblown?

_____Act competent and controlled in some situations but extremely out of control in others?

_____Verbally abuse others, criticizing and blaming them to the point where it feels brutal?

_____Act verbally abusive toward people they know very well, while putting on a charming front for others? Can they switch from one mode to the other in seconds?

_____Act in what seems like extreme or controlling ways to get their own needs met?

_____ Do or say something inappropriate to focus the attention on them when they feel ignored?

_____Accuse others of doing things they did not do, having feelings they do not feel, or believing things they do not believe?

If You Learn They Have BPD

People who care about someone with Borderline Personality Disorder are usually flabbergasted when they learn that BPD may be at the root of this person's erratic, hurtful, and confusing behavior. We call this moment of shocking realization the "lightbulb effect." People often wonder why they haven't heard of BPD before—especially if they've sought help from the mental health system.

There are several possible explanations for why BPD is not widely recognized. First, the American Psychiatric Association didn't formally recognize BPD in its *Diagnostic and Statistical Manual* (a standard reference for the diagnosis and treatment of psychiatric illnesses) until 1980. Many mental health professionals miss signs of BPD in their patients simply because they're not educated enough about the disorder. Also, some clinicians disagree with the information in the *DSM*; a few do not even believe that BPD exists. Some professionals dismiss the diagnosis as a catchall designation or a new fad to describe difficult patients. Other clinicians believe that BPD is so stigmatizing that they will not label patients with the disorder for fear they will become outcasts within the mental health system. Also, many clinicians make a formal diagnosis of BPD on patients' charts, but choose to keep it a secret from the patient. Or, they mention it briefly but do not explain it.

One last possibility is that, as of this writing, no celebrity has admitted to having the disorder (although many show the traits). Rightly or wrongly, issues like eating disorders, domestic violence, AIDS, and breast cancer do not step to the forefront of U.S. national consciousness until they affect someone famous.

To Tell or Not to Tell?

After reading the previous sections, you may be eager to talk about BPD with the person you think has it. This is understandable. Learning about the existence of BPD is a powerful, transformational experience. It seems logical that others will benefit from the information as well. The fantasy goes like this: The person will be grateful to you and will rush into therapy to conquer their demons.

Unfortunately, this doesn't usually happen. Almost everyone we interviewed told us that their loved one instead responded with rage, denial, and a torrent of criticism. Frequently, the possible borderline accused the family member of being the one with the disorder. (We will explain the reasons for this in chapter 3.)

The complete opposite may also happen: the possibly borderline person may feel such shame and despair that they attempt to hurt themselves. Or, they may use the information to deny responsibility for their behavior—"I can't help myself; I'm borderline."

In our interview with John M. Grohol, Psy.D., he said, "You cannot force someone to want to change their behavior. After all, they are not just 'behaviors' to the person suffering from the disorder—they are coping mechanisms they have used all their life." Keep this in mind when talking with a BP. The issues here are extremely complex. Don't rush into anything. Discuss your thoughts with a qualified therapist who is experienced in treating people with BPD. Generally, it's preferable that the person learn about BPD from a therapist—not from you. If the person is an adult and is currently seeing a therapist, the therapist probably will not discuss BPD with you because of confidentiality reasons. You can, however, find out if they are familiar with treatment of BPD and discuss your concerns with them (see appendix A).

Finally, be aware that other people in the BP's life may also respond with denial and accusations—especially the borderline's family of origin (mother, father, siblings). Keep in mind that it is not your job to convince anyone of anything. When a person is ready to learn, a teacher usually appears.

The Exception

There is a situation where you might carefully discuss BPD with the potential borderline in your life: if they are actively look-ing for answers as to why they feel the way they do; if the two of you are not playing the "blame game"; and if you can do so in a caring, loving way and assure the person that you plan on stick-ing with them through years of treatment. Do not make this promise lightly. Making it and breaking it can be worse than not making the promise at all.

When You Know and They Don't

The eggshells become even more fragile when you are aware of a possible BPD diagnosis and the other person is not. Sam, for example, says that because he can't discuss BPD with his possibly borderline wife, Anita, she won't take responsibility for her actions. Talking about treatment, obviously, is not an option. He also feels like he's being dishonest because he uses a separate mailing address to receive printed information about BPD.

Wesley says, "Since finding out about BPD, my interactions have become softer and more compassionate—but certainly just as frustrating. At times, it feels like the tremendous volume of information I have gained has been killing me."

Most people expect a high degree of intimacy in their close relationships. This is hard to achieve when you can't talk about something as significant as BPD. So if you feel that you must make your loved one aware that you suspect BPD, be forewarned that your immediate situation may get worse—not better. We suggest that you finish this book first, and then explain your situation to a qualified mental health professional and discuss how to proceed. Make sure you choose this therapist using the guidelines in appendix A.

Another alternative is to de-emphasize the diagnosis. Instead, help the person see that in any relationship both people bear responsibility for the way things are. (You may feel that the BP is responsible for all the problems, but set this aside for now.) The message should be that when there are problems in relationships, both people need to work on them together.

If the person with BPD is not yet at the point where they can take a cooperative approach for the good of the relationship, you may wish to simply focus on setting limits (chapter 6). As you will see, asking them to observe your limits doesn't depend on their willingness to admit having problems.

Remember, the other person may or may not have BPD. And even if they do, that may not totally explain their behavior. Switch the focus from figuring out the possible causes of their actions to problem solving around issues involving the results of their actions. Here, you can be more effective.

How to Use This Book

This book is packed with information. Read slowly, and don't try to absorb it all at once. It is meant to be digested in small bites.

Go Step-by-Step

We suggest you read this book in order, rather than skipping around. The knowledge you gain in one chapter will be needed in the next. This is especially true of the chapters in part 2. We have reiterated some fundamental concepts in different chapters; this is to help you not just to know them but truly to integrate them into a new way of thinking about yourself and this relationship.

Understand Terms

We have created some new terms and definitions in order to make this book more readable. We strongly suggest that you become familiar with these before you read the rest of this book.

Non-Borderline

The term "non-borderline" (non-BP) does *not* mean "person who doesn't have BPD." Rather, it is shorthand for "relative, partner, friend, or other individual who is affected by the behavior of someone with BPD." Non-BPs can be in any type of relationship with someone who has BPD. Non-BPs we interviewed were married partners, unmarried partners, friends, children, parents, siblings, daughter-in-laws, aunts, cousins, and co-workers of people with BPD.

Non-BPs are a diverse group of people who are affected by BPs in a variety of ways. Some non-BPs are very supportive of people with BPD in their lives; some may be verbally or physically abusive. Non-BPs may have mental health concerns of their own, such as depression, substance abuse, Attention Deficit Disorder, and Borderline Personality Disorder. People with BPD are also considered non-BPs if they are coping with someone in their life who also has BPD (see appendix B).

One important note: Some people with BPD were sexually, physically, and emotionally abused by their parents. Others had very good parents who have dedicated their lives to getting treatment for their borderline children. The parents we interviewed for this book are in the latter category. They were not perfect parents. But their behavior was in no way abusive. For this reason, in this book when we discuss non-borderline parents we mean ordinary parents who make ordinary mistakes, not abusive ones. Any exceptions will be noted as such.

Borderline

In this book, we use the term "borderline" (BP) to mean "a person who has been diagnosed with Borderline Personality Disorder or who seems to fit the definition for BPD in the *Diagnostic and Statistical Manual IV (DSM-IV)* (1994), published by the American Psychiatric Association."

You may never know for sure if the person you care about really has BPD. They may refuse to be evaluated by a mental health professional—in fact, they may deny that they are having difficulties. Or, they may be seeing a therapist but choose not to share their diagnosis with you.

If the BP has been under the care of several mental health professionals, it's quite possible that each one has a different opinion about their diagnosis. This is common because BPD is often misdiagnosed and because it frequently coexists with other mental health concerns.

In the absence of a formal diagnosis—or even a consensus of opinion—you may feel uncomfortable calling this person borderline. Even reading this book may seem like a betrayal of the person you care about. This feeling is especially common among children of borderline parents—many of whom have been keeping their parent's behavior a family secret for many years.

You should not diagnose people based on information in a book. A diagnosis can only be made by a professional who is experienced in assessing and treating people with BPD. However, this book is about you, not the BP. Whatever your circumstances, you have the right to seek help. And if you are being confronted with behavior patterns like those listed on the previous pages, you will be able to benefit from the strategies in this book regardless of the presence or absence of the BPD diagnosis.

Borderline Versus Person with BPD

Some professionals prefer the phrase "person with BPD." They believe that calling someone a "borderline" implies that they are their diagnosis. These clinicians assert that the longer phrase "person with BPD" should always be used.

We agree that the term "person with BPD" is less stigmatizing than the noun "borderline." However, our goal is to produce a book that is readable, succinct, and concise, as well as respectful to people with mental disorders. Unlike other books that focus primarily on the person with the disorder, we will examine the complex interactions between BPs and non-BPs. To do this, we must constantly differentiate between them—sometimes several times in the same sentence. This is a challenge that other books about BPD have not encountered. Therefore, when using the longer phrase would make this book hard to read and overly verbose, we will use "borderline" or "BP" instead.

Remember Our Focus

As you read, it may seem as if we are holding the person with BPD responsible for all the problems in the relationship. But actually, we are not discussing the relationship as a whole at all. Our focus is very narrow: coping with BPD behavior.

In real life, relationships are multifaceted. Hundreds of factors unrelated to BPD affect them. We do not address these factors because they are beyond the scope of this book. We believe the BP is responsible for 50 percent of the relationship and the non-BP is responsible for the other half. At the same time, each person is responsible for 100 percent of their own 50 percent.

Know There Is Hope

BPD is probably the most misunderstood psychiatric diagnosis. And the biggest misperception is that people with BPD never get any better. In reality, new research suggests that BPD behavior may be associated with disturbances in neurotransmitters (chemical messengers) within the brain. Medications are helping reduce depression, moodiness, and impulsivity. Cognitive-behavioral treatment has been shown to be effective in empirical research. And we have met many recovered borderlines who no longer feel compelling urges to hurt themselves, who feel good about themselves, and who give and receive love joyfully.

What if the BP refuses help and treatment? There's still hope, because although you can't change the person with BPD, you can change yourself. By examining your own behavior and modifying your actions, you can get off the emotional roller coaster you're on and reclaim your life.

2

The Inner World of the Borderline: Defining BPD

Trying to define BPD is like staring into a lava lamp: what you see is constantly changing. The illness not only causes instability but symbolizes it.

> —Janice Cauwels, *Imbroglio: Rising to the Challenges of Borderline Personality Disorder*

Understanding Personality Disorders

According to the *DSM-IV*, a personality disorder is an enduring pattern of inner experience and behavior that deviates markedly from the expectation of the individual's culture, is pervasive and inflexible (unlikely to change), is stable over time, and leads to distress or impairment in interpersonal relationships.

The very definition of a personality disorder is that it causes distress for both the person who has the disorder and those who interact with them. Since the description of BPD seems so negative, people diagnosed with BPD often feel very stigmatized. It's crucial to keep in mind that Borderline Personality Disorder and the person who has it are not the same thing. Borderline Personality Disorder is something people have, not something they are.

When you're living with someone with BPD, however, it can be difficult to separate BPD from the person who suffers from it, though you may know they're not the same thing. Borderlines recover. Troublesome symptoms such as moodiness, rage, and self-mutilation can be greatly alleviated or may disappear with the right medication and therapy.

Ultimately, the only person who can control the thoughts, feelings, and behaviors of the person with BPD is the borderline themselves. Coming to a gut-level understanding of this is vital for their recovery—and your own.

The *DSM-IV* Criteria for BPD

The *DSM-IV* diagnostic criteria for Borderline Personality Disorder reads as follows:

> A pervasive pattern of instability of interpersonal relationships, self-image, and affects [moods], and marked impulsivity beginning by early adulthood and present in a variety of contexts, as indicated by five (or more) of the following:

> 1. Frantic efforts to avoid real or imagined abandonment. Note: Do not include suicidal or self-mutilating behavior covered in (5).

> 2. A pattern of unstable and intense interpersonal relationships characterized by alternating between extremes of idealization and devaluation.

> 3. Identity disturbance: markedly and persistently unstable self-image or sense of self.

> 4. Impulsivity in at least two areas that are potentially self-damaging (e.g., spending, sex, substance abuse, shoplifting, reckless driving, binge eating). Note: Do not include suicidal or self-mutilating behavior covered in (5).

5. Recurrent suicidal behavior, gestures, or threats, or self-mutilating behavior.

6. Affective instability due to a marked reactivity of mood (e.g., intense episodic dysphoria, irritability, or anxiety usually lasting a few hours and only rarely more than a few days). [Dysphoria is the opposite of euphoria. It's a mixture of depression, anxiety, rage, and despair.]

7. Chronic feelings of emptiness.

8. Inappropriate, intense anger or difficulty controlling anger (e.g., frequent displays of temper, constant anger, recurrent physical fights).

9. Transient, stress-related paranoid ideation or severe dissociative symptoms.

Following is a further explanation of the *DSM-IV* criteria, as well as examples from people with BPD and their family members. We will explain lack of identity and feelings of emptiness (3 and 7) in the same section because we believe they are related. Conversely, we have separated self-mutilation and suicide (5) because we believe that the motivations for each are very different.

DSM-IV Criterion 1

Frantic efforts to avoid real or imagined abandonment.

Imagine the terror that you would feel if you were a seven-year-old lost and alone in the middle of Times Square in New York City. Your mom was there a second ago, holding your hand. Suddenly the crowd swept her away and you can't see her anymore. You look around, frantically, trying to find her. Menacing strangers glare back at you.

This is how people with BPD feel nearly all the time. Isolated. Anxious. Terrified at the thought of being alone. Caring, supportive people are like friendly faces in the middle of the crowd, offering smiles, help, and warm hugs. But the moment they do something that suggests an imminent departure—or do anything that the BP interprets as a signal that they're about to leave—the BP panics and reacts in a variety of ways, from bursting into rage to begging the person to stay.

It takes very little to trigger fear of abandonment—one borderline woman refused to let her roommate leave their apartment to do laundry. The fear of abandonment can be so strong that it can overwhelm the BP and lead to outrageous reactions. For example, when one man told his BP wife that he had a potentially fatal illness, she raged at him for seeing the doctor.

Sometimes the person with BPD will tell you outright that they are afraid of being abandoned. But just as frequently, this fear will be expressed in other ways—rage, for example. Feeling vulnerable and out of control can be an anger-provoking situation.

If a BP was neglected as a child or raised in a severely dysfunctional household, they may have learned to cope by denying or suppressing their terror at being abandoned. After many years of practice, they no longer feel the original emotion. When the BP in your life becomes upset or angry, it may help to think about whether anything has happened that might be triggering their fears of abandonment.

Armin (non-BP)

If I'm five minutes late coming home from work, my wife will call me to find out where I am. I have to carry a beeper for work, and she pages me constantly. I can't go out by myself with friends anymore because she reacts so strongly—she'll even page me while I'm watching a movie. It's so stressful that I've stopped going out with friends unless she feels like coming along.

Tess (BP)

When I feel abandoned I feel a combination of isolation, terror, and alienation from everyone around me. I panic. I feel betrayed and used. I think I'm going to die.

One night I called my boyfriend and he said he would call me back because he was watching something on TV. So I did my ironing to pass the time. He didn't call. I waited. He didn't call. This terrible feeling of being abandoned came over me again. I couldn't help it. It hurt so bad because the day before, had started to believe that he really loved me.

By the time the phone finally rang at 10 P.M., I had decided to break up with him—get rid of him before he could get rid of me. It turned out that he had still been watching the movie. I felt so ridiculous, but the pain, the fear, and the gut-wrenching poker in my gut were very real.

DSM-IV Criterion 2

A pattern of unstable and intense interpersonal relationships characterized by alternating between extremes of idealization and devaluation.

People with BPD look to others to provide things they find difficult to supply for themselves, such as self-esteem, approval, and a sense of identity. Most of all, they are searching for a nurturing caregiver whose never-ending love and compassion will fill the black hole of emptiness and despair inside them.

Beverly (BP)

I used to approach every friendly looking person with a deep hope that they would take care of me. Then I began to realize (with a lot of pain) that none of them were able to nurture me the way that I wanted because although I felt like a child inside, I looked like an adult on the outside.

The intense neediness of people with BPD can put a strain on any relationship—even when the non-BP is a parent and the BP is their child.

Roberta (non-BP)

Parenting my eighteen-year-old daughter (with BPD) has always been a twenty-four-hour-a-day job, every day. She is depressed and needs to be comforted. She needs help in thinking through solutions to every- day problems. She comes in my bedroom at midnight, crying and bleeding from self-inflicted cuts. I love her very much, but I just see no end to this and I don't know what to do. All of my time and energy goes to her, and my other children resent it.

For someone with BPD, the potential loss of a relationship can be like facing the loss of an arm or leg—or even death. At the same time, their sense of self-esteem is so low that they really don't understand why anyone would want to be with them. People with BPD are hypervigilant, looking for any cues that might reveal that the person they care about doesn't really love them after all and is about to desert them. When their fears seem to be confirmed, they may erupt into a rage, make accusations, sob, seek revenge, mutilate themselves, have an affair, or do any number of destructive things.

This leads us to the central irony of Borderline Personality Disorder: People who suffer from it desperately want closeness and intimacy. But the things they do to get it often drive people away from them. As torturous as this can be for you, imagine what it's like for the person who has the disorder. You can take a break and get away from it for awhile—have fun, go to a party, read a book, take a long walk on the beach. But the BP lives with the fear and panic twenty-four hours a day.

Many BPs fluctuate between extremes of idealization and devaluation, called "splitting." People with BPD perceive other people as either a wicked witch or a fairy godmother, a saint or a demon. When you seem to be meeting their needs, they cast you in the role of superhero. But when they perceive that you've failed them, you become the evil villain.

Because people with BPD have a hard time integrating a person's good and bad traits, their current opinion of someone is often based on their last interaction with them—a little bit like "Mr. Short-Term Memory" on the TV show *Saturday Night Live*. The central joke was that each moment was brand new to Mr. Short-Term Memory; during lunch he would continually reintroduce himself to his dining partner and order his food again and again and again. The emotional memory of people with BPD is a bit like that.

Jerold J. Kreisman (1989) explains splitting this way:

> Normal persons are ambivalent and can experience two contradictory states at one time; borderlines characteristically shift back and forth, entirely unaware of one feeling state while in another. . . . A child emotionally, the borderline cannot tolerate human inconsistencies and ambiguities; he cannot reconcile another's good and bad qualities into a constant coherent understanding of another person. At any particular moment, one is either "good" or "evil"; there is no in-between, no gray area. Nuances and shadings are grasped with great difficulty, if at all. . . . Intended to shield the borderline from a barrage of contradictory feelings and images—and from the anxiety of trying to reconcile those images—the splitting mechanism often achieves the opposite effect: The frays in the personality fabric become full-fledged rips; the sense of his own identity and the identities of others shift even more dramatically and frequently.

All-or-nothing thinking may appear in other areas of the BP's life—not just relationships. When there is a problem, some people with BPD may feel as if there is only one solution. Once action is taken, there's no turning back. For example, when one borderline woman was given new work duties she disliked, her solution was to quit her job. Also, a BP's effort may be all or nothing. For example, a borderline college student became so involved with a political campaign that he flunked all his classes. The next semester, he dropped out of all his political activities to focus on his classes. He was unable to balance his time and do a little of both.

People with BPD may feel that relationships must be clearly defined. Someone is either their friend or their enemy, their passionate lover or a platonic buddy. This is one reason why people with BPD may have a hard time being platonic friends after a romance ends. This need for definition does not just apply to others; people with BPD also see themselves in black and white. In his self-help book for borderlines, Richard Moskovitz (1996) writes:

> You [the person with BPD] may strive valiantly for perfection and feel, at times, that you have achieved it, only to condemn yourself when the smallest flaw appears. When you are good, you may feel entitled to special treatment and live outside the rules made for others. You may feel entitled to take whatever you wish and have everything good for yourself.
>
> When you are bad, you may feel entitled to nothing. You may feel responsible for all that is evil and expect punishment. If punishment does not come, you may invite it from others or inflict it yourself.

The practice of splitting can become an ongoing cycle. It is very difficult, if not impossible, to fulfill all the borderline's needs and expectations. For one thing, they may never be explicitly stated—either because the person with BPD has trouble articulating them or because the BP doesn't even know they exist. Or, once you take steps to meet the borderline's needs, they may decide they want something else. Your role may change from hero to villain several times in one day, or it can take years for the person with BPD to cycle through the saint/sinner pattern. Sometimes the BP may find a new "love object" once the old one has proven to be "flawed," only to repeat the cycle with someone else.

When this happens, it's your job to maintain a consistent, balanced view of yourself at all times. This can be difficult because the BP is so sure that you have done something terrible—and as a result can be very convincing. It's not an act. They believe it. It's also crucial that you maintain a rational perspective when the person with BPD views you in glowing, positive terms. This will help you stay on an even keel during those times when you're in the doghouse.

Partially because of their habit of splitting, people with BPD—especially those who were abused as children—find it extremely difficult to trust others. This lack of trust causes a great deal of turbulence in relationships; for example, while they are seeing you as a villain they may accuse you of not loving them or of having an affair.

Non-BPs in this situation often try harder to show their trust-worthiness, but often to no effect. That's because the feelings of mistrust lie within the person with BPD, and often have nothing to do with the specific actions of the BP.

Jenice (BP)

I always had this insatiable hunger for something I couldn't define, except to call it the bottomless pit of need. Something that made me different and ashamed. Something that made me scared to get close to anybody for fear they'd discover I was rotten and disturbed. So I diversified. I had lots of friends and didn't get too close to any one of them. If I let my guard down and one friend found out how weird I was and they backed off—well, I had fifty-nine others.

But now a romantic relationship has kicked in. And with it, closeness. The stakes are high, with one person meaning so much. And the need within me wells up like water behind a weak dam—it takes all I have not to let it burst through. Ah, but this is different—the guy needs me, too. So maybe it's safe here. So I knock a chunk of rock out of the dam that holds back the raging waters. And it sweeps me in its currents, tosses me around in every direction, bouncing like a pinball. Spinning. I can't control it—it's got a life of its own. Be with me, please. Every day and every night. Look at me, listen to me. I'm here. See me? I'm here! I'm here! I'm here . . . Oh, this is incredible! Finally, finally, the one person who can take all of this need! What a relief! Hey . . . wait a minute! He's resisting this—says he wants to watch TV in peace, says he's got something else to do. What the hell do I do now? Needus-interruptus! Ooohhh, am I frustrated . . . Damn it. I hate this guy! I let my guard down—doesn't he know how hard it was for me to do that? How dare he rather watch TV than talk to me? How dare he rather be out with his friends than be right here, right now? How dare he find out what kind of a completely disturbed person I am? I'm furious. And I'm embarrassed as hell. I've been caught with my pants down—he's seen the bottomless pit of need. He's made a fool of me! Embarrassed, I lash out. Let him have it! Let the jerk know just who he's toying with. Hey, guess what buddy—I don't care about you. Nope, don't give a damn about you at all! Take this—take that! See, I'm cool. I'm a tough chick. I don't need a damned soul and I certainly don't need you! I rage, I scream until I collapse in exhaustion. And then I wake up and I see how much I've hurt him. And I despise myself more than I could ever imagine. I'm scared to death. Because he's gonna walk, I just know he's gonna walk. I'm so vulnerable. I'm not tough. Please don't leave—honestly, I'm not the tough chick. I do need you! How can I show you?

I cry, I beg, I tell him what an incredible man he is, how patient he is. I just know you hate me! You should hate me! I'd be better off dead. You'd be better off without me! No, I mean it—I wish I were dead . . . He's relenting a bit. Oh, please, let me make it up to you. Let's make incredible love anywhere, anytime! Let me cook you a delicious twelve-course meal, be your charming concubine—let me show you the best side of my passion. Whew! He's back. He's still around. Thank God I didn't blow it permanently. It feels so good to be with him. He cares. I need him.

When I realize that I've caused irrevocable damage—when the cycle has repeated itself so often I'm convinced that I've irrevocably blown it—whether or not he has reached this conclusion—I cut the cord and find somebody else. And go through the whole damned thing again.

DSM-IV Criteria 3 and 7

Identity disturbance: markedly and persistently unstable self-image or sense of self.

Chronic feelings of emptiness.

By the time people reach their 20s and 30s, their self-image is usually fairly consistent. Some people also go through a midlife crisis in their 40s, when they question the choices they've made. But most of us take certain things for granted, such as our likes and dislikes, our values, our religious beliefs, our positions on important issues, and our career preferences.

But the searching never ends for people with BPD. They lack an essential sense of themselves, just like they lack a consistent sense of others. Without a sense of self to cling to, they are like passengers on the deck of a ship during a typhoon, getting tossed about and battered. In the midst of the fury, they frantically look around, searching for something—anything—to hold onto. But all they see are other passengers wearing life jackets, lashed to poles for security. As another wave roars over the deck, they grab onto someone else's pole and hang on for dear life. But the life jacket is only big enough for one person. And the pole can't withstand the combined weight and is starting to crack.

Robert J. Waldinger (1993) discusses the issue of identity diffusion, a characteristic that leads to feelings of emptiness:

> Identity diffusion refers to borderline patients' profound and often terrifying sense that they do not know who they are. Normally, we experience ourselves consistently through time in different settings and with different people. This continuity of self is not experienced by the person with BPD.
>
> Instead, borderline patients are filled with contradictory images of themselves that they cannot integrate. Patients commonly report that they feel empty inside, that there is "nothing to me," that they are different people depending on whom they are with.
>
> A sense of inner emptiness and chaos renders the borderline patient dependent on others for cues about how to behave, what to think, and how to be; whereas being alone leaves them without a sense of who they are or with the feeling that they do not exist. This, in part, accounts for these patients' frantic and often impulsive effort to avoid being alone, as well as their descriptions of panic, crushing boredom, and [dissociation].

While a BP may have difficulty with self-definition, they also feel that, no matter what their identity, they're never good enough. In the section on splitting, we explained that people with BPD may base their opinions of others on their most recent interaction. They may have no conception of the relationship as a whole; it's always, "But what have you done for me lately?"

People with BPD do the same with themselves, basing their self-worth on their latest achievement—or lack of it. And they judge themselves as harshly as they judge others, so whatever they do is never good enough. Because of this, some people with BPD become extremely successful at what they do. They become known for their achievements at work, in their community, or at home. But they often feel like actors reciting their lines. When the audience goes home, they cease to exist.

Perhaps as part of their identity dilemma, some people with BPD often see themselves as helpless victims of other people—even when their own behavior has affected the outcome of a particular situation. For example, during group therapy a borderline man complained that his landlord had evicted him and he had no place to live. After twenty minutes of commiseration, group members began asking him why this had happened. It turned out that the man had violated many apartment rules, including parking in the landlord's space. Another borderline woman repeatedly battered her husband, had numerous affairs, and had her husband falsely arrested for possession of drugs after she planted them in his suitcase. Eventually, she filed for divorce. Her ex-husband began dating a woman he worked with. Yet, when the woman described the breakup to her friends, she told them that her husband deserted her for a co-worker. These two BPs refused to recognize their role in the situations.

Some people with BPD may play the role of victim because it draws sympathetic attention, supplies an identity, and gives them the illusion that they are not responsible for their own actions. Borderlines with abusive backgrounds may be replaying scripts from the past. They may feel continually victimized because they've been conditioned to expect cruel behavior from people they trust. As children, they may have felt responsible for their abuser's behavior. They may have come to believe that something about them causes people to act in a heartless or abandoning way. So as adults, these formerly abused children expect the worst from people. They interpret normal behavior as cruel or abandoning and react with intense rage, despair, or shame. The people around them are confused because they can't see what's really triggering the behavior.

Another role common among people with BPD is that of helper or caretaker. This more positive role may help provide them with an identity, heighten feelings of control, and lessen feelings of emptiness.

Salia (BP)

I have a chameleonlike ability to take on the coloring of the individual I am with. But the act is done more to fool me than to fool them. When I "become" a persona it's not worn over the real me as a cloak. For the time being, I have become who I'd like to be.

I am not some kind of a Machiavellian manipulator with nothing better to do than ruin lives. The process isn't even really conscious. It's been going on for so long now that I don't even know who I really am. I feel unreal—like a phony. If I had any true control over it, I would simply revert back to "myself" whenever I felt threatened. But I don't know who that is.

DSM-IV Criterion 4

Impulsivity in at least two areas that are potentially self-damaging (e.g., spending, sex, substance abuse, reckless driving, binge eating).

Everyone has urges they would love to indulge if they could: eat every chocolate in the box, buy a great new sweater in every color, drink one last glass of champagne to toast in the New Year. Most people have varying abilities to control impulses and delay immediate gratification. They're aware of the long-term consequences—in this case, weight gain, a massive credit card bill, and a nasty hangover. But some people with BPD find it very hard to resist or control these impulses. If a person feels empty and anxious most of the time, pleasant activities are a welcome diversion. Mood-altering drugs provide an even more immediate relief and therefore can be a powerful distraction. Harmful activities may be a way of expressing rage or self-hate.

People with BPD may also try to fill the emptiness and create an identity for themselves through impulsive behaviors such as bingeing and purging, indiscriminate sexual activity, shoplifting, compulsive shopping, drinking, or substance abuse.

BPD and substance abuse disorders often go hand in hand (Oldham et al. 1995). Another study (Links et al. 1988) reported that about 23 percent of borderline patients had a diagnosis of substance abuse. Borderline substance abusers are likely to abuse more than one drug (a frequent combination is drug and alcohol abuse), are more likely to be depressed, have more frequent suicide attempts and accidents, have less impulse control, and seem to have more antisocial tendencies (Nance et al. 1983) (Links et al. 1995). If the BP in your life is actively abusing drugs and alcohol, it can be difficult to determine what behavior is related to BPD and what is related to substance abuse.

DSM-IV Criterion 5

Recurrent suicidal behavior, gestures, or threats.

According to the *DSM-IV* about 8–10 percent of all people with BPD commit suicide. This does not include BPs who engage in risky behavior that results in death, such as drinking and driving. Marsha M. Linehan (1993) explains that suicide (and other impulsive, dysfunctional behaviors) are seen as solutions to overwhelming, uncontrollable emotional pain:

> Suicide, of course, is the ultimate way to change one's [moods]. . . . Other, less lethal behaviors can also be quite effective [in changing the borderline's mood]. Overdosing, for example, usually leads to long periods of sleep; sleep in turn, has an important influence on regulating emotional vulnerability. . . .
>
> Suicidal behavior, including suicidal threats, is also very effective in eliciting behaviors from the environment—help that may be effective in reducing the emotional pain. In many instances, such behavior is the only way an individual can get others to pay attention to and try to ameliorate her emotional pain.

Tony (non-BP)

My wife came home crying, desperate because her boyfriend had dumped her. Incredibly, she felt that I shouldn't be angry about the affair, and that I should support her because of the pain she was feeling. When I wasn't supportive enough, she started threatening suicide in front of our ten-year-old son, who has become extremely cynical about his mother's behavior.

Self-mutilating behavior

Self-mutilation is another BPD behavior that is very difficult for family members to understand. Examples include cutting, burning, breaking bones, head banging, needle poking, skin scratching, pulling out hairs, and ripping off scabs—all without suicidal intent. Sometimes, dangerous or compulsive behavior can be a type of self-mutilation—overeating to the point of obesity, for example, or provoking physical fights with others.

Self-injury is a coping mechanism that BPs use to release or manage overwhelming emotional pain—usually feelings of shame, anger, sadness, and abandonment. Self-mutilation may release the body's own opiates, known as beta-endorphins. These chemicals lead to a general feeling of well-being.

Borderlines' reasons for self-mutilation vary tremendously and include:

- To feel alive, less numb, and empty

- To feel more numb

- To express anger at others

- To punish themselves or express self-loathing (probably more frequent among BPs who have been abused)

- To somehow prove that they are not as "bad" as they think they are

- To relieve stress or anxiety

- To feel in control of their pain

- To bring back a sense of reality

- To feel "real"

- To seek relief from emotional pain, frustration, and other negative feelings by focusing on physical pain

- To communicate emotional pain to others or ask for help

Here are some words from BPs on self-mutilation:

- "To tell you the truth, I think I did it so someone would notice that in fact I needed help."

- "When I cut, I don't have to try to explain how bad I am feeling. I can show it."

- "When I get angry at someone, I want to destroy, hurt, or kill them. But I know that I can't really hurt that person. So I take out the anger by cutting myself or pulling out my hair. It makes me feel better at the time, but later on I am ashamed of myself and I wish that I had not done it."

- "When my father stopped abusing me, I had to make up for the hurt that suddenly disappeared."

- "For me, the scars were just outside paintings of what my parents did."

Self-harm may be planned in advance or done impulsively. It may be performed intentionally or unconsciously—almost as if the person is in a haze and doesn't realize what they're doing. A person who mutilates themselves may or may not feel pain while they're doing it. Some people hide their self-mutilation, only disfiguring areas that are normally hidden by clothing. Some people we interviewed even learned to sew up their wounds so they wouldn't have to seek medical attention and reveal their secret. Other people are more open about the results of their self-injury—perhaps because it's a way of asking for help or a method of communicating their pain.

The people with BPD we interviewed were often very aware of their own reasons for self-injury. But an intellectual understanding didn't make it any easier to stop. Most felt that self-mutilation had become a coping habit, much like smoking, and the urge to do it can be just as powerful as a smoker's urge for another cigarette.

There is a misperception that all people with BPD harm themselves or are suicidal. Many high-functioning BPs do not. BPs who hurt themselves, however, may seek professional help more often than those who don't.

DSM-IV Criterion 6

Affective instability due to a marked reactivity of mood (e.g., intense episodic dysphoria, irritability, or anxiety usually lasting a few hours and only rarely more than a few days).

When most people feel bad, they can take steps to feel better. They can also control, to some extent, how much their moods affect their relationships with others. People with BPD have a hard time doing this. Their mood may swing from intense anger to depression, depression to irritability, and irritability to anxiety within a few hours. Non-BPs often find this unpredictability exhausting.

Dina (non-BP)

Living with my borderline husband is heaven one minute and hell the next. I call his personalities Jovial Jekyll and Horrible Hyde. I walk on eggshells trying to please someone who blows up just because I spoke too soon, too quickly, in the wrong tone, with the wrong facial motions—whatever!

DSM-IV Criterion 8

Inappropriate, intense anger or difficulty controlling anger.

If you care about someone with BPD, you are probably very familiar with this trait. Borderline rage is usually intense, unpredictable, and unaffected by logical argument. It is like a torrential flash flood, a sudden earthquake, or a bolt of lightning on a sunny day. And it can disappear as quickly as it appears.

Some borderlines, however, have the opposite problem: they feel unable to express their anger at all. Marsha M. Linehan (1993) writes that borderline individuals who underexpress anger "fear they will lose control if they express even the slightest anger, and at other times they fear that targets of even minor anger expression will retaliate."

Jane G. Dresser, RN, who specializes in BPD, told us in an interview that she believes that people with BPD feel all emotions intensely, not just anger. She theorizes that anger was highlighted in the *DSM* criteria because anger is typically the feeling that causes the most problems for people close to the borderline. Linehan echoes this belief, saying, "People with BPD are like people with third degree burns over 90 percent of their body. Lacking emotional skin, they feel agony at the slightest touch or movement."

If you are being attacked verbally or physically by someone with BPD, keep in mind that even experienced mental health professionals may, at times, take borderline rage personally and become upset. We explain how to take steps to protect yourself in chapter 8.

Jeremy (BP)

When I feel I cannot control my surroundings, I become nervous and angry. It gets much worse when I am under stress. Everything negative comes in full blast and overwhelms me. When triggered, I can go from perfectly calm to full-blown, white-hot rage within a fraction of a second. I feel as if I'm under siege and that everyone else is just daring me to ventilate my anger so I can get into trouble.

I think that my temper comes from the abuse I suffered when I was a child. At some point, I decided that I didn't have to take my parents' abuse anymore. Raging back became a matter of survival.

So now, it's hard for me to feel concerned about the other person's feelings—in fact, I want them to hurt because they've hurt me. I know this sounds bad, but that's the way I feel when I'm in the middle of an outburst. I'm just trying to survive the best way I know how.

Laura (BP)

I think that borderlines are concerned of only one thing: losing love. When cornered, I get very scared and I show that by getting angry. Anger is easier to feel than fear and makes me feel less vulnerable. I strike before being struck.

No borderline will admit that the anger is really fear of being hurt. When I'm mad, all the intellectual understanding in the world doesn't help. The only thing that helps is when my husband says to me, "I know you are scared and not angry." At that moment my anger melts away and I can feel my fear again.

Real anger—the anger normal people feel when they've been treated unjustly—I don't feel at all. That would require a self; a complete being. Since I don't have a self—or since I put away my own self so deep that I can't reach it anymore—I can't get angry.

DSM-IV Criterion 9

Transient, stress-related paranoid ideation or severe dissociative symptoms.

Have you ever arrived home from work without remembering how you got there? You've traveled the route so many times that your brain had its own little adventure while your eyes and reflexes do the driving. This "out of it" feeling is a mild type of dissociation.

People who are severely dissociating, however, feel unreal, strange, numb, or detached. They may or may not remember exactly what happened while they were "gone." The degree of dissociation can vary from the car-trip-home variety to the extreme dissociation characterized by Multiple Personality Disorder (this is why it is now called "Dissociative Identity Disorder").

People with BPD may dissociate to different degrees to escape from painful feelings or situations. The more stressful the situation, the more likely it is that the person will dissociate. In extreme cases, people with BPD may even lose all contact with reality for a brief period of time. If the borderline in your life reports memories of shared situations quite differently from you, dissociation may be one possible explanation.

Karen (BP)

Sometimes I feel like a robot going through the motions. Nothing seems real. My eyes cloud over and it's like there's a movie going on all around me. My therapist says I look lost, like I am off in a place where even she can't reach me. When I come back, people tell me that I did or said certain things that I can't remember.

Additional Traits Common to BPD

People with BPD may have other attributes that are not part of the DSM definition but that researchers believe are common to the disorder. Many of these may be related to sexual or physical abuse if the BP has experienced abuse earlier in life.

Pervasive Shame

John Bradshaw's (1998) book *Healing the Shame That Binds You* is not about Borderline Personality Disorder, yet his explanation of toxic shame and the resulting feelings and behaviors epitomizes BPD. Bradshaw writes:

> Toxic shame is experienced as the all-pervasive sense that I am flawed and defective as a human being. It is no longer an emotion that signals our limits; it is a state of being, a core identity. Toxic shame gives you a sense of worthlessness, the feeling of being isolated, empty, and alone in a complete sense. Exposure to oneself lies at the heart of toxic shame. A shame-based person will guard against exposing his inner self to others, but more significantly, he will guard against exposing himself to himself.

Bradshaw sees shame as the root of issues such as rage, criticism and blame, caretaking and helping, codependency, addictive behavior, excessive people pleasing, and eating disorders. In their typical all-or-nothing way, people with BPD may either become consumed by their shame or deny to themselves and others that it even exists. Shame is also a core issue for many non-BPs—especially those who remain in chosen, abusive relationships.

Undefined Boundaries

People with BPD have difficulty with personal limits—both their own and those of others.

Tom (BP)

I was brought up thinking that the perfect intimate relationship had no boundaries. Boundaries only meant a rift between people. Boundaries meant I had to be alone, separate, have an identity. I didn't feel good enough to have a separate identity. I needed either total enmeshment or total isolation.

We will further discuss boundary issues in chapter 6.

Control Issues

Borderlines may need to feel in control of other people because they feel so out of control with themselves. In addition, they may be trying to make their own world more predictable and manageable. People with BPD may unconsciously try to control others by putting them in no-win situations, creating chaos that no one else can figure out, or accusing others of trying to control them. Conversely, some people with BPD may cope with feeling out of control by giving up their own power; for example, they may choose a lifestyle where all choices are made for them, such as the military or a cult, or they may align themselves with abusive people who try to control them through fear.

Bradshaw believes that shame also leads to oversteering:

Those who must control everything fear being vulnerable. Why? Because to be vulnerable opens up one to be shamed. All my life I used up my energies by always having to be guarded. The fear was that I would be exposed. And when exposed, all would see that I was flawed and defective as a person. . . . Control is a way to insure that no one can ever shame us again. It involves controlling our own thoughts, expressions, feelings, and actions. And it involves attempting to control other people's thoughts, feelings, and actions. Control is the ultimate villain in destroying intimacy. We cannot share freely unless we are equal.

Lack of Object Constancy

When we're lonely, most of us can soothe ourselves by remembering the love that others have for us. This is very comforting even if these people are far away—sometimes, even if they're no longer living. This ability is known as object constancy.

Some people with BPD, however, find it difficult to evoke an image of a loved one to soothe them when they feel upset or anxious. If that person is not physically present, they don't exist on an emotional level. The BP may call you frequently just to make sure you're still there and still care about them. (One non-BP told us that every time her boyfriend called her at work, he introduced himself using both his first and last name.) The BP may keep a photo of you nearby or carry something you gave them to remind them of you, in the same way that children use teddy bears and blankets to remind them of their parents' love. This strategy is often suggested by therapists to help the BP understand and better cope with fears of abandonment. Letters, pictures, colognes (scents that remind the BP of their partner) are typically used. Non-BPs need to understand that these strategies help the BP, often reducing their anxieties and fears. Usually, the result is less clinging behavior, which often brings some relief to the non-BP.

Interpersonal Sensitivity

Many individuals have noticed that some people with BPD have an amazing ability to read people and uncover their triggers and vulnerabilities. One clinician jokingly called people with BPD psychic.

Interpersonal sensitivity can best be understood by the non-BP in terms of the BP's astute ability to identify and use social and nonverbal cues of others. BPs can empathize well with others and often understand and respect how others feel, and they can use these skills to "see through others." It is thought that many adults who were repeatedly physically and/or sexually abused as children developed these "social and emotional antennae" as a survival strategy. This helped them predict and therefore prepare themselves (usually by dissociating) for what their abusers were about to do. As adults, BPs continue to use these social antennae to uncover triggers and vulnerabilities in others that they can use to their advantage in various situations. Therapists who work with BPs can attest that BPs have a "gift" for knowing how their therapist is doing that day (e.g., tired, worried, sad, or angry) and will often bring this up during the session.

Situational Competence

Some people with BPD are competent and in control in some situations. For example, many perform very well at work and are high achievers. Many are very intelligent, creative, and artistic. This can be very confusing for family members who don't understand why the person can act so assuredly in one situation and fall apart in another. This ability to have competence in difficult situations while being incompetent in seemingly equal or easier tasks is known as situational competence.

By way of explanation, one borderline woman says, "We know deep within that we are defective. So we try so hard to act normal because we want so much to please everybody and keep the people in our lives from abandoning us." But this competence is a double-edged sword. Because they can appear so normal, high-functioning borderlines often don't get the help they need.

Narcissistic Demands

Some people with BPD frequently bring the focus of attention back to themselves. They may react to most things based solely on how it affects them. Some people with BPD draw attention to themselves by complaining of illness; others may act inappropriately in public. These self-involved characteristics are defining components of narcissism; narcissistic behavior can be especially taxing on non-BPs, as the BP may not even consider how their actions affected the non-BP.

Jack (non-BP)

My mother's perception of me, my brother, and my father were as an extension of her. All my relationships were perceived to be about her, affecting her either by creating a reflection of her (good or bad) as a mother or by threatening my availability to provide her with emotional support and validation.

My mom also saw all of my friends as threats to her. She did everything she could to sabotage my friendships. The only "acceptable" people were ones who could never be really close friends, such as those who weren't in our faith (we were a very religiously conservative family).

Manipulation or Desperation?

It's no secret that non-BPs often feel manipulated and lied to by their borderline loved ones. In other words, they feel controlled or taken advantage of through means such as threats, no-win situations, the "silent treatment," rages, and other methods they view as unfair. We believe that, in most cases, the BP's behavior is not intentionally manipulative. Rather, this kind of behavior can be seen as desperate attempts to cope with painful feelings or to get their needs met—without the aim of harming others.

The Non-BP Point of View

Susan Forward (1997) defines emotional blackmail as a direct or indirect threat by someone to punish someone if they don't do what the person wants. "At the heart of [emotional blackmail] is one basic threat, which can be expressed in many different ways: if you don't behave the way I want you to, you will suffer." Forward explains that people who use this technique—which is widely used by all types of people, not just BPs—can skillfully mask the pressure they're applying to people, who often experience it in ways that make them question their perception of what's happening.

Almost universally, non-BPs say they feel manipulated by the BPs in their lives. If the non-BP doesn't do what the BP wants them to do, BPs may threaten to break off the relationship, call the police, or even kill themselves.

The BP Point of View

The terms "manipulation" and "emotional blackmail" imply some sort of devious, planned intent. While this may be true for some people, borderlines who appear to be manipulative usually act impulsively out of fear, loneliness, desperation, and hopelessness—not maliciousness. Marsha Linehan (1993) writes:

> People with BPD do influence others, such as through the threat of impending suicide or through communications of intense pain and agony. But this, by itself, is not evidence of manipulation. Otherwise, we would have to

say that people in pain or crises are "manipulating" us if we respond to them.

In our interview with psychiatrist Larry J. Siever, he said:

Although [people with BPD] can be apparently manipulative, they don't think about the behavior as such. They're trying to meet their needs in the only way they know how. Somebody has to relieve their anger or anxiety or distress or sense of impending annihilation right now. They are trying to elicit a response to soothe them, to help them feel better.

Degrees of Awareness

In our experience, people with BPD have varying degrees of conscious awareness that their behavior could be perceived as manipulative—just like most people do.

A. J. Mahari (BP)

My days and thoughts are not consumed by plans of how to push which button in whom. My actions are about survival and preserving my identity; they are not some preplanned sporting activity.

Petrova (BP)

Often I realize my motivations only after the incident is over. Once, I was so upset that my husband was ignoring me at Christmas that, right in front of him, I began destroying all the gifts he had just given me. My husband stopped me as I was about to rip apart the gift I loved most: a book of love poetry. When I saw the book, it dawned on me that I never would have ruined it. I was more interested in seeing my husband try to stop me. If I had been living alone, the whole episode would have never happened. So why did I do it? The answer was ugly and harsh, shameful and disgusting. Manipulation. I felt deeply ashamed.

Laurey (BP)

While others might feel manipulative, I feel powerless. Sometimes I just hurt so bad from the mean things that people do to me, real or perceived, or I'm so desperately feeling abandoned, that I withdraw and pout and go silent. At some point people get pissed off and fed up with that crap and they go away and then I'm left with nothing all over again.

It is important that you understand the differences between manipulation and desperation. The BP's behavior is more about them than you. For example, it may help to be able to look at a self- mutilating BP's behavior as self-punishment, rather than as a way to "trap" the non-BP into a relationship. In chapter 7, we will explain communication techniques that can be used to respond to behavior that you perceive as manipulative.

High Functioning, Low Functioning

People with BPD vary a great deal in their functionality: that is, in their ability to live a normal lifestyle, work inside or outside the home, cope with everyday problems, interact with others, and so on.

Some people with BPD are so incapacitated by their illness that they are unable to work. They may spend a great deal of time in the hospital because of self-mutilation, severe eating disorders, substance abuse, or suicide attempts. BPD makes it very hard for them to form relationships, so they may have a weak support system. They may be so incapable of dealing with money that they have no cash for food or a place to live.

People who are close to low-functioning borderlines often find themselves living from crisis to crisis. They often feel manipulated by self-mutilation and suicide attempts. However, because the borderline is obviously ill, non-BPs usually receive understanding and support from family and friends.

High-functioning borderlines act perfectly normal most of the time. Successful, outgoing, and well-liked, they may show their other side only to people they know very well. Although these borderlines may feel the same way inside as their less-functional counterparts, they have covered it up very well—so well, in fact, that they may be strangers unto themselves.

Non-borderlines involved with this type of BP need to have their perceptions and feelings confirmed. Friends and family members who don't know the borderline as well may not believe stories of rage and verbal abuse. Many non-BPs told us that even their therapists refused to believe them when they described the BP's out-of-control behavior.

Of course, there's a lot of room in between high-functioning (sometimes referred to as the "borderline" borderline) and low-functioning BPs. Stressful life events are most likely to trigger dysfunctional coping mechanisms, such as those explained in the next chapter.

Acting In, Acting Out

Most borderline behavior is about one thing: trying to cope with internal anguish. However, people with BPD may do this in different ways. In our experience, the behavior of people with BPD tends to fall into two general categories: "acting out" and "acting in." These are not official, empirically researched categories. Rather, they are a convenient, real-world way of looking at differences.

Acting-out behaviors are attempts to alleviate pain by dumping it onto someone else—for example, by raging, blaming, criticizing, making accusations, becoming physically violent, and engaging in verbal abuse. Acting-out behaviors cause direct anguish for friends, family members, and partners. For example, one borderline woman, Kiesha, became very angry when she felt that her husband was ignoring her at an office Christmas party. So she went up to him, threw her drink in his face, and stalked out.

Acting-in behaviors mostly hurt the person with BPD, although non-BPs are also affected. Someone with BPD who mostly acts in may feel extremely guilty over imagined transgressions. They may mutilate themselves, try to hold in their anger, and blame themselves for problems that are not their fault. Suicide is also a possibility.

Denise (BP)

I remember feeling different in grade school. I decided not to tell anyone, because I didn't want people to think I was crazy like my grandmother. She ended up in a mental institution. I learned to control my inner rages by seventh grade. Some people thought I was moody, but no one found out about my internal agony. As my rage turned to suicidal feelings, every day became a struggle to stay alive. It still is.

Some BPs seem to mainly act in. Some mainly act out. And some both act in and act out. Take Kiesha, for example; after she embarrassed her husband at the Christmas party, she felt very guilty. She walked home from the party, a distance of several miles. When she arrived home, she grabbed several ornaments from the tree and crushed them with her hands, causing a great deal of bleeding.

Myths and Realities about BPD

Myth 1: People with BPD never get better.

Reality: Many people with BPD report success with proper treatment.

It is true that ingrained personality traits are not easy for people to change. But BPD behavior that has been learned can be unlearned. And many symptoms of BPD that are biological or chemical in nature can be treated effectively with medication.

Why is it, then, that this myth persists—in spite of the fact that researchers have demonstrated effective treatments? The problem is the stigma of BPD and the lack of awareness. The research on effective BPD treatment is so new that many seasoned clinicians weren't exposed to it during their training. In addition, clinicians are bombarded with contradictory research on BPD treatment, which may leave them confused about which treatment approaches are most effective.

Since many mental health professionals find working with borderline patients arduous and exhausting, promising new studies often go unnoticed by clinicians who don't specialize in BPD. It becomes a vicious circle: clinicians don't read studies that could help them work with borderline patients because they believe that borderline patients are always going to be difficult to work with.

Another problem is that many insurance plans won't cover BPD treatment—again, because of the myth that treatment rarely works. This acts as a barrier for clinicians to learn about state-of-the-art BPD treatments. Clinicians then rely on outdated information, misleading statements, and false information about BPD they've heard from their associates. (See appendix A for more information about BPD treatments.)

Myth 2: BPD is a "wastebasket definition." That is, clinicians give patients this diagnosis when they can't figure out what's wrong with them.

Reality: BPD should be diagnosed only when patients meet the specific clinical criteria.

Janice Cauwels (1992) wrote:

BPD is still a wastebasket diagnosis, a label slapped on patients by therapists trying to pretend that their illness is understood. It is also used to rationalize treatment mistakes or failures, to avoid prescribing drugs or other medical treatments, to defend against sexual issues that may have arisen in therapy, to express hatred of patients, and to justify behavior resulting from such emotional reactions.

In other words, some clinicians use the word "borderline" like some schoolyard bullies use the word "cooties." But the fact that BPD is used as a wastebasket definition doesn't make it a wastebasket definition, any more than calling grapefruit a fat burner makes it a fat burner. A patient should be diagnosed as borderline only if they meet the clinical criteria and only after a clinician has worked with the patient over time to verify that the BPD symptoms are persistent, extreme, and long standing.

Myth 3: Women have BPD; men have Antisocial Personality Disorder.

Reality: Although BPD is diagnosed in women much more frequently, men have it as well.

According to the *DSM-IV*, about 75 percent of those diagnosed with BPD are women and that most people diagnosed with Anti-social Personality Disorder (APD) are men. But although the personality disorders have some external similarities (i.e., difficulties with relationships, tendencies to blame others), their internal states are strikingly different. Borderlines feel shame, guilt, emotional distress, and emptiness; people with APD generally do not.

So why are more women diagnosed with BPD than men? No one knows, but several theories have arisen:

- Sexual abuse, which is common in childhood histories of borderline patients, happens more often to women than men.

- Women experience more inconsistent and invalidating messages in this society.

- Women are more vulnerable to BPD because they are socialized to be more dependent on others and more sensitive to rejection.

- Clinicians are biased. Studies have shown that mental health professionals tend to diagnose BPD more often in women than men, even when patient profiles are identical except for the gender of the patient.

- Men seek psychiatric help less often.

- Men are more likely to be treated only for their alcoholism or substance abuse; their borderline symptoms go unnoticed because BPD is assumed to be a woman's disorder.

- Female borderlines are in the mental health system; male borderlines are in jail.

Myth 4: There is no such thing as BPD.

Reality: More than three hundred research studies and three thousand clinical papers provide ample evidence that BPD is a valid, diagnosable psychiatric illness.

Clinicians may claim that BPD doesn't exist for several reasons. They may not have kept up-to-date with the research and are misinformed. They may believe that BPD is not a separate disorder, but part of another illness such as Bipolar Disorder or Post-Traumatic Stress Disorder. They may simply reject the idea of labeling anyone as "borderline" because they think it is too stigmatizing, or they may find nearly all psychiatric diagnoses limiting and misleading.

In this chapter, we've explained BPD as the *DSM-IV* describes it. We've also illustrated other traits that people with BPD seem to have in common, but that are not mentioned in the *DSM-IV*. As you've seen, BPD is pervasive: it impacts the way the sufferer feels, thinks, and behaves. But BPD doesn't exist in a vacuum. In the next chapter, we'll discuss what happens when you enter the picture.

3

Making Sense Out of Chaos: Understanding BPD Behavior

Borderlines and non-borderlines live in two different worlds that coexist in the same space, but not always in the same time. Comprehending the "real" world, for me, is as formidable as the task of understanding the borderline world is for you.

—A. J. Mahari (BP) (taken from the non-BP Internet support group)

In the last chapter, we defined the pieces of the puzzle that make up BPD. In this chapter, we'll put those pieces together and explain why some people with BPD seem to:

- Experience reality differently than you do.
- Make untrue accusations.
- Blame you for things that aren't your fault.
- Criticize you all the time.

- Change their wants and opinions at lightning speed.

- Put you in no-win situations.

- Push you away just when you are feeling close.

- Act in ways that feel manipulative to you.

- Deny the effects of their behavior on others.

- Deny that their behavior is problematic.

Keep in mind, however, that each person with BPD is unique. If something you read rings true for you, consider it carefully. If it doesn't seem to apply in your situation, don't try to make it fit.

In addition, remember that people with BPD, like everyone else, will sometimes have reactions that are either greatly exaggerated or seem to have no basis in reality. However, don't blame everything on BPD. Before you conclude that BPD alone is responsible for your loved one's strong response, we recommend that you first ask yourself if your behavior has triggered a natural human reaction. For example, let's say you have decided to cope with BPD behavior by spending as much time as possible away from home. You work late, and when you come home you barely speak to the person with BPD. You may be trying to protect yourself, which is understandable. However, if your distancing triggers abandonment fears and acting out, you may need to take a look at how your own actions are affecting the situation. You both play a part in what is happening. To ignore your contribution and dismiss the other person's feelings is counterproductive.

Then ask yourself if there is any truth to what the person with BPD is saying. People with BPD can be very intuitive. Many are extremely sensitive to tone of voice and body language. They may even pick up something you are feeling before you are aware of it. Acknowledging and owning up to what is truly your responsibility can often defuse a potentially explosive situation. However, you should only take responsibility for what is your doing. It is very unlikely that your actions were the sole cause of the problem. However, you can be a healthy role model to the BP by acknowledging that your behavior may have contributed to the problem.

The BP World

Most people find it hard to understand BPD behavior because they assume that people with BPD think and feel the way they do. It's an understandable mistake. High-functioning borderlines can act quite normal when their BPD behaviors are not being triggered. They don't look or sound like they have a disorder. Trying to reconcile the seemingly malevolent Mr. Hyde aspects of their personality with their friendly Dr. Jekyll exterior can be like playing hide-and-seek with a chameleon.

Some people with BPD—usually those in therapy—can have an excellent intellectual understanding of BPD. They can recite the *DSM* criteria backward and forward and pinpoint which traits describe them. When not overcome by intense emotions, they may understand that their feelings don't always reflect reality as others see it.

But that knowledge doesn't fill the aching hole inside them. Understanding the causes of their pain doesn't necessarily make them feel any better, and it may not make it any easier for them to change their behavior. It also doesn't prevent them from feeling hopelessly misunderstood when exasperated non-BPs tell them, "Just pull yourself together."

In order to understand borderline behavior, you have to leave your own comfortable world and journey into theirs. And you should, since you're asking the BP in your life to come into yours. As you read, keep in mind that these behaviors are usually unconscious. They are designed to shield the person with BPD from intense emotional pain—not to hurt you.

Common BP Thinking

When you travel to another country, it's important to know the local customs. Similarly, when you're interacting with someone with BPD, it's crucial to understand that their unconscious assumptions may be very different from yours. Keep in mind that these do not reflect the thinking of every person with BPD. You must judge what is pertinent in your individual circumstances.

Their assumptions may include:

- I must be loved by all the important people in my life at all times or else I am worthless. I must be completely competent in all ways to be a worthwhile person.

- Some people are good and everything about them is perfect. Other people are thoroughly bad and should be severely blamed and punished for it.

- My feelings are always caused by external events. I have no control over my emotions or the things I do in reaction to them.

- Nobody cares about me as much as I care about them, so I always lose everyone I care about—despite the desperate things I try to do to stop them from leaving me.

- If someone treats me badly, then I become bad.

- When I am alone, I become nobody and nothing.

- I will be happy only when I can find an all-giving, perfect person to love me and take care of me no matter what. But if someone close to this loves me, then something must be wrong with them.

- I can't stand the frustration that I feel when I need something from someone and I can't get it. I've got to do something to make it go away.

Feelings Create Facts

In general, emotionally healthy people base their feelings on facts. If your dad came home drunk every night (fact) you might feel worried or concerned (feeling). If your boss complimented you on a big project (fact) you would feel proud and happy (feeling).

People with BPD, however, may do the opposite. When their feelings don't fit the facts, they may unconsciously revise the facts to fit their feelings. This may be one reason why their perception of events is so different from yours.

Let's look at Minuet (BP) and her husband Will. One Friday afternoon, Will calls his wife to say he'll be home late because he's having a beer with the guys after work. Minuet feels anxious, rejected, and jealous. Minuet's emotions are confusing and overwhelming to her. In order to make sense of them, she concludes that Will must be doing something to bring them on. She might accuse Will of having a drinking problem. She might tell him that he's a terrible person for wanting to be with friends instead of her after a hard work week. She unconsciously revises the facts so that her feelings make sense.

Extreme Defense Mechanisms

Like everyone else, people with BPD use defense mechanisms. Defense mechanisms are unconscious processes that protect people from anxiety and painful ideas or impulses. People with BPD, however, use some of them more frequently and with much greater intensity than most of us.

Denial

Denial is one common defense mechanism. For example, if a woman feels a lump in her breast but is afraid to get it examined because it might be cancer, she might choose denial and decide it's nothing and quickly forget about it. Or, a family member may deny that the behavior of a person with BPD is out of the ordinary.

Rationalization

Rationalization is another common defense mechanism. You know you should exercise, but it seems like too much trouble. So you tell yourself that you're too busy to work out—even though you always have enough time to watch your favorite TV programs. Some family members use rationalization to explain a BP's behavior—for example, "He's just acting this way because he's so stressed out at work."

It's possible that some people with BPD developed these intense defense mechanisms early in life, when they were useful in warding off fear, shame, and other negative emotions. In adulthood, however, these strategies don't work anymore because it prevents the BP from confronting and conquering their fears. It is hard, however, to give up rationalization and other coping mechanisms because they have become so automatic and they worked in the past.

Splitting

In the last chapter, we explained that people with BPD may have a hard time seeing gray areas. To them, people and situations are all black or white, wonderful or evil. This process of splitting serves as another defense mechanism. Peter, who has BPD, explains: "Dividing the world into good or evil makes it easier to understand. When I feel evil, that explains why I am the way I am. When you are evil, that explains why I think bad things about you."

Alexandra (non-BP)

Months after I split up with a borderline boyfriend, he called and asked me to have lunch with him. When I got to the restaurant he bombarded me with photos of us just to remind me of all the "good times" we'd had together. Then he asked me to tell him exactly what he had done wrong in our relationship.

I explained patiently that I didn't feel it was my place to tell him about his problems, rather that it was his job to explore his own behavior. But no, he begged me—needed me—to explain what happened for his own good.

Finally, I told him exactly what I thought. Pretty much unedited. He took it like a man—that is, straight-faced, earnest, and without too much comment. We parted on somewhat peaceful terms.

Of course, two days later I got the most scathing, hateful letter I'd ever received from him, turning it all around on me and letting me know what a witch I was and telling me how I'd contributed to the demise of the relationship. Somehow I wasn't surprised.

Tag, You're It: A Game of Projection

Some people with BPD who act out may use a more compli-cated type of defense mechanism—we've named it "Tag, You're It"—to relieve their anxiety, pain, and feelings of shame. It's more complex because it combines shame, splitting, denial, and projection.

Tag is a fun game for a six-year-old. But it's not a game for people with BPD. Lacking a clear sense of who they are, and feeling empty and inherently defective, people with BPD feel like "it" all the time. Others seem to run away from them, which is lonely and excruciatingly painful. So borderlines cope by trying to "tag" someone else. This is called projection.

Projection is denying one's own unpleasant traits, behaviors, or feelings by attributing them (often in an accusing way) to someone else. In our interview with Elyce M. Benham, M.S., she explained that projection is like gazing at yourself in a hand-held mirror. When you think you look ugly, you turn the mirror around. Voila! Now the homely face in the mirror belongs to somebody else.

Sometimes the projection is an exaggeration of something that has a basis in reality. For example, the borderline may accuse you of "hating" them when you just feel irritated. Sometimes the projection may come entirely from their imagination: for example, they accuse you of flirting with a salesclerk when you were just asking for directions to the shoe department.

The BP's unconscious hope is that by projecting this unpleasant stuff onto another person—by tagging someone else and making them "it"—the person with BPD will feel better about themselves. And they do feel better, for a little while. But the pain comes back. So the game is played again and again.

Projection also has another purpose: your loved one unconsciously fears that if you find out they're not perfect, you will abandon them. Like in the *Wizard of Oz*, they live in constant terror that you'll discover the person behind the curtain. Projecting the negative traits and feelings onto you is a way to keep the curtain closed and redirect your attention on the perfect image they've tried to create for themselves.

Your task is to examine what the person with BPD is saying and determine whether or not they have an accurate point. Remember, not everything is projection. But, if the borderline is projecting, you need to stop playing the game and decline to be "it" in a respectful way. We'll explain how to do this in the second part of this book.

How the Game Is Played

When someone with BPD tags you, they're unconsciously trying to transfer their own behaviors, feelings, or perceived traits onto you. When projecting their traits onto you, the person with BPD thinks they're defective, so they accuse you of having something wrong with you. Sometimes the flaw they see in others is the identical flaw they fail to see in themselves. Sometimes it's not.

Sharon (BP)

I hate myself so much I can barely see straight. When I am drowning in hate it floods over everyone and everything, and I feel so justified for feeling such loathing toward everyone—mostly my husband. He seems so utterly disgusting; so pitifully stupid.

Here are some projections of traits, followed by the unconscious painful thoughts and feelings underlying the projection:

- You're a horrible person. No one will ever love you but me. (I am such a rotten person that anyone who would love me must be defective, too.)

- You're such a suck up, it's no wonder Mom loved you best. (I feel so flawed that not even my own mother loves me.)

- You are such a terrible parent that you shouldn't even be around our kids. (I feel like a terrible parent.)

- You two are the worst parents in the world. It's no wonder I have BPD. (I feel like the worst kid in the world.)

- I do not have BPD. You do! (The thought that I might have BPD terrifies me.)

- You made me have this affair and get pregnant because you're such a lousy husband. (I had this affair because I think I'm a lousy wife and don't deserve to be loved.)

When projecting behaviors, the BP may accuse you of doing something that they are actually doing. Or, they may use your real or imagined behavior to absolve themselves of responsibility for their own actions, or keep themselves from feeling shame for having engaged in the behaviors.

Here are some typical behavioral projections, followed by the painful thoughts and feelings that unconsciously underlie the projection:

- You made me do it. (I did it for reasons I don't understand.)

- You think I'm controlling? You're the one who's so controlling! (I feel like I'm losing control right now and it scares me.)

- Stop screaming at me! (I am so angry that I need to scream at you right now.)

- You never consider my needs. You're always thinking about yourself. (My needs are so overwhelming to me that I can't think about yours.)

- You're the one who left this marriage. You're not the person I fell in love with anymore. (I've shown you my real, flawed self and it scares me so much that I have to reject you before you reject me.)

- If you had taken my calls at work, I wouldn't have had to call you at three o'clock in the morning at home. (I need to talk with you so badly that I'll do anything to reach you.)

The other way a person with BPD can project onto you is to accuse you of having feelings and thoughts that really belong to them.

Ellen (BP)

When I accused my psychiatrist of hating me and telling me to "snap out of it," it was because I hated myself and I wished that I could snap out of it. My deepest fears and feelings of self-hatred were those I would project onto someone else because they were too frightening and disturbing to acknowledge within myself.

Here are more examples of BPs projecting their feelings:

- You hate me. (I hate myself.)

- You don't think I'm good enough. (I don't think I'm good enough.)

- When you said "it's cold outside," you really meant to criticize the way I dressed the children for school this morning. (I have such a low opinion of myself that I question my parenting abilities.)

- You spend so much time at work because you don't want to be around me. (I don't want to be around myself, so why would anyone else want to be around me?)

How can people with BPD deny that they are projecting when it is so obvious to everyone else? The answer is that shame and splitting may combine with projection and denial to make the "Tag, You're It" defense mechanism a more powerful way of denying ownership of unpleasant thoughts and feelings. How does this process, which can take place in only a few seconds, work? Some people with BPD feel shame—defective at the core of their being. Like every-one else, people with BPD have negative feelings, behaviors, and traits. But because of splitting—black-and-white thinking—they often deny any flaws, because that would make them less than perfect. And if they're not perfect, they're worthless. Projection then completes the picture.

The BPD logic goes like this: There seems to be a problem. It's not my fault. Therefore, the problem must be yours.

There's one more piece of "Tag, You're It" that's important for you to understand. After many games of tag, you may actually come to believe the accusations of the person with BPD. You may even start to behave in such as way as to make the borderline's accusations true. This is called projective identification.

Let's say that in order to cope with her own feelings of shame and worthlessness, Edith (BP) constantly tells her five-year-old daughter, Joanie, that she's a horrible person and she'll never have any friends. Eventually, Joanie concludes that she is a horrible person. Convinced that she is innately flawed, she avoids contact with other people. When they reach out to her, she rejects them before they reject her.

Projective identification brings to mind the political cliché, "If you repeat a lie often enough, people will believe you." It's also a bit like a self-fulfilling prophesy: Edith's prediction has come true: Joanie has no friends, not because she's a loathsome person, but because she feels like she is. Children are especially vulnerable to projective identification because they're still forming their own identities. In fact, on a subconscious level they may feel that they may lose their parent's love if they don't do whatever mom or dad seemingly expects of them—including act badly. Projective identification may also have more of an impact on those adults whose self-esteem is low and whose own identities are weak.

In our interview with Elyce Benham, M.S., she explained, "Even as adults, we give credence to what others tell us about ourselves. If we find ourselves in an important relationship with someone who constantly undermines what we know or believe about ourselves, we'll start to believe it." Here are some adult examples of projection and projective identification:

- Your BP girlfriend accuses you again and again of not loving her and wanting to abandon her. For years, you try to get her to see that this isn't true, but nothing works. Exhausted, you realize that the relationship is over and you need to get on with your life—thereby "abandoning" her.

- Your teenage borderline son accuses you of not loving him enough to let him live at home. When he comes home for a visit from the residential facility, he's physically violent.

He brings drug-dealing friends into the house and threatens his sister with a knife. You lie awake at night, vowing to never let him live at home again—thereby seeming to fulfill your son's accusation.

- Your borderline sister accuses you of "sucking up" to Mom and Dad, who always "loved you best." You spend more time with your folks because you enjoy being with them and they enjoy being with you. They love your sister, but rescuing her from her reckless behavior has put a terrible strain on them. As time goes on, you wonder if your parents do indeed prefer being with you.

Some adults who enter into relationships with borderlines feel brainwashed by the BP's accusations and criticisms. Says Benham: "The techniques of brainwashing are simple: isolate the victim, expose them to consistent messages, mix with sleep deprivation, add some form of abuse, get the person to doubt what they know and feel, keep them on their toes, wear them down, and stir well."

The person with BPD gains more from projective identification than a repository for their painful feelings. When the BP's negative predictions come true, the person with BPD may "benefit" in other ways. For one, the BP is now justified in their feelings. Edith feels upset because as Joanie grows up, she no longer seems to need her as much. Because of Joanie's projective identification, Edith has a more socially acceptable reason to be upset: Joanie is depressed and is a social misfit. Projective identification may also allow the BP to feel better when the roles are reversed. Edith no longer has to be "it" in the game of tag. Now Joanie can be "it." A side effect is that Joanie is now more emotionally dependent on Edith, since she lacks other people in her life. Edith feels less abandoned.

Finally, projective identification may allow the BP to feel more in control. If Edith feels that the world is against her, the fact that her daughter has problems may confirm her view of herself as victim—paradoxically allowing her to feel more in control. Her role as victim is validated by the "fact" that her daughter has problems. If this leads to attention and sympathy from others, the victim role may be reinforced. Your projective identification is caused unconsciously on the part of the person with BPD. The BP may feel extremely guilty and sorrowful when they realize how their actions have affected you.

Everything Is Your Fault

Continual blame and criticism is another defense mechanism that some people with BPD who act out use as a survival tool. The criticism may be based on a real issue that the person with BPD has exaggerated, or it may be a pure fantasy on the borderline's part. Family members we interviewed have been raged at and castigated for such things as carrying a grocery bag the wrong way, having bedsheets that weighed too heavily on the BP's toes, and reading a book the BP demanded they read. One exasperated non-BP said that if by some chance he didn't make an unforgivable error one day, his wife would probably rage at him for being too perfect. Another family member asked, "If a non-BP is standing out in the woods making a statement—and their borderline partner isn't around to hear it—is the non-BP still wrong?"

Like "Tag, You're It," this defense mechanism may really be about abandonment. The borderline's unconscious thinking process may go like this: "If there is just one thing wrong with me, then everything is wrong with me. If everything is wrong with me, I really am as defective as I feel. And when people find out I'm defective, they will abandon me. So there just can't be anything wrong with me—it has to be someone else's fault!" Often, what seems like angry, impulsive, and manipulative behavior is really a misguided attempt to elicit involvement and caring.

Patty (BP)

Sometimes I criticize my fiancé's every move, telling him that if he loved me he wouldn't do that. When I belittle and blame him I feel that I might be abandoned or embarrassed, or that he is somehow not showing me love. I feel fearful—so much so that my whole face changes. I am so upset that I yell and scream and knock over objects. My decision making is poor.

Just yesterday I threw my engagement ring in the garbage during my rage at him. Today, I realized I would be lost without him. He has to constantly prove his love to me. He cannot tell me he loves me enough. I expect him to cheat on me though I have no logical reason to. I look through his pockets and his bankbook. I surprise him at work to make sure he's there. When I find things are fine, I feel very reassured and embarrassed and swear to myself I won't ever feel that way again. But I always do.

If you object to the criticism or try to defend yourself, your loved one may accuse you of being defensive, too sensitive, or unable to accept constructive criticism. Since their very survival seems to be at stake, they may defend themselves with the ferociousness of a mother bear protecting her cubs.

When the crisis has passed and the person with BPD seems to have won, they may act surprised that you're still upset. From their point of view, their response has prevented you from seeing their hollow inner core. They may think that this should draw you closer to them or at least prevent you from withdrawing. They may also have been dissociating, which would make them genuinely remember things differently.

You, of course, feel worse. Only now, you also feel baffled because the person with BPD doesn't seem to understand the impact of what they've done. You may also feel frustrated because they never seem to accept responsibility for their own behavior. This cycle happens again and again.

When Blaming Becomes Verbal Abuse

When the person with BPD lashes out at you, they're consumed with their own needs. They may also be displacing rage and anger onto you that are the result of abuse they suffered in the past. If they seem controlling, they may be trying to gain control over their own life—not yours.

And even when they seem to have won an argument, they've really lost. For one thing, they've damaged their relationship with you—someone they're terrified will leave them. When things calm down, the person with BPD may feel ashamed of the way they behaved toward you. This adds to the downward spiral of shame, guilt, and low self-esteem. They may apologize and beg for your forgiveness, then deny that they ever admitted that their behavior was out of line.

But even though their behavior is not really about you, excessive criticizing and blaming can cross the line and become verbal abuse. Beverly Engel (1990) writes:

> Emotional abuse is any behavior that is designed to control another person through the use of fear, humiliation, and verbal or physical assaults. It can include verbal abuse and constant criticism to more subtle tactics like intimidation, manipulation, and refusal to ever be pleased.
>
> Emotional abuse is like brainwashing in that it systematically wears away at the victim's self-confidence,

sense of self-worth, trust in her perceptions, and self-concept. Whether it be by constant berating and belittling, by intimidation, or under the guise of "guidance" or teaching, the results are similar. Eventually, the recipient loses all sense of self and all remnants of personal value.

Engel categorizes verbal abuse in several ways. Some of these definitions read like the criteria for BPD from the *DSM-IV* although Engel's book never refers to the disorder. As you read, keep in mind that we are not discussing the intentions of the person with BPD. We are talking about the effects of their coping strategies on you.

Domination: The person resorts to threats to get their own way.

Verbal Assaults: This includes reprimanding, humiliating, criticizing, name calling, screaming, threatening, excessive blaming, and using sarcasm in a cutting way. It also involves exaggerating your faults and making fun of you in front of others. Over time, this type of abuse erodes your sense of self-confidence and self-worth.

Abusive Expectations: The other person makes unreasonable demands and expects that you will be their first priority—no matter what. This includes denouncing your needs for attention and support.

Unpredictable Responses: This includes drastic mood changes or sudden emotional outbursts. Living with someone like this is extremely anxiety provoking. You may feel frightened, unsettled, and off balance. This hypervigilance can even lead to physical distress.

Gaslighting: This involves the other person denying your perceptions of events and conversations.

Constant Chaos: The BP may deliberately start arguments and is in constant conflict with others. They also may be addicted to drama, since it creates excitement. (Many non-BPs also may be addicted to drama.)

BPD Behavioral Patterns

No-Win Situations

Most family members we've interviewed say they feel like the person with BPD puts them in no-win situations.

Jack (non-BP)

If I asked her about her unhappiness, I was told I was too sensitive and paranoid. If I ignored the unhappiness, I was told I didn't care about her.

If I praised her, she thought I was up to something. If I criticized her, I was trying to hurt her.

If I spent time talking to her four-year-old, she wanted to know what I was asking him. If I played a simple game with him, I was criticized if I won.

If I wanted to have sex, she wanted it to be her idea—later. If I didn't want to have sex, I was a homosexual.

If I spent time alone, I was "up to something." If I spent too much time with her, I was needy.

If I wasn't thirty minutes early, I was late. If she wasn't ready and I sat down to read, I was rushing her.

Some of the people with BPD we've interviewed gave some possible reasons for this behavior. Paige (BP) suggested that it may be a variation of "Everything Is Your Fault," saying, "Putting other people in no-win situations allows me to self-validate, when validation has been in short supply in my life. So maybe it's a way to grab something I've felt I haven't gotten before, even though it alien-ates others and harms me in the long run."

Another possible explanation for the creation of no-win situations is that the person with BPD may be dissociating. Someone who is dissociating or under a great deal of emotional stress may not remember what they have said or done previously. Many people with BPD we interviewed had no memory of putting their friends and family members in no-win situations—even though the non-BPs we interviewed could cite many examples.

The person with BPD may be inconsistent, thus causing seemingly no-win situations, because they have an inconsistent sense of self. In order to state their preferences, a person must be able to clearly identify their feelings and beliefs. Only then can they communicate these to others. But as you know, some people with BPD have an inconsistent sense of self. When the BP tells you what they want, it probably is what they want—at that moment. Later, they may want something else. But they may not be able to admit to you—or to themselves—that they're being inconsistent because of shame and splitting. They may even try to portray you as the one who's hopelessly mixed up.

Fear of Abandonment, Fear of Engulfment

Sometimes it may seem as if the BP is wanting you to "keep your distance a little closer." This impossible request is not a defense mechanism like "Tag, You're It" and "Everything Is Your Fault." Rather, it is a behavior pattern that results from two primary and conflicting fears: the fear of being abandoned and the fear of being engulfed or controlled by others.

As infants, all people experience fear of abandonment. Babies have two primary needs: to feel safe and secure and to develop a sense of trust in their caregivers. When they cry, they need to know that someone will respond with love, food, or a diaper change. When mommy or daddy leave, they need to know that a parent will return.

As people grow up, they balance their dependency needs with another objective: becoming independent and venturing away from the protective womb of the family. You can see this in the two-year-old who proudly runs on the playground, falls, and comes crying to mommy and daddy. As time goes by, the need to run back to parents diminishes and the need to distinguish a separate identity becomes more important. The teen years are the most distinct time of testing, as adolescents try out new adult roles under the steadily decreasing guidance of school and family. Ideally, adulthood brings an independence that is not dominated by fears of abandonment or engulfment.

People with BPD are still struggling daily with the issues of engulfment and abandonment. Torn between the urge to merge and the desire for independence, they may feel—and look—like a walking contradiction. Their actions may not make sense because half the time they seek closeness and nurturing and the rest of the time they seem compelled to drive you away.

Here's what's happening: Borderlines may begin to feel engulfed or afraid of losing control when people get too close to them. They don't know how to set healthy personal limits, and genuine intimacy may make them feel vulnerable. They may be afraid you might see the "real" them, be repulsed, and leave them. So they begin to distance themselves to avoid feeling vulnerable or controlled. They may pick a fight with you, "forget" to do something important, or do something dramatic or explosive. But then the distance makes them feel alone. Feelings of emptiness worsen and their fear of abandonment become stronger. So they make frantic efforts to get close again and the cycle repeats.

During an argument, it might take your loved one only seconds to bounce from abandonment to engulfment. Or the cycle might take days, weeks, months, or years. External events often play a part; for example, going off to college could easily trigger abandonment fears in an adolescent borderline, while an ill, elderly borderline parent moving in with an adult child might feel engulfed. In addition, as the level of intimacy rises, so does the severity of the abandonment/engulfment issues, which results in more dramatic behaviors. This is one reason why people who don't know a borderline as well as you do may not believe your accounts of their behavior.

Testing Your Love

The back and forth dance of "keep your distance a little closer" is incredibly frustrating for friends and family.

Beth (non-BP)

The harder I try to placate the wild beast inside my borderline husband, the fiercer his reaction becomes; the moment I give up and start to walk away, he turns into a clinging vine. It's like that old burlesque routine of the clown trying to pick up his hat. Every time he bends to grab it, he accidentally kicks it further away. Finally, he gives up in disgust. And as he walks away, the wind blows his hat after him!

Herein lies yet another irony about BPD: from your point of view, the person with BPD is in control. They're the choreographer of the abandonment/engulfment dance and you're just being whirled around, getting progressively dizzier and dizzier. But from their point of view, you're the one with all the power.

They can't predict how you're going to react to their behavior. Will you keep moving to the music? Will this be the time you give up and go home—for good? Not knowing may make them feel unsafe and insecure. (And keep in mind that they feel unsafe and insecure already.)

Remember, to people with BPD, everything is all or nothing. Once the dance stops, it stops forever. And once you're gone, they cease to exist because they have no identity of their own. Feeling helpless in the face of both their own emotions and your unpredictable reactions, they may try to grab control in the only way they know how: by acting out in ways that, to you, feel intensely manipulative. They may threaten suicide. Then, once you've capitulated, the music starts and the dance begins anew.

Some people with BPD may also seek to gain control of the dance by constantly testing you to see how much you really care about them. The logic goes like this: If you really love them, you should be willing to put aside all your own desires and concentrate on filling the black hole of need inside them.

For example, if you and the other person have agreed to meet at a certain time and place, they may show up an hour late. If you "fail" the test by becoming irritated, or giving up and going home, the person with BPD may feel that their unworthiness has been confirmed. This makes the world more predictable, and therefore safer.

If you "pass" the test by tolerating their actions, they may escalate their behavior (perhaps by showing up many hours late next time) until you finally blow up in anger. Then *you* become the bad guy and they become the helpless victim.

You may be wondering, "What kind of test is this? No matter what happens, we both fail!" You're right. It doesn't make any sense in your world. But it does in the borderline world.

A Childlike World View

Many adult borderlines—especially those with young children—have noticed that their view of the world can be very child-like. Splitting, object constancy problems, abandonment/engulfment issues, identity issues, narcissistic demands, seeming lack of empathy, and seeming manipulation are all borderline thinking patterns that mimic developmental stages in children.

Laura (BP)

When my two-year-old wants something, she wants it now, not tomorrow. When I am shopping I am like that. I can't tell myself no, so I buy it, even though I'm in debt.

To a child, the most important thing is security and safety. Me, too. For me, safety means being what others want me to be so they won't reject me. The inside stays hidden—even to me. But under all the civilness and politeness hides an angry, frightened toddler.

My husband wants the damaged little girl inside me to set

priorities by saying, "Yes, I'm angry, but when I talk to you I'm going to try to be reasonable." You wouldn't ask that from a real two-year-old, so don't ask that from me, either. It's not that I don't want to. I just can't.

Some people with BPD feel patronized or insulted when people point out these similarities.

Janet (BP)

I definitely feel like a child, I just don't want to admit it! People say to me, "Grow up." They accuse me of being a crybaby and of having temper tantrums. Do they think I want to act this way? Do they think it's fun to have your emotions rule you? Do they really believe I can mature twenty years in a few minutes?

Heidi (BP)

I felt insulted when I first read the comparisons between children and people with BPD. But then again, my family never had any respect for children. It was an inferior thing to be.

In therapy, however, I learned that there is nothing shameful about being childlike. Children are cherished. And when people we love understand the way we are, they can take our actions less personally and try to forgive us instead of condemn us.

The borderline world differs markedly from your own in several ways. People with BPD may unconsciously revise facts in order to justify their feelings. Some people with BPD use defense mechanisms to manage their painful feelings. In addition, people with BPD may feel alternatively abandoned and engulfed, which may cause them to intermittently change their behavior 180 degrees. Finally, in many ways, some people with BPD see the world through the eyes of a child. But they have the ability to affect the world in more serious, adult ways.

In chapter 4, we'll explain the effects of BPD behavior on you.

4

Living in a Pressure Cooker: How BPD Behavior Affects Non-BPs

For years I believed with an open heart
Now I'm just lookin' for the easy part.

> —Carrie Newcomer, "Streamline,"
> from *An Angel at My Shoulder*

Living with a BP is like living in a pressure cooker with thin walls and a faulty safety valve.

Living with a BP is like living in a perpetual oxymoron. It's a seemingly endless host of contradictions.

I feel like I've been through the spin cycle on a washing machine. The world is whirling around and I have no idea which way is up, down, or sideways.

> —From the non-BP list

Filled with self-loathing, people with BPD may accuse others of hating them. Terrified of being abandoned, they can become so critical and easily enraged that people eventually want to leave them. Then, unable to confront the cause of their pain because it would make them feel so bad about themselves, people with BPD may blame others and put themselves in the role of victims.

BPD is not really infectious. It is not like the measles. But people who are exposed to these behaviors can unwittingly become an integral part of the disorder. Friends, partners, and family members usually take these behaviors personally and feel trapped in a toxic cycle of guilt, self-blame, depression, rage, denial, isolation, and confusion. They try to cope in ways that do not work in the long term or even make the situation worse. Meanwhile, the borderline's unhealthy behaviors are reinforced because the non-BP accepts responsibility for the feelings and actions that really belong to the borderline.

In this chapter, we'll discuss some common ways non-BPs react to BPD behavior. Then we will provide you with some questions to help you determine how BPD behavior might be affecting you personally.

Common Non-BP Thinking

These beliefs do not reflect the thinking of every person with a borderline in their life. You must judge what is pertinent in your individual circumstances.

- I am responsible for all the problems in this relationship. (Actually, each person is responsible for 50 percent of the relationship.)

- The actions of the person with BPD are all about me. (The BP's actions may have nothing to do with you.)

- It's my responsibility to solve this person's problems, and if I don't do it no one else will. (Each of us must take the lead in solving our own problems. And by trying to take charge of the borderline's life, you may be giving them the message that they can't take care of themselves.)

- If I can convince the person with BPD that I am right, these problems will disappear. (BPD is a serious disorder that profoundly affects the way people think, feel, and behave. You can't talk someone out of it no matter how persuasive you are.)

- If I can prove that their accusations are false, they will trust me again. (Lack of trust is a hallmark of BPD. It has nothing to do with your behavior; it has to do with the way people with BPD view the world.)

- If you really love someone, you should take their physical or emotional abuse. (If you love yourself, you won't let people abuse you.)

- This person can't help having BPD, so I should not hold them accountable for their behavior. (The borderline in your life didn't ask to have BPD, it's true. But with help they can learn to control their behavior toward others and may already know how to do so under certain circumstances.)

- Setting personal limits hurts the person with BPD and is wrong. (Setting personal limits helps both you and the BP.)

- When I try to do something to help my situation and it doesn't work, I should keep trying the exact same thing until it does work. (If you examine your behavior, you may realize that you've behaved as if you believe this. A better plan is learning from your mistakes and trying something new.)

- No matter what the BP does, I should offer them my love, understanding, support, and unconditional acceptance. (There is a big difference between loving, supporting, and accepting the person and loving, supporting, and accepting their behavior. In fact, if you support and accept the behavior you may be encouraging it to continue.)

- If I ignore the warning signs, everything will be all right. (You probably know the answer to this one already. BPD behavior won't go away on its own.)

Non-BP Grief Over Borderline Behavior

Non-BPs being devalued by someone with BPD cherish clear and powerful memories of the times when the borderline loved them unconditionally and thought they could do no wrong. Some family members say they feel like the person who loved them has died and that someone they do not know has taken over the BP's body. One non-BP said, "Help! The aliens have taken over my wife's body!" Another non-BP said, "If I had cancer, at least I would die just once. This emotional abuse ensures that I die many, many times and that I will always live on the edge, waiting for the next senseless bomb."

Elisabeth Kübler-Ross (1975) outlined five stages of grief, which are appropriate for people who care about someone with BPD. We have adapted these stages to directly discuss BPD issues.

Denial

Non-BPs make excuses for the BP's behavior or refuse to believe that their behavior is unusual. The more isolated the non-BP, the greater the chances they will be in denial. This is because without outside input, non-BPs lose their sense of perspective about what is normal. People with BPD can be skillful at convincing others that their behavior is the non-BP's fault. This helps keep non-BPs in a continual state of denial.

Anger

Some non-BPs respond to angry attacks by fighting back. At first, this can help the non-BP deflect blame, criticism, and accusations. But these arguments have no real resolution and are repeated again and again. They may escalate, leading to violence on the part of either person.

Other non-BPs maintain that anger is an inappropriate response to borderline behavior. Some say, "You wouldn't get mad at someone for having diabetes—why would you be angry when they have BPD?" People who feel guilty about anger and other negative emotions may then channel them into more "acceptable," but potentially more harmful, emotions such as depression.

Feelings don't have IQs. They just are. Sadness, anger, guilt, confusion, hostility, annoyance, frustration—all are normal, and to be expected by people faced with borderline behavior. This is true no matter what your relationship is to the person with BPD. This doesn't mean that you should respond to the BP with anger. But it does mean that you need a safe place to vent all your emotions and feel accepted, not judged.

Bargaining

When applied to borderline/non-borderline relationships, this stage is characterized by the non-BP making concessions in order to bring back the "normal" behavior of the person they love. The thinking goes, "If I do what this person wants, I will get what I need in this relationship." We all make compromises in relationships. But the sacrifices that people make in order to satisfy the borderlines they care about can be very costly. Furthermore, the concessions are never enough. Before long, more proof of love is needed and another bargain must be struck.

Depression

Depression sets in when non-BPs realize the true cost of the bargains they've made: loss of friends, family, self-respect, hobbies, etc. The person with BPD hasn't changed. But the non-BP has.

Sarah (non-BP)

For three years he told me the problem was me—that my shortcomings ruined everyhing. And I believed him. I turned my back on some of my good friends because he didn't like them. I rushed home after work because he said he needed me. I constantly watched the way I said things, so he didn't take them as an insult. Then we had a big fight, and now I'm lonely and depressed because I don't have anybody else to turn to.

Dreams die very hard. The child of a borderline parent may spend decades trying to win their love. When nothing ever seems good enough, it may take years for them to mourn the loss of unconditional parental love they never really had.

Fran (non-BP)

I spent many years grieving for my borderline son when I realized the dreams I had for him might never come true. I began mourning in earnest when my son's therapist asked me what I would do if my son needed to live in a residential facility for the rest of his life. I just started sobbing. The therapist explained that the child I thought I had had died, along with the future I had pictured for him. But when I was done grieving, I would have a new child, and I would have new aspirations for him.

Acceptance

Acceptance comes when non-BPs integrate the "good" and "bad" aspects of the borderlines they care about and realize that the BPs are not one or the other, but both. Non-BPs in this stage have learned to accept responsibility for their own choices and hold other people accountable for their choices as well. Each can then make their own decisions about the relationship with a clearer understanding of themselves and the person with BPD.

Non-BP Responses to Borderline Behavior

Borderline behavior causes many reactions in non-BPs. Some of the more common responses are addressed in this section.

Bewilderment

Phil (non-BP)

At first everything looks and sounds as normal as apple pie. Then, unexpectedly, strange twists and reversals of reality occur; off-kilter shifts in the time-space continuum hurl me onto the floor. Suddenly, I realize I've crossed into the Borderline Zone!

Loss of Self-Esteem

Beverly Engel (1990) describes the effect of emotional abuse on self-esteem:

> Emotional abuse cuts to the very core of a person, creating scars that may be longer-lasting than physical ones. With emotional abuse, the insults, insinuations, criticism, and accusations slowly eat away at the victim's self-esteem until she is incapable of judging the situation realistically. She has become so beaten down emotionally that she blames herself for the abuse. Emotional abuse victims can become so convinced that they are worthless that they believe that no one else could want them. They stay in abusive situations because they believe they have nowhere else to go. Their ultimate fear is being all alone.

Feeling Trapped and Helpless

The borderline's behaviors cause a great deal of anguish, but leaving seems impossible or improbable. Nothing the non-BP does seems to have any lasting positive effect. Non-BPs may feel trapped in the relationship because they either feel overly responsible for the safety of the BP or they feel overly guilty for perhaps "causing" the BP to feel and behave the way they do. The BP's threat of suicide or threat to harm others can, at times, paralyze the non-BP and make them feel as if leaving the relationship is too risky.

Withdrawal

The non-BP may leave the situation, either emotionally or physically. This could include working long hours, remaining silent for fear of saying something wrong, or terminating the relationship. This may result in the person with BPD feeling abandoned and acting out more intensely. Also, the non-BP may leave children alone with the BP for longer periods of time. If the BP acts abusively toward the children, the non-BP isn't there to try to protect them.

Guilt and Shame

Over time accusations can have a brainwashing effect. Non-BPs may come to believe that they are the source of all the problems. This is extremely damaging when applied to children, who look upon parents as God-like figures, and who do not have the capacity to question an adult borderline's accusations or assumptions.

Parents of people with BPD are also vulnerable to this. They believe that they have been horrible parents when they simply made the same mistakes that most parents make. Some parents we interviewed berate themselves endlessly, putting their mistakes under a microscope in an effort to figure out what they did to cause their children's disorder. When they can't find the "smoking gun," they conclude that the problem must be biological. But that doesn't take them off the hook either, since they then feel responsible for the child's "flawed" biological heritage (unless the child was adopted).

Adopting Unhealthy Habits

This includes excessive drinking, overeating, substance abuse, and so on. These unhealthy habits are typical ways many people, not just non-BPs, try to cope with stress. Initially, drinking, overeating, and substance abuse soothe anxiety and stress. As these coping strategies become more habitual and ingrained, the non-BP will begin to experience the negative consequences of the habit, which are then mixed in with the original stressors, compounding the situation.

Isolation

The unpredictable behavior and moodiness of people with BPD can make friendships difficult. Making excuses or covering up the borderline's behavior can be so emotionally exhausting that some people find it's not worth the effort to sustain friendships. Many non-BPs say that friends often suggest solutions that are simplistic or unacceptable, which leaves the non-BPs feeling misunderstood. Some say they lose friendships because their friends disbelieve them or grow tired of hearing about their struggles.

Frequently, non-BPs become isolated because the BPs in their lives insist that they cut off their ties with others. Too often, the non-BP complies. Once a non-BP becomes more isolated, several things can happen. They may become more emotionally dependent on the BP. Because they are out of touch with the real world, the outrageousness of BPD behavior may seem normal, once there is nothing to compare it to. Friends can no longer observe the relationship and talk to the non-BP about unhealthy components of the relationship. With things bottled up inside, the non-BP is left to deal with their problems with the BP on their own.

Hypervigilance and Physical Illnesses

It is very stressful to be around someone who may severely berate you at any moment with no visible provocation. In an attempt to gain some control over what appears to be very unpredictable BP behaviors, non-BPs often find themselves "on alert" to forecast or predict the occurrence of the distressing behaviors of the BP. If one can forecast or predict when these behaviors will occur, then the non-BP can prepare to either defend themselves or avoid being overrun by the rage and acting out. However, being on alert requires a heightened sense of arousal both physically and psychologically that, over time, can wear down the body's natural defenses against stress. As a result, physical symptoms of stress begin to manifest in the form of headaches, ulcers, high blood pressure, and other illnesses.

Adoption of BPD-like Thoughts and Feelings

The moodiness and "matching" of emotions that non-BPs experience is the result of their inability to identify or utilize more effective strategies to separate, protect, and nurture themselves in the face of these intense emotions and stress. Non-BPs often begin to see things in black and white and see all-or-nothing solutions to problems. Moodiness is also extremely common in non-BPs, since they're often in a good mood when the borderline is up and a bad mood when the BP is down. In a way, the person with BPD takes the non-BP with them on the roller-coaster ride that is their life. If this happens to you, you may wish to use this experience to glimpse what it's like to actually have BPD.

Codependence

The non-BP often performs valiant and heroic acts of kindness, no matter what the price to themselves. In an effort to help the person they love, they swallow their anger, ignore their own needs, accept behavior that most people would find intolerable, and forgive the same transgressions again and again. This is a common trap for non-BPs—especially if the borderline had an unhappy childhood and the non-BP is trying to make up for it.

Many non-BPs assume that by subordinating their own needs for the sake of the BP (or simply for the sake of avoiding a fight), they are helping. While the non-BP's motives are commendable, this actually enables, or reinforces, inappropriate behavior in the person with BPD. Borderlines learn that their actions will have few negative consequences; therefore, they have no motivation to change.

Also, continuing to put up with BPD behavior rarely makes the BP really happy. And even if the non-BP endures this behavior, the BP may become isolated because other people won't stand for it. Furthermore, how long will the non-BP be able to keep this up? One family member who smoothed things over for years in order to make up for his borderline wife's terrible childhood said,

"I was concentrating on not abandoning her, no matter what she did. One day, I realized that instead, I had abandoned myself."

Dean (non-BP)

I felt like such a failure in this relationship. I thought that if I could just persuade my wife to get the help she needed, everything would be all right.

Despite the abuse, I felt like I couldn't leave. How could I abandon someone who'd already suffered so many misfortunes in life? I thought that if I just tried a little harder, I could fix her and make up for all the abuse she suffered when she was a kid. This was confirmed to me once when I did try to leave. I'll never forget the look on her face as she told me with big sad eyes that she was happy I came back. "Why are you glad?" I asked. She responded, "Because who else is going to make my life better?"

I decided to see a counselor, and told the whole story to him over many months. One day he said to me, "Aren't you being a bit pompous? Who do you think you are, God? Well, you're not God. You are not responsible. And you just can't fix this. Your job is to accept that fact. Live with it. And make the decisions you have to make to live your life."

Effects on the Relationship

Borderline behaviors such as verbal abuse, perceived manipulation, and defense mechanisms often shatter trust and intimacy. They make the relationship unsafe for the non-BP, who can no longer trust that their deep feelings and innermost thoughts will be treated with love, concern, and care.

Susan Forward and Donna Frazier (1997) explain that targets of emotional blackmail may become very guarded about certain subjects and stop sharing major parts of their lives, such as embarrassing things they've done, frightened or insecure feelings, hopes for the future, and anything that shows that they're changing and evolving.

What's left when we must consistently walk on eggs with someone? Superficial small talk, strained silences, lots of tension. When safety and intimacy are gone from a relationship, we get used to acting. We pretend that we're happy when we're not. We say that everything is fine when it isn't. What used to be a graceful dance of caring and closeness becomes a masked ball in which the people involved are hiding more and more of their true selves.

Is This Normal?

It can be very hard to determine what kind of behavior is normal and what isn't. The following questions may help. The more "yes" answers you give, the more we recommend that you take a hard look at how the behavior of the BP in your life might be affecting you.

- Do people in healthy, happy relationships tell you that they don't understand why you are still putting up with the BP's behavior? Do you try to avoid contact with these people?

- Do you feel the need to cover up some of the BP's behavior? Have you betrayed other people or told lies to protect the BP or your relationship with them?

- Are you becoming isolated?

- Does the thought of spending time with the BP give you unpleasant physical sensations? Do you have other possibly stress-related ailments?

- Has the BP ever expressed their anger at you by attempting to cause you legal, social, or financial difficulties? Has this happened more than once?

- Are you becoming clinically depressed? Signs of depression include: becoming less interested in normal activities, taking less pleasure in life, gaining or losing weight, having sleep difficulties, thinking of suicide, having feelings of worthlessness, feeling tired all the time, and having trouble concentrating.

- Have you considered suicide? Do you think that friends and loved ones would be better off without you? (If yes, seek help immediately.)

- Have you acted in ways that go against your fundamental values and beliefs as a result of your relationship with the borderline in your life? Are you no longer able to take a stand for what you believe in?

- Are you concerned about the effects of this person's behavior on children? Have you ever interceded to prevent abuse from occurring?

- Have you or the BP ever put each other in physical danger or in a situation where physical danger was possible or likely?

- Are you making decisions mainly out of fear, obligation, and guilt?

- Does your relationship with the BP seem to be more about power and control than kindness and caring?

Now that we have discussed the ABCs of BPD, we will give you some steps in part 2 for getting off the emotional roller coaster and taking charge of your life. You can apply these steps even if the person with BPD does not change.

You will need to complete certain steps in part 2 before you can begin others. As an example, you must determine your personal limits before you can explain them to anyone else. Other steps are part of a lifelong journey and need to be practiced on an ongoing basis—for example, depersonalizing the BP's actions, taking good care of yourself, and understanding yourself and your own behavior.

As you read, it is important to keep in mind that we are discussing how to cope with borderline behavior—not the borderline person themselves.

Jamie (BP)

It's important that friends and family members of people with BPD realize that we are much more than our behavior. We are not "things" that have to be "dealt with" or "handled," as in "how do you handle a borderline?" People should put themselves in our shoes and try to feel empathy, because borderline behavior and feelings are just bizarre exaggerations of normal behavior and feelings.

PART 2

TAKING BACK CONTROL OF YOUR LIFE

5

Making Changes Within Yourself

Denying our problems is a coping mechanism that helps us borderlines keep the pain and fear under our control. The larger the fear, the larger the denial will be. Please, please, please, don't try to rip away the denial from borderlines who aren't ready to face the blackness inside. It may be all that's keeping them alive.

> —A BP's words to the non-BP Internet support group

No one can make you feel inferior without your consent.

> —Eleanor Roosevelt

Lately all I've been praying for is some kind of grace
To accept what I cannot change as I meet it face to face
And conjure up some kind of courage as I'm walkin' lightly here
Taking things for what they are and not what they appear to be.

> —Carrie Newcomer, "Some Kind of Grace," from *Visions and Dreams*

You Can't Make the BP Seek Treatment

Here is the good news: You have a right to all of your opinions, thoughts, and feelings. Good or bad, right or wrong, they are part of you. They make you who you are. And here is the bad news: Everyone else has a right to their opinions, thoughts, and feelings, too. You may not agree with everyone else, and they may not agree with you. But that is okay. It is not your job to convince everyone else to see things your way.

It can be frustrating and heartbreaking to watch someone you love act in ways that hurt themselves and others. But no matter what you do, you can't control anyone else's behavior. Moreover, it's not your job—unless, of course, the person with BPD in your life is your minor child. Even then, you can only influence the child's behavior—not control it. Your job is to know who you are, to act according to your own values and beliefs, and to communicate what you need and want to the people in your life. You can always encourage people to do what you want through subtle or blatant rewards and punishments. But it is still their decision how to act.

Reasons for a BP's Denial

It may be obvious to you that the person in your life with BPD needs help. But it may not be obvious to them. For people with BPD, admitting that anything about them is less than perfect, let alone acknowledging that they may have a personality disorder, can send them into a spiral of shame and self-doubt.

Imagine feeling empty, virtually without a self. Now think about admitting that what little self you can recognize has something wrong with it. To many people with BPD, this is like ceasing to exist—a terrifying feeling for anyone.

To avoid this, people with BPD may employ a powerful and common defense mechanism: denial. They may maintain that nothing is wrong with them, despite clear evidence to the contrary. They would rather lose things very important to them—jobs, friends, and family—than lose themselves. (Once you understand this, you will truly appreciate the courage of people with BPD who do seek help.)

Look at it another way. Think about something you accomplished that seemed insurmountable. Getting a college degree, perhaps, or losing thirty pounds. Try to remember how your intense desire to achieve this goal made it all possible. Now, imagine that your intense need was to *avoid* this goal. How likely is it that someone else can make you get that degree or lose that weight?

In much the same way, people with BPD may seek to avoid confronting problems other people want them to face. They may ask for help or try to alter their behavior—but not on your schedule. If they change, it will be in their own time and in their own way. In fact, it could be detrimental to force someone to admit having problems before they're ready to do so.

Lynn (BP)

Ignoring and denying my problems was a coping mechanism that enabled me to keep the fear and pain under control. If you care about someone with BPD, don't underestimate their pain. Don't under- estimate their fear. The more we fear, the more we deny.

Nichelle (BP)

I can see what kind of hell living with a BP could be. I can understand how much non-BPs would want to nudge that person, do anything humanly possible to get that person to change. After all, it would help the relationship and make life less painful for the borderline. But denial is a funny thing. What some of us might see as "the bottom" can be denied repeatedly—ad infinitum in some cases.

So, the BP has destroyed a relationship? She moves on to the next one and the next one after that and so on and so forth. A BP loses a job over his behavior? He blames the boss and moves on to the next one, then the next. She loses custody of her children? It's the damned court system.

The fear of change and the fear of the unknown are quite compelling. Thus, denial can be extremely powerful. And in the case of the borderline, the fears are so vast, so encompassing, and so overwhelming that denial can be absolute.

When Will the BP Seek Help?

What motivates people with BPD to seek help? In general, people alter their behavior when they believe that the benefits of doing so outweigh the obstacles to change. People with BPD are the same as everyone else in this regard.

The specific catalysts for change, however, vary greatly. For some people, the unbearable emotional turmoil of living with BPD is worse than the fear of change. For others, it is realizing how their behavior is affecting their children. Some face their demons after losing someone important to them because of their behavior.

Laura (BP)

Until I really understood personal responsibility, I believed that everything that happened to me was someone else's fault. While I was pushing the limits of appropriateness at every turn, I felt annihilated when people tried to convince me that I had control over my crazy behavior. I resisted the thought and became enraged.

Eventually, in therapy, I realized that I hated and judged other people because that's how I felt about myself. If I couldn't respect myself, I couldn't respect others. Consequently, it was easy to devalue them and to hit out at them. By searching for the middle ground and accepting responsibility, I was able to greatly decrease a lot of imagined rejection, abandonment, and fears.

Diane (BP)

As a former borderline, I believe that there does have to be some kind of shock or jolt that serves as a catalyst for change. At various times in my life, I was forced into therapy. I didn't have a sincere desire to change; I just didn't want to lose something. And that just isn't enough.

My own shock was the look in my four-year-old son's eyes when I lost it and began smacking him until his thighs and face were red. He hadn't done anything wrong. I was beating him for being a kid when I didn't feel like being a mother. Echoes of my past. And when he initially started bawling with all his might, it fed my frenzy and made me angrier. I hit him harder and used my dad's old phrase, "I'll give you something to cry about."

Ultimately, he stopped crying. He was terrified of what I might do next. And in his eyes, opened wide in a look of utter terror, I saw the reflections of my own eyes from years ago—reflections I had spent a lifetime running away from.

That was my shock. I couldn't blame it on anyone else. I couldn't blame it on a university administration that was too parochial and authoritative. I couldn't blame it on a husband who wasn't making enough money, or because he wasn't this-or-that-or-the-other-thing enough for me. I couldn't blame it on a power-hungry boss, bitchy neighbors, or any of the scores of people I was convinced had it out for me. Looking in my son's helpless and horrified eyes, I could see it was me. Completely me. And I knew that I had to change things or die. Because I could no longer live with the person I had become.

What You Can Do

There is nothing wrong with wanting to change the person with BPD in your life. You may be right: they might be a lot happier and your relationship with them might improve if they sought help for their BPD. But in order for you to get off the emotional roller coaster, you will have to give up the fantasy that you (and only you) can or should change someone else. When you let go of this belief, you will be able to claim the power that is truly yours: the power to change yourself.

The example of a lighthouse, which someone on the Internet sent to us, illuminates the difference between providing someone with support and taking responsibility for their recovery.

Consider a lighthouse. It stands on the shore with its beckoning light, guiding ships safely into the harbor. The lighthouse can't uproot itself, wade out into the water, grab the ship by the stern and say, "Listen, you fool! If you stay on this path you may break up on the rocks!"

No. The ship has some responsibility for its own destiny. It can choose to be guided by the lighthouse. Or, it can go its own way. The lighthouse is not responsible for the ship's decisions. All it can do is be the best lighthouse it knows how to be.

Stop Taking All the Borderline's Actions Personally

Borderlines see the world in black and white. More than that, they assume everyone else sees things the same way. In the face of this, people who have a consistent sense of their own self-worth have an easier time maintaining their own sense of reality. No matter how the BP feels about them at any given moment, these non-BPs can be happy and secure in the knowledge that they're neither a goddess or a demon. Most people, however, need some guidance in staying clear and focused when the BP splits.

Alternate Interpretations

Non-BPs don't usually ask for help when the BPs in their lives sing their praises. But it's important to remember that the up side of splitting (idealization) also has its down side (devaluation). This doesn't mean that you should discount the good things the BP is saying—by all means, enjoy them. But be careful about positive overstatements and exaggerations that are hard to live up to. Also, be cautious about declarations of love and commitment that come too soon, for they may be based on the BP's image of you rather than the real you. It's important to keep your interpretation of things in mind, since the BP's may often be too negative or too idealized.

Sometimes it's not the actual event but the borderline's interpretation of that event that prompts splitting. Consider an emergency department physician who treats a child who has been in a very bad car accident. They try to save the child's life, but she was already near death when the paramedics brought her in. Clearly, there is nothing they could have done. The doctor goes to the waiting room and tells the girl's parents that the child has died. The father does not take it well.

"You incompetent fool!" he shouts. "She wasn't badly hurt at all! You should have been able to save her. If our family doctor had been treating her, she would have survived. I'm going to report you to the authorities!"

Although no one likes to be threatened, most physicians would realize that the trauma and shock of his daughter's death could cause the father to lash out and blame them. They probably wouldn't take his words personally because they have comforted dozens of grieving relatives and they know that this type of reaction is not uncommon. In other words, they would not take responsibility for the father's feelings. They would realize that his reaction had everything to do with the situation and little to do with them.

In this example, the incident that caused the father's response is external, obvious, and dramatic. A child died. With BPD, the cause of an argument is not necessarily the actual event but the borderline's interpretation of that event. As you probably know, you and the person with BPD may come to very different conclusions about what was said and done. Following are two such examples:

Robert (non-BP) says:	I have to work late. I'm really sorry, but I'm going to have to cancel our plans.
Kathryn (BP) hears:	I don't want to go out with you this evening because I don't love you anymore. I never want to see you again.

Kathryn says (in either an angry or tearful tone of voice):	How could you! You never loved me! I hate you!
Tom says:	I'm so proud of my daughter! Yesterday she hit a home run and won the game. Let's go to a movie tonight to celebrate.
Roxann hears:	I love my daughter more than you. She is talented and you are not. From now on, I'm going to give all my love and attention to her and ignore you.
Roxann thinks:	He realizes that I'm flawed and defective. So now he's going to leave me. But no, I'm not flawed and defective. Nothing is wrong with me. So he's got to be the defective one.
Roxann says:	No, I don't want to go to a movie! Why don't you ask me what I want to do? You never think of me. You are so incredibly selfish and controlling!

We don't know why Roxann and Kathryn interpreted the men's comments in the ways they did. Perhaps they're afraid of being abandoned. Or, perhaps BPD behavior like this is caused by faulty brain chemistry. Thus, although we can see what triggered the behavior—Tom and Robert's comments—the cause may be unknown.

Triggers Versus Causes of BPD Behavior

Understanding the difference between causes and triggers of borderline behavior is crucial to taking the behavior less personally. You can trigger borderline behavior quite easily as you go about your day. That doesn't mean, however, that you caused the behavior.

Imagine that you're having a very bad day. You get to work and realize you left your expensive new umbrella on the bus. You spill coffee on your new outfit. Your boss tells you that the president just canceled your pet project. And when you turn on your computer, you find that a virus has destroyed all your files. You were supposed to back them up, but you could never find the time.

Just then, your happy-go-lucky officemate walks in with a big grin on his face. "Wow, what a beautiful day it is today!" he exclaims. "Kind of makes you glad to be alive, doesn't it?"

"Not really," you snarl. "I'm trying to work. Can you keep it down?"

Your officemate triggered your rude retort. But he didn't cause it. If you care about someone with BPD, you may need to accept that sometimes they will act in ways that make no sense to you. This is something that people with BPD and the more obviously mentally ill have in common. Christine Adamec (1996) says:

> Once you begin to accept that a mentally ill person will sometimes behave irrationally, you alleviate some of your own internal stress and strain ... once you do so you can begin to develop more effective coping mechanisms. No longer burdened by the "what-ifs" and "shoulds" in your mind, you can deal with the way things really are. And you seek out what works.

Seek Support and Validation

You probably don't know anyone else who cares about someone with BPD or has even heard of BPD. So you may have little or no support and no one to do "reality checks" with. For this reason, we created a support group on the Internet called the non-BP mailing list (see appendix D). People on the list share their stories and talk about having someone with BPD in their lives. For most of them, it is the first time they have connected with another person in the same situation. Here is an excerpt of a post from Joellen to Bill, which the two shared with the rest of the list members. (Joellen quotes Bill's previous statements by putting them between the "<<<" ">>>" marks, which is standard practice on the Internet.)

Joellen (non-BP)

Bill, you said:
<<<*One day I'd be labeled by her as the most loving, genuine, sincere, gentle lover, and the next day I'd be reduced to being the evil, satanic, fascist, hooligan pig. No matter how available I was or how loving I tried to be, there was simply nothing I could do to fill the bottomless pit of need or to stop the emotional hemophilia. I began to walk on eggshells and would fear ever expressing my true opinion on anything for fear of starting an argument.*>>>

This is exactly what's happening to me. You don't know how glad I am to find someone else who has been in the same situation that I'm currently in. It's reassuring to me to know that I'm not alone. I am constantly berated if I don't drop everything in an instant and comply with his demands. He likens me to his ex-wives and past girlfriends and says that, just like them, I have my own hidden agenda and always have an excuse. Say what?!

The other night I was going to the doctor and he blew up because I wouldn't drive him to a friend's house. He's still angry about that, although not much is said now. All the reasoning in the world about how long I had been waiting for the appointment and how I needed to be on time doesn't help because, he says, I'm just not reliable.

<<<Later, I began to realize that by the end of work, I'd get an upset stomach knowing that in a couple of hours, I would have to go and see my wife.>>>

That's the worst of it. As you experienced, I never know now what I'm walking into. If he looks angry, I want to be anywhere but there because I know what's coming. And, if an argument occurs, I leave because I just can't stand how crazy with rage he makes me feel inside. At that point, I'm labeled a "coward" or I'm told that I'm constantly deserting him. When he talks, my gut starts to twist and tense up. Hell, I just don't want to fight anymore over what are stupid, silly little things. Nor do I want to be psychologically and verbally abused any longer.

<<<If, by chance, I would try and express a boundary or need, I would more often than not be viciously attacked for my "needy, controlling behavior." In short, I was living with Dr. Jekyll and Mr. Hyde, and I was damned if I do and damned if I don't.>>>

Exactly. Catch-22. A no-win scenario. I keep saying to myself, "I can't win, I can't break even, I can't even quit the game." I feel like I'm a passenger on this BPD bus from hell, and I just wish the damn thing would break down or stop so I can get off. But if I do get off the bus, I'll be alone again with my self-esteem in the gutter. Unfortunately, after almost four years of this, I've become accustomed to it.

Therese (non-BP)

I kept thinking that I was the problem, because the man with BPD I dated told me I was. I kept thinking that if only I could say or do the right thing at any given moment, the rages wouldn't be triggered, the criticism would stop, the arguments would lessen. The problems would just magically go away. Things got really rough *for me, and I had to realize that no matter what I did or said or didn't say or didn't do, the BPD behaviors were not going to stop or even lessen. It wasn't about how perfect or responsive I was. This was a real behavioral problem with my mate that had little to do with me at all.*

Many members of the group tell us that the list, more than anything else, has enabled them to depersonalize the behavior of the people with BPD in their lives. The stories are so similar that it really sinks in that the behavior is not about them. Many people find this a big relief. Joining a local or Internet support group can help you depersonalize the person's behavior. If that isn't possible, perhaps a friend or family member can lend a willing ear. However, it's best to talk with someone who will not feel put in the middle of you and the BP in your life.

Don't Take BPD Behavior Personally

A woman who found out that her borderline husband had been having an affair asked us, "How can I not take it personally when my husband says he has been unfaithful and lying about it for the duration of our marriage? Am I supposed to feel good when he tells me he's going to leave me for her?" We explained that there is a big difference between working through your grief and not taking things personally.

Imagine if you were planning to have your wedding reception at the nicest hall in town, but two days before the wedding lightning struck the hall and it burned to the ground. When you tried to find another site, you found that every other hall was booked. Naturally, you would be very upset and angry. You would need to let off some steam, perhaps cry or call all your friends to complain. If you end up in the high school gym, you would still need to mourn the loss of the perfect wedding reception you had anticipated.

But you wouldn't feel personally attacked, as if the lightning bolt knew you and was deliberately trying to make your life miserable. You wouldn't spend hours trying to figure out what you did to cause the fire. You wouldn't try to change the laws of nature. In short, you wouldn't blame yourself for things beyond your control. But that is precisely what many people do when faced with the actions of a person with BPD. They spend years assuming they're the source of the lightning when, in fact, they're only the lightning rod.

Keep a Sense of Humor

Many family members find that having a sense of humor helps.

Hank (non-BP)

It was October and my BP wife and I were going to a Halloween party given by my friend, Buck. I was dressed as Charlie Brown, complete with striped shirt and stuffed beagle. She was Lucy. In one hand she carried a football, and in the other a sign that said, "Psychiatric Advice, Five Cents." (Ironic, isn't it?)

Buck opened the door and a terrible realization came over me: this was not a Halloween party! Everyone else had on sweaters and jeans. The three of us—me, my wife, and her friend—all realized my mistake at exactly the same time. My wife immediately became very angry and started carrying on about how stupid I was. Ordinarily, I would react to her rages and verbal abuse with fear, anxiety, and confusion. However this time I just couldn't stop laughing! So while my wife raged, the two of us just cracked up. I thought about the episode the next time my wife lost it, and it made me feel better to realize I had a choice about how I was going to react.

Take Care of Yourself

The person in your life with BPD didn't ask to have the disorder. And you never asked for someone in your life to have BPD. But if you are a typical non-BP, you have taken on a huge chunk of the blame for the other person's problems, and you probably feel that you—and only you—can solve them.

Many non-BPs—especially those who have chosen their relationship with the borderline—go through life trying to fix things for other people and rescue them. This gives them the illusion that they can change someone else. But it is just a fantasy that shifts responsibility away from the only person who has the power to change the borderline's life—the BP themselves.

You can spend twenty-four hours a day feeling your loved one's pain for them. You can put your life on hold, waiting for them to come around to your way of thinking. You can let your entire emotional life be dictated by their mood of the moment. But none of that will help the person with BPD.

In our interview with Howard I. Weinberg, Ph.D., he said, "People with BPD need their friends and family members to be stable and clear—not to reject them and not to smother them. They need you to let them take care of themselves and to not do things for them that they can do for themselves. The best way to do this and help them is by working on yourself."

Patricia (BP)

For those of you who have decided to stay with your BPD family member, thank you, thank you! We so need your love and support. We need you to believe in us and encourage us in our recovery. But if you stay, seek therapy for yourself if necessary and make sure you don't lose yourself in the process. You can't lose your own identity. You must come first. Because if you lose it, then the borderline doesn't really have a supporter. She just has another person in her life with a lot of problems.

Detach with Love

Some family members practice detaching with love, a concept promoted by Al-Anon, an organization for people whose lives are affected by someone who abuses alcohol. Al-Anon developed a statement about personal limits that is also appropriate for non-BPs, if you substitute "BPD behavior" for "alcoholism." The original reads, in part:

In Al-Anon we learn individuals are not responsible for another person's disease or recovery from it.

We let go of our obsession with another's behavior and begin to lead happier and more manageable lives, lives with dignity and rights.

In Al-Anon we learn:

- Not to suffer because of the actions or reactions of other people.

- Not to allow ourselves to be used or abused by others in the interest of another's recovery.

- Not do for others what they could do for themselves.

- Not to create a crisis.

- Not to prevent a crisis if it is in the natural course of events.

Detachment is neither kind nor unkind. It does not imply judgment or condemnation of the person or situation from which I am detaching. It is simply a means that allows us to separate ourselves from the adverse effects that another person's alcoholism [substitute "BPD behavior"] has upon our lives.

Detachment helps families look at their situations realistically and objectively, thereby making intelligent decisions possible.

Take Your Life Back

Don't delay your own happiness. Grab it right now. There are many things you can do today to take your life back. Take some time off to reflect. Even combat soldiers get R and R (rest and recuperation). It can remind both you and the person with BPD that you are two separate individuals. The BP will learn that they can live through a temporary separation and that you will still care about them when you return. Encouraging retreats actually builds the relationship.

Also, do not try to be the person's therapist. That is not your role. If the person with BPD wants that kind of help, suggest that they see a mental health professional. If you no longer have contact with the BP, don't spend hours psychoanalyzing them. It is not your job anymore—actually, it never was to begin with.

Memorize the three Cs and the three Gs:

I didn't cause it.

I can't control it.

I can't cure it.

Get off their back.

Get out of their way.

Get on with your own life.

Be good to yourself. Visit an art gallery, buy an outrageously expensive chocolate truffle, or get a massage. Become less isolated. Seek out friends and family. Realize that no one person—illness or no illness—can fulfill all of your needs. If you have let friendships falter, "unfalter" them. And when you go out, do not spend all your time talking about the person with BPD. See a movie. Try a new food. Relax and enjoy yourself! Have fun. The world will not stop if you take some time for yourself. In fact, you will be able to come back refreshed and with a broader perspective.

If you are eating or drinking too much or engaging in other unhealthy coping mechanisms, stop. Seek professional help if you need to. Maintain realistic expectations. Borderline behavior takes years to develop; it is ingrained. Don't expect miracles. Celebrate small steps in the right direction and appreciate the things you enjoy about the person with BPD.

Tanya (non-BP)

It helps to remind myself that I can't fix everything. There really is only so much I can do. I keep reminding myself that being in a situation where I feel helpless doesn't mean I'm a failure.

My therapist told me not to feel guilty about taking care of myself. It's going to take some time to really feel that that's okay. I know I need to grieve. I know I have to deal with my own feelings. But sometimes I long to have my own life back for a little while.

Bolster Your Identity and Self-Esteem

If the person in your life blames and criticizes you, your self-esteem may be in the gutter. If you had low self-esteem to begin with, the situation may be critical. Some non-BPs we spoke with—especially adult children of borderlines—let others take advantage of them because they felt they didn't deserve better. They stayed in abusive work situations or unknowingly sabotaged themselves, as if to confirm the BP's low estimation of their worth.

Many people with BPD are able to be supportive of their children and other people in their life. But some are not. If the relationship with the BP in your life is damaging your self-worth, take immediate steps to repair it. Don't depend on the person with BPD to affirm or validate your worth, because they may not be able to. It's not that they don't care about you—it's just that at this time, their own issues may be getting in the way.

Chapter 6 discusses the issues of setting limits and responding to rage, blame, and criticism. Read it carefully and practice the communication techniques with a friend before using them in a real life situation. You do not have to listen to anyone else tell you that you're an awful, terrible person. You have a choice.

Do things on your own that you can feel proud of. Take up a new hobby. Volunteer or become politically involved in something bigger than yourself. Strive for success at school or work. Don't let yourself drift. Set reasonable goals and work toward them. Reward yourself for even small movement in the right direction.

Finally, seek therapy to deal with the stress of living with someone who has BPD. In a survey we conducted of non-BPs, 75 percent of the non-BPs said they had sought therapy themselves.

Take Responsibility for Your Own Behavior

You may feel like a crumpled newspaper in a tornado, buffeted about at the whim of the person in your life with BPD. But you have more control over the relationship than you probably think you do. You have power over you own actions. And you control your own reactions to troublesome BPD behavior. Once you understand yourself and the decisions you've made in the past, it is easier to make new decisions that may be healthier for you and the relationship in the long run.

Susan Forward (1997) discusses how even avoidance is an action taken:

> Every day, we teach people how to treat us by showing them what we will and won't accept, what we refuse to confront, and what we let slide. We may believe that we can make another person's troublesome behavior disappear if we don't make a fuss. But the message we send is "It worked. Do it again."

Some non-BPs find this step of owning up to their own responsibility difficult because they hear the critical voice of the BP in their head saying, "See, everything *is* your fault. I *told* you that something is wrong with you." To these non-BPs, taking this step almost seems like agreeing with the BP's criticisms. If this describes you, silence those voices right now. We are not suggesting that you provoked or caused the person's behavior—rather, we are proposing that you may have unwittingly given the BP permission to repeat behaviors that have worked in the past.

Also, when you hear the BP's blaming voice in your head, consider whether *you* might be splitting—buying into the belief that one of you must be "wrong" or "bad" and the other is "blameless" and "perfect." Remember, in chapter 4 we explained that splitting and other BPD behavior can be "catching."

Consider How the Relationship Meets Your Needs

In our interview with Howard I. Weinberg, Ph.D., he said, "If you care about someone with BPD, remember that you did not choose the borderline because you are sick. You chose this person because they were important to you."

You wouldn't be reading this book if the relationship was completely negative. You would just walk away. So something about the relationship may be meeting your needs. Following are some conscious and unconscious reasons why some adult non-BP's get into and stay in relationships with adult BPs—even when it causes them a great deal of pain. These reasons may vary depending upon whether you are in a chosen relationship (friend, lover) or unchosen relationship (relative) with someone with BPD.

Many people stay in relationships with borderlines because the person with BPD is incredibly interesting, engaging, bright, charming, funny, witty, and alluring. One woman said that when she met her borderline boyfriend, she felt like she was meeting a member of her own species for the first time.

Diane (BP)

I can understand why non-BPs engage in discussion about the pathologies, the rages, and the rotten things borderlines can do. A BP has the capacity to destroy themselves and anyone close to them. It's healthy to vent this pain.

But sometimes, in the course of the books and the discussion and the clinical terminology, these reasons why you began the relationship become lost. You didn't fall in love with a borderline because you had some hankering to be destroyed. You did it because there were good qualities about the person. And they are just as characteristic of the person as the bad ones.

When the destructive bad qualities began to manifest themselves, you got through it by telling yourself that in the end, these good qualities supersede the bad ones. Well, maybe they will, maybe they won't. Non-BPs aren't masochists, they're optimists—which may or may not turn out to be warranted. It is hard to give up on that optimism and let go of a relationship that's so good otherwise.

Stop Making Excuses and Denying the Severity of the Situation

Remaining hopeful is essential. And it's true that everyone has good and bad qualities. But hope must be tempered with a realistic view of the situation and an assessment of the likelihood of change.

Kevin's girlfriend Judy was bright, talented, and very attractive. Best of all, she loved him. So Kevin overlooked behavior that would have been a wake-up call for others. For example, one day Judy showed up at his workplace and began screaming at him in front of his boss and co-workers. Several days later, he still couldn't figure out why she had been angry. Judy also impulsively bought luxury items like crystal vases and designer clothing, even though she was on public assistance and lived with Kevin and her nine-year-old son in a roach-infested apartment. She would leave her son alone at home to go shopping.

Each time Judy and Kevin had a disagreement, she would throw him out of the apartment and destroy some of his possessions. This became so routine that he began leaving his treasured belongings with his parents. When Kevin's friends tried to convince him that Judy's behavior wasn't normal, Kevin would shrug his shoulders and say, "Oh well, nobody's perfect. Every relationship has problems."

Kevin is using denial as a way of keeping the relationship going and coping with painful feelings of his own. At this point, Kevin is likely to do anything to avoid conflict in the relationship. However, his denial of problems only enables and reinforces the negative behaviors of Judy. Kevin will need the support and perspective of his friends to begin to address these problems and address why he allows Judy to treat him so poorly. Kevin will also need to address why his relationship with Judy is so important that he allows her to treat him badly.

Understand the Effects of Intermittent Reinforcement

Let's say that you have a rat in a box with a lever. You teach the rat to press the lever. Every fifth time he presses the lever, he is rewarded with some food. The rat quickly learns to press the lever five times so he can claim his reward. But if you stop giving the rat food, he will quickly abandon the exercise and go back to doing whatever it is that rats do.

Now let's say that you intermittently reinforce the rat with food; that is, you vary the reward schedule. Sometimes you reward the rat after two lever presses. Sometimes you wait until the fifteenth press. You alternate the reinforcement so he never knows when to expect the food. Then, once more, you take away all the food pellets. But the rat keeps pressing the lever. He presses it twenty times. No food. He presses some more. He thinks, "Perhaps the human is waiting for the ninety-ninth press this time."

When a behavior is intermittently reinforced, extinguishing the behavior takes a lot longer once the reward has been removed.

Intermittent reinforcement can work both ways. You are intermittently reinforced when the BP is in a good mood. You can't predict when it will occur next—but you know it could be soon. The BP can also be intermittently reinforced when you occasionally cave in to their demands when they act in or out.

Molly says, "I am caught right now in Sondra's charming behavior. I am thinking 'Ah! This is the person I used to know.' My logic tells me not to reconnect with her. But my emotions are telling me another thing."

If you feel "addicted" to the BP despite their harsh treatment of you, consider whether intermittent reinforcement is playing a part in the relationship.

Recognize the Exhilaration of the Roller-Coaster Ride

Many people say that when things are good, they're really good. The flattery, attention, and obsessiveness are very exhilarating to the ego. To feel so important to someone can be very exciting and empowering. The exhilaration can be recognized immediately, especially if the non-BP has not been in this position of being an "idol" before. The non-BP may also begin to look for the exhilaration—anticipate the flattery and attention. And, after awhile, when the flattery begins to gradually fade, the non-BP will miss it and make attempts to get the BP to idolize them again. The law of intermittent reinforcement applies here again, since the BP may intermittently engage in the obsessiveness and flattery throughout the relationship. This in turn reinforces the non-BP's commitment to the relationship.

Jim (non-BP)

I found my wife's initial obsessiveness with me very flattering. I mean, I never thought I was worth that kind of attention. Other women didn't pay much attention to me. But she worshipped me. It's easier to feel good about myself when I'm around someone who idolizes me.

But our relationship was like an addiction. I kept going back for more, in spite of myself, filled with self-contempt and even a sort of subtle shame: "I hate myself for loving you."

I saw her as a charming rogue who fed my desperate fantasies; only half-disbelieving her flattery, I preened under the unexpected, intense light of her full and dazzling attentions. So began our roller-coaster relationship; living vicariously through the sublime, dizzying heights, I was shaken by the sudden, despairing drops, the switchbacks, the topsy-turvy illogical loops, the stunning stops, and later, the absence, the silence, the flatness at the end.

Stop Trying to Resolve Childhood Issues Through Relationships

In our interview with Paul Hannig, Ph.D., he said (to all non-BPs), "If you find yourself involved with a BP, you can bet that you have unfinished business with a parent."

A few times in their lives, adult children of borderlines have managed to please their BPD parents. So they hang around their aging parents, sometimes enduring emotional abuse, and try repeatedly to do something that will please the parents again. Sometimes, rather than (or in addition to) trying to please the actual parent, adult children of BPs choose a BPD partner who acts like their parent. It is an unconscious bid to duplicate the experience in order to resolve unfinished business with the parent. Unfortunately, the adult child usually feels trapped and abused in the same way that they did when they were a kid.

Reenactment of the parental relationship through the BP partner is an unconscious process. The typical drive for this behavior is the need to gain a sense of control or mastery over a situation. This occurs very frequently with people who have been physically or sexually abused. They essentially put themselves in a position to reenact the abuse in an effort to find a better solution or response to the abuse. The mantra "If only I had done something different" often underlies the drive to reenact. However, because this is unconscious it is difficult to recognize. It is usually supportive siblings, family members, friends, or therapists who suggest reenactment as a reason for the problematic relationship. Defensiveness and denial are the typical first reactions to this suggestion. However, over time, with support and assistance, non-BPs may begin to accept this possibility and explore their relationships with both their partner and parents.

Make Decisions for Yourself

Acknowledging that you have the authority to make your own decisions is the first step toward making new choices and changing your life for the better.

Some non-BPs think they are helpless in their relationship when, in actuality, they are feeling scared. Fear and anxiety are not the same as being helpless. Non-BPs are typically fearful that their efforts toward limit setting and change will be met with rage and anger. Therefore, in an effort to avoid negative reactions of BPs, non-BPs will describe themselves as "helpless." Moreover, believing you are helpless may also serve the purpose of ridding yourself of any responsibility for making changes or for creating a better life for yourself. You may think that if you're "helpless" that means you're a "victim"—a person that others can't blame for their situation.

You must understand that you do have the power to change your relationships and your life, but it is likely going to be frightening at first. The alternative is to live a fairly unhappy and unsatisfying life in which fear dictates your choices and their relationships.

Here are two questions that could be helpful in making your first steps to change:

- Do you expect that changes in the relationship are the sole responsibility of the BP in your life?

- If you have a victim role in the relationship, do you receive any special attention from others for this?

Believe You Don't Deserve to Be Treated Badly

Do you sometimes think that being in an emotionally abusive relationship is better than being in no relationship at all? It sometimes feels easier to be hurt than to be alone, but in the long run abusive relationships can cause you to lose yourself, which is the ultimate loneliness. People with self-esteem problems are very vulnerable to blame and criticisms. They come to believe they deserve this treatment. They think that if they leave, no one else will want them. Even emotionally healthy people can begin to question their own self-worth.

Alex (non-BP)

I had to examine why I would spend years in abusive relationships. I had to overcome my fears, my "you don't deserve to be happy" voices, and my tendency to beat up on myself. I had to learn that I am worthy of being in relationships with people who are good to me and who genuinely love me as I am—without putting me on a pedestal or tossing me into the gutter.

John (non-BP)

I realized that one of the major reasons I got involved and stayed in this relationship so long was that I thought I deserved that kind of pain and anguish. It was unconscious, but I thought that I deserved that kind of treatment and found women to give it to me to reinforce my lack of worth. Now I'm working on this so I won't be attracted to women like that in the future. Two hurricanes are enough.

All people, not just non-BPs, have the right to healthy relationships. However, after months or years of enduring excessive criticism, blame, and borderline rage, most non-BPs may begin to question whether they deserve to have a healthy relationship. Do you believe that you have the following rights?

- To feel respected as a person
- To get your physical and emotional needs met
- To be appreciated and not taken for granted
- To communicate effectively with your partner
- To have your privacy respected
- To not constantly fight for control
- To feel good about yourself and your relationship
- To trust, validate, and support each other
- To grow within and outside of the relationship
- To have your own opinions and thoughts
- To either stay in or leave the relationship

As you may know, rights are neither respected nor acknowledged unless someone stands up for them. So ask yourself, are you ready to stand up for your rights?

Face Your Own Issues about Being Needed

Codependence expert Melody Beattie (1987) developed a list of questions for people who feel like they must rescue others. Paraphrased, they include:

1. Do you feel responsible for other people's thoughts, actions, and feelings?
2. When someone tells you about a problem they have, do you feel it is your duty to solve it?

3. Do you swallow your anger in order to avoid conflict?

4. Do you find getting more difficult than giving?

5. Do you somehow seem to enjoy life more during interpersonal crises? Have you avoided choosing partners
   whose lives seem to go too smoothly because you
   become bored?

6. Do people tell you that you are a saint for putting up
   with something or someone? Does part of you enjoy
   this?

7. Is it more tempting to concentrate on the problems of
   others than to solve difficulties in your own life?

Examine Your Beliefs about Marriage and Family

Many non-BPs stay in abusive relationships because they
believe that marriage is a lifetime commitment or because they do
not want their children to have divorced parents. However,
spouses who take this position often must endure some of the
most extreme behavior from people with BPD. The borderline
spouse may realize that no matter how they act, the other person
will remain in the relationship. With no real consequences to their
behavior, the person with BPD may act out in ways most people
would find intolerable. For example, one woman brought home
extramarital sex partners while her husband was in another room
of the house.

Non-BPs who are married and have children with an abusive
borderline say they feel like they are in a no-win situation. If they
stay, they will be emotionally or physically abused, but at least
they can attempt to protect their children from any harmful
behavior. If they leave the marriage, they fear that their partner
will get custody and try to impede their relationship with the children—or worse, that in their absence, the acting out will more
severely affect the children.

If this is your situation, ask yourself if the other person is
presently acting abusive toward the children. If they are, then the
crisis is already an immediate one. Seek assistance from mental
health professionals, social service agencies, and law enforcement
if needed. The number one priority at this time must be the protection of the children regardless of the effect on the marital

relationship. If not, has the BP really given you a good reason to believe that this might happen?

Focus on Your Own Issues

Some people find that trying to change someone else is easier than changing themselves and that focusing on the problems of others helps them avoid their own problems. Do you have a firm sense of who you are apart from the person with BPD? Are you where you want to be at this point in your life? Is there anything in your life that you are avoiding that you might have to take a look at if you were not concentrating on your relationship with the BP? How much time do you spend worrying about this relationship, and what would you do with that time if life with this person was perfect?

Nina (non-BP)

Because my boyfriends were so obviously out of line, I tended to overlook my own behavior. So I learned that my responsibility was to admit when I screwed up immediately, to be honest and open—even in the face of BPD rages and blame. Through a solid year of therapy and twelve-step work, I realized that the problems I faced with BPD partners were magnified versions of the problems I had with myself.

I was also hypercritical. I also had a tendency to blame and avoid responsibility. I was out of touch with my true feelings. I had a lot of shame piled up. I had trouble trusting others and communicating honestly. I was a master at holding on to bitterness.

It was shocking to realize that my behaviors had gotten so distorted and out of control. I kept thinking it was just those crazy men in my life, and that if only they would change, everything would be fine. It was a painful realization to wake up one day and notice that I was not a saintly martyr to the cause of BPD and that there were no medals handed out to willing sufferers like me!

Where to Go From Here

Ask yourself:

- How did I end up in this position?

- What have I learned about myself?

- What choices have I made in the past, and are they the best ones for me right now?

- What is keeping me from standing up for myself? What can I do about it?

- What am I responsible for in this relationship? What can I do about it?

Note that we are not blaming you for what has happened to you in the past or for the choices you've made. We are simply pointing out that only you—not the BP, your therapist, your friends, nor this book—can resolve these issues for you. It's truly up to you. Many introspective non-BPs found that what they discovered about themselves was invaluable:

Alex (non-BP)

This was the greatest gift of being around people with BPD. I got to see myself and how I interact with others. As painful as these relationships were, I needed them in order to become the person that I am today.

Marilyn (non-BP)

My saving grace is that I have been able to move from being a person who lived her life unconsciously to a person who now lives a conscious life. Someone said that the unexamined life is not worth living. I am happy to say that my life is very much worth living!

Russell (non-BP)

It really helps to view situations as opportunities for growth and personal education. Rather than see every conflict and tribulation as a crisis of unresolvable proportions, I recognize that I am the one with the problem—I detest this person's behavior—and I'm open to learn more about myself. It becomes more about my choices than about my helplessness. And I can learn a lot from my choices.

In this chapter, we've explored ways to better cope with BPD behavior, simply by making changes within yourself: accepting that you can't make the BP seek treatment, not taking the BP's actions personally, taking care of yourself, and taking responsibility for your own behavior. Next, we'll look at beginning to change the way you interact with the BP in your life.

6

Understanding Your Situation: Setting Boundaries, and Developing Skills

It's no big deal they say
It's just the kind of madness you get used to
But where do you run when fear stalks your dreams
How do you measure the weight of those things?

> —Carrie Newcomer, "The Madness You
> Get Used To" from *My Father's Only Son*

Identify Triggers to Intense Emotional Reactions

When you or the BP have an intense reaction to something, chances are good that one of your triggers or "hot buttons" has been pushed. Hot buttons or triggers are stored-up resentments, regrets, insecurities, angers, and fears that hurt when touched and cause automatic emotional responses. By identifying specific actions, words, or events that seem to trigger emotional reactions—either in you or in the BP in your life—these reactions may be easier to anticipate. Then they may become more manageable.

Keeping Track

Many family members find that keeping a daily log of their loved one's patterns of behavior helps them understand and depersonalize the person's actions. Parents of borderline children, especially, find records extremely useful in helping obtain proper diagnosis and treatment for their child.

Whether you simply observe the BP or jot down notes about their moods and behaviors, your intent is not to make judgments, but to stop reacting to the behavior emotionally and start learning from it. If there appears to be little relationship between your actions and those of the person with BPD, you will see all the more clearly that the person's behavior is not about you.

If it looks like something external to the BP seems to be triggering the behavior, step back and see if you can figure out what's going on. What factors might be involved, such as the person's general mood, the time of day, the presence or absence of alcohol, the immediate environment, and so on? If you can find patterns in the person's behavior, it may become more predictable. Behavior that is predictable is easier to manage.

Portia (non-BP)

Sandy and I are parents of a possibly borderline child. We actually used a spreadsheet to graph our son's moods and behaviors. The scale varied from -10, for extreme despair, to +10, for extreme optimism. A zero indicated a neutral mood. Our son's therapist was blown away by our documenting and it became part of his chart. It also helped them determine if our son had BPD or bipolar disorder.

Henry (non-BP)

I never kept a journal, but over a ten-year period, I realized that Barbara's moods occurred in cycles that seemed to repeat every six weeks. It went kind of like this:

1. Explosive, violent raging that lasted from ten minutes to several hours.

2. Silence that lasted for two to five days.

3. Friendly, cheerful, affectionate behavior that would last three or four days. (When things were going well, Barbara would apologize and even ask me to find out what might be causing her "crazy behavior.")

4. A long deterioration that lasted four to ten weeks. During this period, Barbara became increasingly more critical, condemning, and short-tempered. She would deny her earlier apologetic remarks. Finally, there would be an angry explosion and the cycle would repeat anew.

Once I recognized the patterns, I knew what to expect. This made things feel more manageable for me.

BP Triggers

Certain issues seem to be triggers for people with BPD. Although it's important for you to know what they are, it would be impossible and inadvisable to avoid all of them. The actions of the person with BPD are still their responsibility, not yours. (In chapter 7 we will show you how to keep these triggers in mind when you communicate with the BP in your life.) A discussion of common triggers of people with BPD follows.

Feeling That Others Are Unpredictable

Ironically, although they seem to act unpredictably, people with BPD often crave predictability in others. This may be due to their difficulties with object constancy (discussed in chapter 2).

Experiencing the Inconsistency of Others

Again, while BPs act inconsistently, the more consistent and predictable your behavior, the easier it is for the person with BPD to manage their own feelings and behavior.

Perceiving Abandonment

Sometimes it is easy to anticipate when the person with BPD might feel abandoned. But as you have seen, this trigger is so sensitive that the slightest thing—or even nothing at all—may make a BP's emotional alarm bells ring. Looking at a situation from their perspective instead of your own may help you see when fear of abandonment is playing a part in the person's reaction.

Feeling Invalidated

An invalidating response is something that denies the person's feelings, thoughts, or behaviors, such as, "You should not feel that way," or "You are overreacting." Of course, sometimes it seems like the person with BPD should not feel or act that way or is overreacting. So the challenge is to search for the underlying meaning or feeling within the borderline response (more on how to do this in chapter 7).

When a BP feels invalidated, non-BPs can ask for clarification from the BP so the non-BP can understand better what they are experiencing. Accepting some responsibility for not understanding fully is usually a safe way to start (for example, "I'm sorry, I probably misunderstood what you meant when you said [did, expressed] that. Can you tell me more about it?")

It is difficult to know what to do when a BP feels invalidated. Even saying, "I know how you feel," can anger someone with BPD because it implies that your feelings are identical to theirs. Chances are that unless you have BPD, you don't really understand how they feel, any more than they can really comprehend what it's like to be in your position.

Receiving Criticism

This can be actual criticism (for example, "I wish you wouldn't call me so often at work") or perceived criticism (for example, you are quiet and the BP thinks, "They must be angry at me—what did I do?"). Either way, feeling criticized can trigger intense emotional reactions.

Being in Situations Where Others Have the Spotlight

Some BPs have a difficult time during family celebrations when all the attention is focused on someone else. These BPs may try to draw the attention back to themselves by acting in or acting out. Several non-BPs told us that when they were going through a crisis— a death in the family, for example—the BP in their lives became furious at them and accused them of being overly needy and manipulative.

Having Every Reaction Attributed to BPD

BPs who accept their BPD diagnosis can be triggered when people attribute everything that they do to BPD. As one BP said, "People with BPD feel angry, depressed, and afraid for the same reasons everyone does. Our wallet gets stolen. We have a bad day at work. We're worried about a sick cat. Yes, sometimes we are too sensitive. Sometimes we read too much into things. But don't blame everything on BPD. It robs us of our right to be human."

Being Labeled and Stigmatized

We have discussed how difficult it is for someone with BPD to seek treatment. We recommend that you never use BPD as a weapon against the other person in the heat of a disagreement, as in "You're not making any sense, that's just the BPD talking!" After all, would you yell at a loved one with a fear of heights, "Just stop complaining and walk across this suspension bridge"? Later, in a calmer moment, you can discuss (in a caring rather than a blaming way) whether or not BPD may have contributed to the person's reaction.

Wendy (BP)

Sometimes I get angry that I've had to wrestle with this demon (BPD). No one likes a borderline. Society doesn't. Shrinks don't. We are chaotic, aggressive, manipulative, and angry to the world. But look inside the soul of a borderline (if you can get there) and you'll find something very different. Fear. Desperation. Abandonment. Incredible sensitivity.

Majida (BP)

It's hard enough to admit that you suffer from depression. People tend to look askance at you after such a revelation, as if they expect you to lunge for the nearest loaded gun. So try explaining BPD to someone. You might as well burn a swastika on your forehead and start humming "Helter Skelter."

Being Told to "Snap Out of It"

While BPD behavior can be alleviated with professional help, it is not something that goes away quickly or easily. Asking the BP to just act different is like asking a diabetic to just make more insulin.

Jacob (BP)

A lot of times I think my family and friends still don't get that something wrong is going on in my brain. They seem to think I act this way at will and can change my moods at random. They keep telling me to try an herbal remedy or get a hold of myself or just not think a certain way, and they don't understand how hard it is to alter years and years of screwed-up thinking.

Non-BP Triggers

Many non-BPs told us that the people with BPD in their lives seemed to be aware of the non-BP's triggers. When the BPs felt threatened, they consciously or unconsciously protected themselves from painful feelings in ways that pushed these buttons.

For example, one non-BP had very poor self-esteem. She had never dated much, and she and her borderline husband had gotten married during high school. The marriage was very difficult because her husband was emotionally abusive. Whenever she spoke of leaving, however, he would tell her that no one else would have her and she would never be able to support herself because she was not smart or talented enough to get a good-paying job.

Some of the things that the BP in your life says or does may sting very badly. Others may not bother you at all. Rather than just reacting, observe your own responses and examine them. Is the criticism true, or does it have a grain of truth? Remember, you don't have to accept or reject the statement in its entirety. Look for splitting (black-and-white thinking), overgeneralizations ("you always" or "you never"), and illogical connections ("You didn't take me to the party because you hate me.").

As time marches on, certain hot buttons get pushed so many times that even the slightest touch becomes painful. Well-used hot buttons for non-BPs include:

- Being unfairly accused by the BP
- Having needs, feelings, and reactions discounted or denied by the BP
- Being overly admired or adored by the BP (because it may be a set-up for later devaluation and criticism)
- Other situations and conditions that usually precede rages or acting out behaviors (e.g., one woman started trembling whenever the phone rang because she was afraid it was her borderline mother)

FOG—Fear, Obligation, Guilt

Susan Forward (1997) believes that traits that make people vulnerable to emotional blackmail include fear, obligation, and guilt— FOG for short. FOG obscures your choices and limits your options to those the blackmailer picks for you.

- Fear: You may fear losing something: love, money, approval, access to your children, or the relationship itself.

You may be afraid of your own anger or of losing control of your emotions.

- Obligation: Says Forward, "Memory, as employed by the blackmailer, becomes the Obligation Channel, with non-stop replays of the blackmailer's generous behavior toward us. When our sense of obligation is stronger than our sense of self-respect and caring, people quickly learn how to take advantage."

- Guilt: When your normal activities trigger the BP, they play the "Tag, You're It" game discussed in chapter 3 and shift responsibility for their upset feelings onto you. They may accuse you not only of devious behavior but of acting in this way to deliberately hurt them. Instead of questioning their assumptions, you may respond by feeling guilty.

Coping Strategies

Just becoming aware of your triggers can make coping with borderline behavior easier. Other strategies include:

- **Working on yourself.** For example, the woman with poor self-esteem might see a therapist and explore why she thinks so poorly of herself. Or she might take some classes at the local college to improve her professional skills or train for a higher-paying position. This way, she will be in a better position to depersonalize and deflect the BP's criticism.

- **Performing reality checks with others.** If the BP in your life accuses you of being ungrateful or inept, or of having other negative qualities, ask friends if they believe there's any truth to what the BP is saying.

- **Minimizing your exposure to situations that trigger you.** You have the right to take care of yourself.

- **Minimizing any visible reaction.** If the BP knows that the button-pushing is having the desired effect—whether consciously or unconsciously—chances are that the behavior will be repeated.

- **Realizing you can't control what people choose to think.** You can't make everyone happy—least of all someone who is projecting their own unhappiness onto you. Stop taking responsibility for the BP's inner world and start taking responsibility for your own.

Determine Your Personal Limits

Personal limits, or boundaries, tell you where you end and where others begin. Limits define who you are, what you believe, how you treat other people, and how you let them treat you. Like the shell of an egg, limits give you form and protect you. Like the rules of a game, they bring order to your life and help you make decisions that benefit you. Healthy limits are somewhat flexible, like a soft piece of plastic. You can bend them and they don't break. When your limits are overly flexible, however, violations and intrusions can occur. You may take on the feelings and responsibilities of others and lose sight of your own.

On the other hand, when your limits are too inflexible, people may view you as cold or distant. That's because inflexible limits can act as a defense—not only from others, but also from your own feelings. Therefore, you may have a hard time feeling sadness, anger, or other negative emotions. Happiness and other positive emotions may also at times be beyond your grasp. You may feel disconnected from others and your own experiences.

Elena (BP)

I feel like I live inside a castle with enormous walls and a tightly closed drawbridge. Outside, a crowd of people are having a party on the lawn. But I can't hear what it's about and I can't join them, although part of me wants to. So I stand at the window and look outside.

Melody Beattie (1987) believes that setting limits is not an isolated process. She writes:

> Setting boundaries is about learning to take care of ourselves, no matter what happens, where we go, or who we're with. Boundaries are rooted in our beliefs about what we deserve and don't deserve.
>
> Boundaries originate from a deeper sense of our personal rights—especially the right we have to be ourselves. Boundaries emerge as we learn to value, trust, and listen to ourselves. Boundaries naturally flow from our conviction that what we want, need, like and dislike is important.

Personal limits are not about controlling or changing other people's behavior. In fact, they're not about other people at all. They're about you, and what you need to do to take care of yourself. For example, you may not be able to stop nosy in-laws from asking you again and again when you plan on starting a family. But you can control whether or not you answer their questions and how much time you spend with them.

Sometimes you may choose to overlook your personal limits. For example, imagine that your elderly father slips on an icy walkway and asks if he can live with you and your family until he recovers from his injuries. Because you love your dad, you say yes—even though you value your privacy. The key here is that you feel you have a choice. It's like the difference between giving someone a gift and being robbed.

Physical Limits

Healthy physical limits protect you from unwanted intrusion. If someone stands too close to you in an elevator, you move away. If your partner wants to have sex and you don't, you have the right to say no. If you want to be alone, you can go into another room and shut the door.

Many people with BPD have had their physical boundaries violently violated (often repeatedly) through physical or sexual abuse. However, violations of physical boundaries can also be as subtle as a suggestive touch on the shoulder from an inappropriate source. Context matters as well. A passionate kiss from a lover may be appreciated at home, but is out of bounds in the workplace. Or, that same kiss might be wonderful after an, "I love you," but unappreciated after an argument. Physical limits can also be violated by too much distance. Physical affection and touching are expected in some relationships, and problems can develop if they are withdrawn (or were never present at all).

The following are examples of how people with good physical limits act in ways that respect their own thoughts and feelings:

- Pat's husband Bob loses all interest in sex, touching, and cuddling. She doesn't know why. Rather than brood about it, though, she approaches Bob in a nonthreatening way and initiates a discussion.

- Sandy's friend Barbara just landed a fantastic new job. Barbara is so thrilled that she grabs Sandy and gives her a big hug. Sandy is taken aback at Barbara's enthusiasm, but enjoys her friend's happiness—and the hug. She even decides to give Barbara a hug every once in a while herself.

Emotional Limits

Emotional limits are the invisible boundaries that separate your feelings from those of others. These boundaries not only mark off where your feelings end and someone else's begin but also help you protect your feelings when you are feeling vulnerable and provide others with access to your feelings when you are feeling intimate and safe with them.

People with healthy emotional limits understand and respect their own thoughts and feelings. In short, they respect themselves and their own uniqueness. Anne Katherine (1993) says, "The right to say 'no' strengthens emotional boundaries. So does the freedom to say 'yes,' respect for feelings, acceptance of differences, and permission for expression."

The following are examples of how people with good emotional limits act in ways that respect their own thoughts and feelings:

- Martha (BP) and Tom, who are having marital difficulties, have a sixteen-year-old daughter, Tanya. One afternoon, Martha and Tanya were running errands when Martha begins to divulge details about her marital problems to Tanya. The teen immediately asks her mother to confide in a friend instead, saying that she'd rather not know the personal details.

- Dan believes that his father has Borderline Personality Disorder. His younger brother, Randy, disagrees. Dan hasn't seen his father in a year, while Randy has dinner with him once a week. Dan and Randy feel free to discuss their opinions about their father though they have differing viewpoints. And they both enjoy their brotherly relationship, realizing that it's separate from their relationships with their father.

- Roberta's lover Cathy (BP) hates it when Roberta (non-BP) goes out with friends. Cathy is always invited along, but she wants to stay home because she thinks that Roberta's friends are "a complete waste of time."

   "Please don't go," Cathy pleads one evening as Roberta gets dressed to go out. "I'm lonely without you," Cathy says tearfully.

   Roberta gently reminds Cathy that she told her about her plans a week ago, and that Cathy had time to find things to do on her own or with one of her own friends.

But Cathy just keeps on weeping. "You must not love me anymore," she says.

Roberta replies, "It sounds like you feel that I am rejecting or abandoning you. That must be very painful. You can believe that and make yourself feel bad, or you can try to work through why you are always doubting my love for you. Let's talk about it when I get back. I'll see you around eleven o'clock."

The Benefits of Personal Limits

Limits can be difficult to set and keep, but doing so has some invaluable incentives.

Limits Help You Define Who You Are

Limits and the struggle for identity are tightly intertwined. People with weak limits often have poorly developed senses of identity. People with weak or non-existent limits can have difficulty distinguishing between their own beliefs and feelings and those belonging to others. They also tend to confuse their problems and responsibilities with those of others. Left with an uncertain identity, they often take on someone else's or identify solely with one familiar role (e.g., mother, executive, or even borderline).

People with well-developed limits, on the other hand, appropriately distinguish themselves from others. They can identify and take responsibility for their own feelings, beliefs, and values, and see them as important parts of who they are. In addition, people with healthy limits have respect for other people's beliefs and feelings—even if they are different from their own. They understand that another person's values and beliefs are equally important in defining who they are.

Limits Bring Order to Your Life

If you're always at the whim of someone else's desires, your life can spiral out of control. People with BPD tend to change the rules, act impulsively, and demand attention on their schedule, not that of others. Limits can help you deal with these behaviors so that you don't feel like a puppet on a string.

Limits can also help you clarify your relationships with others. If you're a manager and someone you supervise comes into your office and begins discussing their financial or marital problems, the boundaries and roles begin to blur. What was purely a professional relationship has turned personal. While a friendship with a subordinate may be rewarding, it has its potential perils. What happens to the relationship if your subordinate's performance at work deteriorates and you must discipline them? Setting limits ahead of time may help you avoid future problems.

Limits Help You Feel Secure

People who don't have limits are always at the mercy of others. They feel helpless when others act upon them, and they take whatever others dish out. On the other hand, people with limits feel more in control of their lives because they realize they have a choice about the behavior they will tolerate. They take the power that is truly theirs to say no. This provides them with a sense of security and control.

For example, Jane and Ben have been dating for several months. Jane's having a hard time because Ben can't decide how he feels about her. When he loves her, she's elated. When he backs off and "just wants to be friends," she's depressed and confused.

One day he has something to tell her. "I've met someone else," he says. "But I don't know if she's the one. I want to date both of you until I know for sure."

Clear limits will enable Jane to stick up for herself and tell Ben what she wants out of the relationship. Because she has healthy limits, she knows that her needs are just as important as Ben's. Jane can tell Ben how his actions have affected her, and she can evaluate his proposed arrangements based on her own values and beliefs. Jane understands that she has many options, and that one of them is telling Ben that although she cares for him, she needs to leave the relationship because it's not meeting her needs.

Limits Promote Intimacy, Not Enmeshment

The idea used to be that when two people got married, they became one. Today's brides and grooms are more likely to believe that one and one still make two. Many couples acknowledge this at their wedding by having someone read from Kahlil Gibran's *The Prophet* (1976). In the passage on marriage, Gibran urges couples to have spaces in their togetherness. "Stand together yet not too near together: for the pillars of the temple stand apart, and the oak tree and the cypress grow not in each other's shadow."

Gibran is describing healthy limits. The opposite, enmeshment, is comparable to the oak tree and the cypress growing so close together that their branches and roots become entwined.

Soon, there's no room for either tree to grow; parts of each tree die, and neither reaches its full potential.

Unlike compromise, which is a conscious and more equal give and take, enmeshment involves denying who you are or what you need in order to please someone else or keep a relationship.

Anne Katherine (1993) says:

> Enmeshment happens when the individualities of each partner are sacrificed to the relationship. Falling in love is exciting and involving. But the truth is, it's a fairly enmeshed stage of the relationship. It is validating for someone to have thoughts and feelings identical to our own. It feels wonderful. Eventually, though, perceptions will differ. How this is handled is critical for the relationship.
>
> Sometimes people become enmeshed because one partner intimidates the other into giving up their own opinions, perspectives, and preferences. In other cases a partner takes on someone else's view voluntarily because they're so eager to feel close to someone. Denying part of themselves is preferable to being alone—at least at first. But the problem with sacrificing parts of yourself to please someone else is that it doesn't work in the long run. It might take many years, but eventually you realize that while you may have gained a relationship, you've lost yourself. In order to share yourself, you need enough of a sense of your own individuality to have something to present to the other. Even if you have a good sense of who you are, intimacy takes time, openness, a nonjudgmental attitude, listening, and acceptance.

BP and Non-BP Boundary Issues

Some people are lucky enough to have had parents and other role models who taught them about personal rights and limits and why they are important. Unfortunately, many adults grew up with damaged, trampled, or nonexistent boundaries. In many cases, parents routinely violated their children's boundaries and rights or forced them into inappropriate roles.

Different kinds of boundary violations cause different kinds of problems for children when they become adults. If parents or other caregivers encouraged a child to be dependent, as an adult they may believe that they need someone else to make them whole.

Children of distant or abandoning parents may have a hard time connecting emotionally to others. Controlling parents teach their children that others have no rights. Overinvolved parents can make it difficult for their children to develop their own identities.

Some people with BPD have experienced childhood sexual or physical abuse—the most horrific violations of personal limits. The abuse, humiliation, and shame severely damage personal boundaries and leave gaping holes where the violations occurred. Abused children feel confused about what to let others do to them physically, how to let others treat them emotionally, and how to interact with others in socially appropriate ways.

Adults who were abused as children may protect themselves by building strong walls between themselves and others, or they may withdraw physically or emotionally, rarely sharing their emotions. Others do the opposite, becoming too open. They may involve themselves in sexual relationships with people who don't really care about them. Children who experience abuse also learn to deny pain and chaos or accept them as normal and proper. They learn that their feelings were wrong or didn't matter. They focused on immediate survival—on not getting abused—and miss out on important developmental stages. As a result, they have problems developing their own identities.

Kamala (BP)

My mother and father physically, sexually, and emotionally abused me. I remember my father running around the house trying to catch me so he could beat me. My mother was an alcoholic, and when he wasn't hurting me, she was. They never loved me or cared about how I felt, so I never had the opportunity to go through the natural process of individuation and separation.

When I became an adult, I walked out into the "real" world looking and sounding fine. But I had no concept of the "other" and no boundaries whatsoever. To my underdeveloped sense of self, people around me were extensions of me. I hated and abused myself, so I hated and abused them. Since I didn't know where I ended and the world began, the world was me and I was the world.

When I tried to have normal relationships, other people's boundaries were my worst enemy. People with boundaries could say "no." My God, "no" was a certain death; I could feel it in the pit of my stomach. The fastest way to get a rise out of me was to deny me anything for any reason.

People saw me as demanding, unendingly chaotic, grabbing,

controlling, manipulating others. But it was really the cry of an insatiable, terrorized, wounded little girl, still struggling to grow up, and to survive.

When people don't have healthy limits, they need defenses such as control, withdrawal, blaming, rationalizing, intellectualizing, name calling, perfectionism, black-and-white thinking, threats, fighting about false issues, and excessive concern for the other—all defenses that damage intimacy.

"These are all handy ways to avoid feelings and avoid communication," says Anne Katherine. "The healthy alternative is to state your true feelings."

Non-BPs can have weak limits, too, of course. However, they may be expressed in a different way. Whereas the person with BPD may refuse to take responsibility for their own actions and feelings, non-BPs tend to take too much responsibility for what others say and do. This tendency may come from childhood experiences. As children, some non-BPs were expected to act as emotional or physical caretakers for their parents or others. Frequently, they learned to deny their own needs and take on responsibility for other people's feelings, thoughts, and problems.

John (non-BP)

I was eleven-years-old when my brother was born. A year later, my twin sisters came along. Money, which had always been tight, became a real problem. When I was in junior high, my job was to come home right after school to look after my siblings and get dinner started. One day, though, as I got on the bus to go home, I watched the cross-country track team warming up, getting ready to run. I wanted to be there, running with them.

But when I asked my parents if I could join, my mother collapsed. "We need you here to look after the kids, John," my mom said, crying. "If I quit my job to watch them, we'll have to move to a cheaper apartment." My father got angry. "What's the point of running around in your underwear with a bunch of fifteen-year-old jocks?" he said. "You're selfish! Can't you think of anyone else for a change?"

John's parents discouraged him from seeing his needs as separate from theirs. In order to maintain his parents' love, he had to deny his true feelings. And as an adult, he continued to deny his feelings because it felt familiar and safer. Disclosing his real feelings meant risking feeling unloved. John also grew up learning that his feelings didn't count. So when he got into a relationship with a BP as an adult, he had difficulty keeping his limits, which he was not practiced in doing.

Scripts From the Past

Some people with BPD frequently won't accept responsibility, and some non-borderlines accept too much. Unaware that they're replaying painful scripts from the past, the BP tries to persuade the non-BP to become the focus of their pain and rage. Often, non-BPs all-too-willingly oblige.

The "bargain" that the BP and non-BP strike may be rooted in deep, largely unconscious beliefs about what it takes to survive in this world. For the person with BPD, feeling separated from someone else can be frightening. It makes them feel rejected, abandoned, and alone. So, consciously or unconsciously, they may discourage independence or independent thinking in people close to them.

Kamala (BP)

Before I got better, if people didn't have any protection in place for themselves I would aim right at them. Play them effortlessly. Who doesn't want a target that they can sink, so to speak? But what I was doing, and what a lot of borderlines do, is not a game or a way to get kicks. It's about survival. People who had healthy boundaries in place left me feeling too defective, too out of control, and too vulnerable.

In response, many non-BPs avoid doing anything to provoke a negative reaction from the person with BPD—at least at first. They may worry that if they assert themselves, they'll lose the relationship and be unloved and alone. And the person with BPD, who is taking care of their own pain in the only way they know how, can be skillful at convincing the non-BP that they're being selfish, irresponsible, or uncaring. Over time, the non-BP may eventually lose sight of just how far they've gone to accommodate the BP's skewed sense of reality.

Pushing the Envelope

Without limits, BPD behavior can get drastically out of control. Some non-BPs interviewed for this book have willingly not answered their own work phone because their BP wife was afraid of other women calling; tolerated the BP's multiple affairs, including extramarital liaisons that led to pregnancies and sexually transmitted diseases; or not expressed any needs at all, because to do so would lead to accusations of being "needy and controlling."

Other non-BPs have given up rewarding activities and friendships because of criticism from the BP, lied to friends and family members about the behavior of the person with BPD, tolerated regular physical abuse, gone without sex for more than a decade, not left the house for long periods of time because the person with BPD refused to be alone, or allowed the person with BPD to be abusive to their children.

You may have let someone violate your personal limits in the past. But that doesn't give them permission to do it again—not unless you give it to them. First, though, you have to decide what your limits are.

How Limits Help the BP

Setting limits can be frightening at first. So it's crucial to remember that you're not setting them just for your own mental health. When you set and observe personal limits, you are also benefiting the person in your life with BPD. In fact, when you let the BP violate your boundaries, or do not set any for them, you may be making the situation worse. Some non-BPs believe that setting aside all their needs will eventually "fix" the BP they love.

George (non-BP)

I really don't care about how Kim treats me. Yes, she's done things that have caused me a lot of pain. But thanks to all I've learned about BPD, I know her suffering is so much greater than mine. I like knowing that I'm making a difference in her life. Isn't that what life's about—helping other people?

George's motivation is commendable. But giving up his own needs will not benefit his wife—or himself—in the long run. If George accepts responsibility for Kim's feelings and behavior, then she won't have to. If she's not held accountable for what she does, she won't have to look at how her behavior affects herself and those around her. And until she is held accountable by others and by herself and decides to change, she won't get better. In fact, she could get worse.

In addition, how long will George be able to remain in this relationship with Kim? What is he willing to give up in the long term (friends? security? self-esteem?) to have a relationship with someone who causes him a great deal of pain? Will he feel the same way in ten years? How about fifteen? Is this the example he wants to set for their children?

A borderline's greatest fear is being abandoned. If you set and observe reasonable limits, and if you learn how to take care of your own needs and live your own life, chances are much greater that you will be able to stay in a long-term relationship with the BP—and the possibility increases that your relationship will ultimately be happy and successful. By setting and observing limits, you are acting as a role model for the person with BPD and others in your home. Firm, consistent limits on your part will help the person with BPD eventually create limits for themselves.

The Right to Set Limits

Often, non-BPs look outside themselves for confirmation that it is okay to set limits in a certain area. They wonder if they have a right to get angry when one of their limits is not observed. Many people—not just non-BPs—seem to divide their feelings into two groups: justified and unjustified. Let's say that your friend Sue is thirty minutes late for your lunch date. If Sue finally arrives without an explanation and doesn't even apologize, you might call your anger at her justified. But if Sue doesn't show up at all and you find out the next day that this was because she was in a car accident, you might decide that your earlier response was unjustified.

People also spend a great deal of time arguing about who is "right" in how they feel and what they want. When they argue, they endlessly debate whose desires are more "normal." Harriet Goldhor Lerner (1985) explains the fallacy of such thinking:

> Most of us secretly believe that we have the corner on the "truth," and that this would be a much better world if everyone else believed and reacted exactly as we do. Married couples and family members are especially prone to behave as if there is one "reality" that should be agreed upon by all.
>
> But it is our job to state our thoughts and feelings clearly and to make responsible decisions that are congruent with our values and beliefs. It is not our job to make another person think and feel the way we do or the way we want them to. We have to give up the fantasy that we can change or control another person. It is only

then that we can reclaim the power that is truly ours—
the power to change our own selves and take a new and
different action on our own behalf.

Let's go back to the example with Sue. You're angry that she
was late and didn't phone or apologize. Her position is that you
should have gone ahead and eaten without her, and that if you
didn't, then you can only blame yourself for being angry. It's use-
less to debate whether you "should" feel angry, because the fact is
that you do. It's your job to tell Sue how you feel. It's Sue's job to
tell you how she feels. You don't have to—nor should you—feel it
necessary to convince Sue that your way of thinking is best.
Instead, you simply need to protect yourself in the future now
that you know Sue's attitude about tardiness.

Believing that your own needs are selfish is another common
trap that people fall into. Barb, a thirty-two-year-old woman, says,
"I'm not sure I can continue trying to please my mother. My every
minute is consumed with thoughts of helping her, but every now
and then I think, 'Forget it, I can't do any more.' Is this selfish of
me?"

Setting and enforcing boundaries is not selfish. It is normal
and necessary. Some non-BPs label their behavior "selfish" when
they are simply watching out for themselves.

Terrell (non-BP)

*When I was a kid, "selfish" was an insult in my home. It was
something only "bad" people indulged in. But I learned that it was
only when I started taking care of myself that I was really able to
care for others.*

Guidelines for Setting Limits

Patricia Evans (1996) suggests that certain rights are basic in
relationships, including:

- The right to emotional support, encouragement, and good-
  will from the other.

- The right to be heard by the other and to be responded to
  with courtesy and respect.

- The right to have your own view even if the other has a
  different view.

- The right to have your feelings and experiences acknowledged as real.

- The right to a life free from excessive accusations, blame, criticism, and judgments.

- The right to live free from emotional and physical abuse.

Asking yourself questions can help you better understand your personal limits. What hurts? What feels good? What are you willing to give up for the relationship? What are the things that others do that leave you feeling angry and taken advantage of? Are you able to say no to requests without feeling guilty? How physically close can you allow others to get? At what distance do you begin to feel anxious or uncomfortable? Does the BP in your life respect your physical limits?

Don't expect to be able to sit down and answer these questions in one night—or even one month. Setting limits is a lifelong process. As you learn more about yourself, you learn more about your limits. Sometimes boundaries are formed when someone goes too far and you feel uncomfortable or abused, and it may be very difficult to define your boundaries before they are crossed. Because of this, when your personal limits are crossed, you gain an opportunity to learn more about yourself (Linehan 1993).

Defuse Anger and Criticism

Steve (non-BP)

I read a story about a Zen seeker who goes to the master and sits across the table at tea time. The Zen master holds a stick in his hand, and he says, "If you drink your tea, I will hit you with this stick. If you don't drink your tea, I will hit you with this stick." So what do you do? Well, I think I figured it out. Take away the stick.

The depersonalization and detachment techniques outlined in chapter 5 are ways of "taking away the stick." The defusing techniques in this chapter can have the same effect. Practice the skills in this chapter in everyday situations—at first, preferably, with a person who does not have BPD. Don't worry if you get angry or flustered or if you forget these tools in the heat of a real situation. That's expected. Remember that you're accomplishing something that even trained professionals have difficulty with. Reward yourself for every small step forward.

Develop a Noncombative Communication Style

The first step of good communicating is to become a good listener. When it is your turn to listen, really listen. Don't think about what you are going to say. Do not become defensive and tune the person out, even if they are accusing you of things you never did or said. You'll have the chance to address this later.

Pay attention to the person's words, body language, expressions, and tone of voice. This will help you validate the person's feelings. People with BPD are not always in touch with their own emotions, and by listening closely you may be able to hear beyond the words and detect the feelings that lie beneath the surface.

Mary Lynne Heldmann (1990) says:

> Listening takes concentration and mindfulness. You must focus only on the speaker and forget about what you want to say. Whether or not you ultimately decide that you agree with your critic's perceptions, listening gives you the opportunity to learn.

Heldmann believes that things that get in the way of listening include preoccupation with your own point, distracting thoughts, deciding that you already know what the other person is going to say, and twisting the speaker's message to fit your expectations.

Ways to show you are listening include being silent, pausing before speaking, making eye contact (unless this is threatening), physically turning toward the person, uncrossing your arms, and nodding when appropriate.

Paraphrasing and Reflexive Listening

When responding to the BP, make "I" statements, not "you" statements. You can't read anyone else's mind. You may be wrong about their intentions and feelings. But you are an expert on yourself. You're on safe ground when you describe your own emotions and motivations and let others do the same.

Let's say that you and your co-worker, Shelby, must both pitch in to answer the phones at work. But it seems like you're carrying more of the load. Shelby takes long lunches. Shelby leaves the office for hours at a time. And when he is there, Shelby asks you to take messages for him because "he's busy."

So you decide to have a little talk with Shelby. Following are examples of "you" statements, which all make assumptions about Shelby's state of mind:

- "You are so selfish for pushing this off on me."
- "You take long lunches so you won't have to answer the phone."
- "You must think that you're the only one who's busy around here."

No one likes to be told what their intentions are—least of all someone with BPD. Plus, these kinds of statements invite criticism. What if you're wrong about why Shelby is taking long lunches? Even if you're right, what are the chances that Shelby will agree with your statements about his selfishness and over-inflated ego? Remember that feeling invalidated is a key trigger for people with BPD. "I" statements will help avoid this trigger.

Following are sample "I" statements you could use with Shelby. Use a confident voice and physical manner. Do not stammer or act apologetic for having feelings and opinions.

- "I feel like I am answering the phone more often, and this is causing problems for me because I can't get all my work done. Can we sit down and talk about this?"
- "I am having a hard time getting all my work done because I'm answering the phone so often. My understanding is that this is a task we are supposed to split evenly. I'd like to set up a time to talk to you about this."

Generally, "I" statements make people less defensive and more open to exploring a solution to the problem. However, it's possible that the person with BPD will hear a "you" statement even when you're really making an "I" statement. But don't give up. Over time, the person with BPD may begin to hear what you're really saying.

It is also helpful when communicating with a BP to restate their feelings and main points to show that you are actively hearing them. This does not mean that you have to agree with what they are saying. People who work in customer service jobs are often taught that one of the best ways to defuse a customer's anger is to acknowledge that person's feelings. This doesn't mean that the company is admitting fault. It does mean, however, that the company cares that the customer is having a difficult time. Heldmann suggests paraphrasing, or repeating, the key points of the speaker's statements to show that you want to understand what the person is saying. Develop your own style of doing this so it comes across naturally.

Be careful not to interpret what the other person is saying. That may only make the other person angry and defensive. Here's the difference:

BP: "You never call me anymore. I always have to call you. I am really beginning to wonder if you still want to be my friend or if you're going to reject me like everyone else. I'm really hurting bad right now. You're acting just like my ex-boyfriend Rick did when he decided he couldn't cope with a girlfriend who has BPD. You both make me sick. I didn't ask to have this disorder, you know. I hope you both rot in hell."

Non-BP (paraphrasing): "It sounds like you're really upset because you feel like I haven't called you lately. From what you're saying, it seems like you're worried that I don't want to be friends anymore and that I'm behaving just like Rick did a few weeks ago."

Non-BP (interpreting): "It sounds like you're mixing me up with Rick and assuming that because he left you, I will too. You must still be hurt over that and taking things out on me [notice interpreting and "you" statement]."

Reflective listening is another helpful style of communicating, where you give the speaker your impression of what they are feeling in order to show you are listening and that you care. Says Heldmann:

We all have feelings, and there is no point in challenging someone else's feelings or telling the other person not to feel that way. Making a neutral observation about the other person's feelings is, however, a good way to invite someone to open up, to give him or her room. It isn't necessary to be "right" in your statement of what the other person is feeling. Merely making your honest observation is often enough to open the door.

If the other person's feelings are obvious, you may phrase your observation as a statement, such as, "I can see that you're very angry," or "You seem very sad right now." If the feelings are subtle and unstated, it may be better to ask a question, "Are you feeling scared right now that I might want to back out of our marriage?" Avoid excessive probing, though—your goal is to help the other person express their feelings, not analyze them.

Heldmann says, "Reflective listening can be difficult if the speaker is criticizing you. But if you can stay calm and in control, the speaker will have let off some steam and will probably feel better. And by allowing him free expression of his feelings, you have communicated your openness."

BPD-Specific Communication Skills

Some of the following suggestions are adapted from Marsha Linehan's (1993) work.

- **Stay focused on your message.** While you are talking, the other person may attack or threaten you or try to change the subject. This could be happening for many reasons. For example, the person may be trying to divert you because you are touching on a sensitive area. Ignore the attempts to distract you. Just calmly continue making your point and come back to the other subject later if it is appropriate.

- **Simplify.** When you are communicating about a sensitive issue, or if the person with BPD seems upset, simplify your communication. You and the BP may be feeling such strong emotions that there is little energy left for either of you to do much high-level thinking. Make each sentence short, simple, clear, and direct. Leave no room for misinterpretation.

- **Give positive feedback appropriate to the person and your relationship.** One BP says, "I try to focus on what is right about me, but most of the time the people in my life keep reminding me 'You're mentally ill; you're borderline.' I am working hard to see the possibilities and a future in which I can be happy and productive. This is not made easier by those who label me and refuse to recognize my individuality and potential to grow."

- **Ask questions.** Turn the problem over to the other person. Ask for alternative solutions. For example, "What do you think we should do here?" Or, "I'm not able to say yes, and you seem to really want me to. How can we solve this problem?"

- **Be aware of your own voice inflection and nonverbal communication.** These may communicate as much as, or more than, the words you use. Speak calmly, clearly, and confidently. If you're stating what you want or need, don't let your voice rise at the end as if you were asking a question. This is called "uptalk," and it undermines what you are saying.

Responding to Attacks and Manipulation

Sometimes the responses discussed in the previous section are not appropriate because the BP is "snipping" at you rather than initiating an honest conversation about something you said or did that bothered them. In these types of instances, you may feel attacked, manipulated, or undermined. Examples include:

- "Your sister was always prettier than you."

- "I'd be a better kid if you were a better parent."

- "I see you're going out with your friends again" (said in a disapproving way).

- "That's what *you* think."

Heldmann writes that most people respond to criticism with behavior they learned in childhood. She calls them "The Four Don'ts": Defend, Deny, Counterattack, and Withdraw. You want to avoid these types of responses.

- Don't Defend: Trying to prove to others that you really haven't done anything wrong can make you feel foolish, childish, and guilty, even when you haven't made a mistake.

- Don't Deny: You may use denial because you truly haven't been responsible for whatever it is that you're being accused of. But repeated denial can also make you feel like a child again ("Did not!" "Did too!").

- Don't Counterattack: You may strike back at the person with BPD to try to win the argument or vent your feelings. But when you do this, you'll fallen into the projection and projective identification trap that the BP has unconsciously set for you (see chapter 3). As the doomsday computer in the film *War Games* discovered, the only way to win this game is not to play.

- Don't Withdraw: When non-BPs realize that Defend, Deny, and Counterattack don't work, they often Withdraw. Some non-BPs clam up completely. Some leave physically. Some learn to dissociate. There is nothing wrong with leaving if you feel attacked. In fact, there are times when it's a good thing to do (see chapter 8). The damage comes from remaining passive and silent, absorbing the other person's criticism while your sense of personal power and self-esteem deteriorate.

Heldmann advises keeping a log of critical remarks in order to heighten your awareness of them and how they might be affecting your self-esteem. Living with constant criticism and blame can be like dwelling in a smog-filled city: when you're living there, the smog is unnoticeable because you're in the middle of it. Also, keeping a log also distances you from the remarks and enables you to look at them less emotionally and more objectively. Track criticism and blame coming from the person with BPD (and perhaps from others in your life). Note what is said, how it makes you feel, and how you respond. Did you Defend, Deny, Counterattack, or Withdraw?

Defusing Techniques

Following are some of Heldmann's better choices for responding. These disarm your critics and enhance and empower you. If you use these suggestions, speak sincerely, naturally, and neutrally. Avoid being flippant or counterattacking. Also, use them cautiously, since you never know how the other person will respond. The same technique, used on two different days, may spark different reactions.

Agree with Part of the Statement

Criticism: "I see you're going out with your friends again" (said in a disapproving way).

Response: "Yes, I am going out."

Criticism: "When I was your age, I never would have gone on a date looking like that."

Response: "No, you probably wouldn't have" (said in an agreeable way).

Criticism: "I can't believe you won't let me go out with my friends just because you found some pot in my room. If you weren't my mother, my life would be so much better."

Response: "True, I'm not going to let you go out with your friends because you've been smoking pot."

Agree with the Possibility That Your Critic Could Be Right

Criticism: "I had an affair. Big deal!"

Response: "Some people might not think it was a big deal if their husband had a affair. But I'm not one of them."

Criticism: "How can you even suggest not inviting Mom to the party? So she acts a little strange, sometimes. She's still your mother!"

Response: "Yes, she is still my mother. And some people would invite all their relatives, no matter how they act. But I believe that Mom has a choice about how she wants to behave. If she's going to choose to say outrageous things that hurt people's feelings, I don't feel comfortable inviting her."

Recognize That the Critic Has an Opinion

Criticism: "Children belong with their mother, not their father. And I know the judge will see it that way too."

Response: "I can see you have strong opinions about custody. The judge may see it the way you do. Or they may not."

Criticism: "If anyone has BPD, it's you, not me."

Response: "I can see that you disagree with the therapist's opinion that you have BPD."

Use Gentle Humor When Appropriate

Criticism: "I can't believe you forgot to buy charcoal. How are we going to grill the fish?"

Response: "Well, we've always been meaning to try sushi" (said without sarcasm.)

Practice defusing response in less threatening situations first. And no matter what happens, congratulate yourself for your efforts.

In this chapter, we've given you the foundation you'll need in order to make substantive changes in your relationship with the BP. In the next chapter, we'll show you how to actually discuss this with the BP in your life. Make sure that you understand the information presented in this chapter thoroughly before you go on. You should have a clear understanding of the following:

- The factors that can trigger BPD behavior, along with the concept that while you may trigger the behavior you are not to blame for it

- How the BP in your life may trigger you with fear, obligation, and guilt

- How personal limits (boundaries) help relationships

- The personal limits that you would like the BP to observe

- The futility of discussing your "rights" to set limits—the question is not about "rights" but about your personal feelings about how you want to be treated

- Guidelines for good communication

In the next chapter, we will go over how you can begin to effectively assert your needs with the BP in your life.

7

Asserting Your Needs with Confidence and Clarity

I told my borderline wife over and over again how much I loved her, that I would never leave her, that she was a beautiful and intelligent person. But it was never enough. If a female salesclerk's fingers brushed mine as she was giving me change, my wife would accuse me of flirting. Trying to fill the emotional black hole inside a BP is like trying to fill the Grand Canyon with a water pistol—except the Grand Canyon has a bottom.

—From the non-BP Internet support group

You can respond to someone with BPD in two primary ways: like a mirror or like a sponge. It is common for the same person to react both ways—sometimes absorbing, sometimes reflecting.

Stop "Sponging" and Start "Mirroring"

Some non-BPs absorb their BP's projections and soak up their pain and rage (sponging). These non-BPs may be under the illusion that they are helping the borderline. But in fact, by not reflecting the BP's painful feelings back to their rightful owner (mirroring), they are rewarding them for using these defense mechanisms and making it more likely that the borderline will continue to use them in the future.

People who act like sponges say they feel like they are trying to fill a black hole of emptiness inside the BP. But no matter how much love, caring, and devotion they pour into the hole, it is never enough. So they blame themselves and work even more frantically to fill the hole. At the same time, the BP feels the very real and terrifying pain of the aching cavity and urges the non-BP to work even harder and faster at filling the hole. If the BP is the acting-out type, they may castigate the non-BP for being lazy or indifferent to their terrible anguish. If the BP acts in, they may tearfully beg the non-BP to do something—anything—to end their suffering.

But it's all a diversion to keep the BP and non-BP from addressing the real issue: The emptiness belongs to the person with BPD, and the only person who can fill it is the BP themselves.

Stay Focused and Observe Your Limits

Don't get caught up in the borderline's accusations, blaming, impossible demands, and criticism. Instead of soaking up the other person's pain, try to maintain your own sense of reality despite what the other person says. Reflect the pain back to its proper owner—the person with BPD. Express confidence that the BP can learn to cope with their own feelings. It is important that you offer your support, while making it clear that the BP is ultimately the only person who can control their feelings and reactions.

Show by your actions that you have a bottom line: there are limits to the type of behavior that you will and will not accept. Communicate these limits clearly and act on them consistently. You may also need to take steps, if necessary, to protect yourself or your children—not because you are judging or labeling anyone else's behavior, but because you value yourself and your feelings. These steps might include removing yourself or your children from an abusive situation, letting the BP take responsibility for their own actions, asserting your own feelings and wishes, disregarding name calling or provocative behavior, refusing to speak to an enraged person, declining to let anyone else's public behavior embarrass you, or simply saying no.

You must know your own bottom line for different types of situations. It may be helpful to think through what you would do if anyone else besides the BP were to act toward you in the same way. For example, what would you do if a stranger in the grocery store began talking to you in the same way the BP in your life does? If you would take steps to stop a stranger from treating you in this way, why not take steps to stop the BP from doing the same? If you're concerned about the BP's behavior toward a child, what would you do if your child's teacher behaved toward your child like the BP does? Which do you believe is more potentially harmful: abuse from a teacher or abuse from a caretaker? Another way to think about these tough issues is to consider what advice you would give to a friend or loved one in your situation. Then ask yourself: Is any of this advice applicable to you as well?

If you find that you feel helpless in all of these situations, you may wish to work with a therapist to explore and set personal limits. This should help you in all your relationships—not just the one with the BP.

There are some specific strategies that you can use while talking to an upset BP that can help you reflect BPD behavior instead of absorbing its affects. The first is to breathe deeply. When stressed, people have a tendency to take shorter and shallower breaths. The fight-or-flight reaction kicks in and it becomes hard to think logically. This can happen to the person with BPD as well. Taking slow, deep breaths can help you settle down and think logically instead of simply reacting emotionally.

Next, it is important that you keep on seeing shades of gray. Often, non-BPs pick up the borderline defense mechanism of splitting, or seeing things in black-and-white. Keep in mind the subtleties inherent in all situations. For example, avoid the words "all" or "never." Instead of thinking everything is "this way or that way," come up with three more alternatives. Don't get sucked into the other person's extreme reactions; trust your instincts and form your own judgments.

Also, remember to separate your feelings from those of the person with BPD. In chapter 3, we explained that BPs often use projection to try to get others to feel their feelings for them. You may need to keep checking yourself to determine whose feelings are whose. If you start to feel helpless or angry, is it because the other person is projecting their own helplessness or anger onto you? Remember the goal of projective identification. Does it seem like the BP is trying to provoke a certain reaction from you? If you act in this way, will the BP then be proved "right"?

During conversations you should validate yourself, yet keep an open mind. The BP may state "facts" that you know to be untrue or may assert opinions that you strongly disagree with. Yet people with BPD can be perceptive. So objectively consider what the BP is saying. If, after reflecting, you still disagree, then remind yourself that your version of reality is equally as valid as anyone else's. This is called self-validation (your feelings need to be validated just as much as those of the person with BPD). Keep in mind all you have learned about BPD defense mechanisms and depersonalizing.

If you are bringing up a touchy subject, be aware of timing. There are good and bad times to bring up certain subjects. If, for any reason, the BP is feeling rejected, abandoned, or invalidated by other life events, they may react strongly to what you have to say. So you may want to postpone the conversation for a calmer time. In addition, be aware of your own moods. If you are feeling lost, vulnerable, lonely, or sad, you may wish to wait until you are feeling stronger.

Finally, remember that you have a choice about your feelings. Although songs and movies often send out the message that people can make others feel good or bad, the choice of how someone feels is largely up to them. If the BP says, "You're the worst mother in the world," you can choose to believe it and feel guilty, or you can depersonalize these words because you know that tomorrow the BP may tell you that you are the best mother in the world.

Acknowledge Before Disputing

People with BPD may unconsciously revise their version of the facts to fit their feelings about a certain situation. While it may be tempting to argue about the facts with a BP, doing so neglects the real source of the problem: the BP's feelings. Consider the following example of how to address the BP's feelings without agreeing with or arguing over their version of the facts.

Fact: Cynthia, the mother of a borderline teenager,
              Jessie, occasionally has a glass of wine at
              night when a friend comes over for a visit.

Feelings:	When Cynthia has friends over, Jessie feels ignored, depressed, and angry.
Jessie's "Facts":	Because of shame and splitting, Jessie doesn't take responsibility for her own negative feelings. Instead, she accuses her mom of causing them, actually convincing herself that Cynthia has a drinking problem. To Jessie (and other BPs), if an explanation feels right it *is* right. Facts that don't fit the BP's theories are conveniently denied or ignored.

If Jessie accuses her mom of being an alcoholic and Cynthia immediately begins defending herself (a natural response), Jessie will interpret this to mean, "You are wrong and bad for feeling this way." She will then become even angrier at having her feelings invalidated. Furthermore, the real issue—Jessie's feelings of abandonment— would not be addressed. So nothing would be resolved.

By addressing Jessie's feelings before disagreeing with her facts, Cynthia will be able to share her version of reality at a time when Jessie is more open to hearing it. In the example that follows, notice how Cynthia allows Jessie to fully express her feelings before she presents the facts as she sees them. Cynthia doesn't begin by addressing whether she is or is not an alcoholic, because that would be dealing with facts. In Jessie's borderline world, feelings are all that are important right now.

Jessie (angrily):	You've been drinking out here on the porch with your friends for hours. You're just a drunk!
Cynthia:	You seem angry and upset.
Jessie:	You bet I am! How would you feel if your mother was an alcoholic?
Cynthia (sincerely):	I wouldn't like it at all. It would make me feel scared and worried that she wouldn't be able to take care of me. Is that how you feel?
Jessie:	I'm just mad! I am calling the child abuse hot line tomorrow. I'm telling them that my mom lies around the house drunk all day!
Cynthia:	No one would want a mom who lies around the house drunk all day. It sounds like that's

what you think I do. You have a right to
your own feelings and opinions. I see things
differently, though, and I also have a right to
my feelings and opinions. The way I see
things, I am quite busy all day, and I drink
pretty infrequently. And when I do, I don't
do it to a state of drunkenness. I don't feel
drunk right now, and I don't believe I'm
acting drunk either.

Jessie: You've had too much to drink. You're acting
just like Grandpa when he is drunk. Why do
you need to sit around the house with your
friends? I hate your friends. They're just a
bunch of stuck-up bitches.

Cynthia: I know you don't like my friends. You have
a right to your opinions about them. We
don't always have to like the same people.

Jessie: I don't see why they have to come over all
the time.

Cynthia: I know that it seems to you like they're here
all the time. Actually, I haven't seen Ronnie
and Marta for several weeks. I have a good
time with them, and I also have a good time
with you when we go shopping and do stuff
together. Like yesterday, when we went to
pick up your dress for the prom and stopped
for hamburgers and milk shakes. We had a
good time, remember?

Jessie (calmer):   Yeah. But I just wish you didn't have to
drink with them.

Cynthia   Yes, I know you don't like it.
(understandingly):

Notice that Cynthia reflects Jessie's feelings without agreeing
that drinking is the same as being drunk. Of course it's frustrating
to be the subject of wild accusations that don't make any sense.
It's not fair. Cynthia may go upstairs and grit her teeth with a
knot inside her stomach. She may wish that Jessie lived somewhere else. But she has succeeded in talking with her daughter

about the real issue that's upsetting her. In addition, Cynthia has expressed her own opinions and observations without invalidating Jessie's. That's quite an accomplishment.

In these kinds of situations, it's helpful to remember the developmental levels that you learned in chapter 3. Jessie looks like a young adult. She sounds like a young adult. But emotionally, Jessie is a small, vulnerable child, feeling forsaken by a mother whom she believes doesn't know or care she exists. But instead of crying for mommy the way a toddler would, Jessie shouts and threatens. Her childlike feelings bring about very real adult consequences. Such is the nature of BPD. You may make things harder for yourself if you expect adultlike behavior from someone who is currently incapable of it, or if you censor your negative feelings and scold yourself for having them.

Expect the unexpected. Accept your feelings for what they are and know that they're normal for people in your situation. See through the BP's exterior and realize that right now, they may not be capable of what most people would consider "normal" behavior.

Prepare for the Discussion

Talking with the BP about your personal limits is something you can and should prepare for. Following are some tips for communicating about your limits:

- **Be specific.** "I would like you to respect me more" is ambiguous. What exactly is respect, and how do you know when you're getting it? "I would like you to stop blaming me for your physical illnesses," is specific and measurable.

- **Communicate about one limit at a time.** The BP may be treating you in a variety of ways you find intolerable. But asking them to stop blaming you for all their problems, to stop raising their voice, and to stop calling you names may be too much for the BP to process all at once. Choose one to start with.

- **Begin with the easy stuff.** Telling someone to stop calling you names may be simpler than asking them to stop being overly blaming. You can increase your chances of success and build your confidence by starting with something easier.

- **Practice with a good friend.** Role-play the situation with a friend. Do this a couple of times, changing the BP's responses each time. Don't feel you have to rush; take as much time as you like to think and respond, both during the role play and the real event. Things will come together and it will get easier. It just takes time.

- **Think about the rewards for maintaining your personal integrity.** These include feelings of strength, self-respect, confidence, hopefulness, and pride.

Determine Your Reality

Often, the truth is not so clear cut. Many non-BPs we interviewed told us they had trouble trusting their own perceptions of reality because the BPs in their lives were so convincing in their insistence that they were right and the non-BPs were wrong.

Let's look at Sara, a non-BP, and her borderline mother, Maria. Sara tells Maria that she will no longer stay on the phone when Maria blames and criticizes her. Sara also puts limits on the number of times per week that her mother may call her.

"I would never do that to my mother!" Maria snaps. "How can you refuse to talk to your own mother on the phone? How can you hurt my feelings like this? How could I raise such an ungrateful, selfish daughter?"

Sara's father, George, agrees. He takes Sara aside and says, "That's just how your mother acts, Sara. She can't help it. Be a good daughter and make things right with your mother."

Sara feels confused. Is she being bad and selfish? Does she owe it to her mother to stay on the phone, even if she feels a horrible tightness in her chest when her mother berates her?

When the BP or other people around them make countermoves, you will need to return to the belief that you have a right to all of your opinions, thoughts, and feelings. Good or bad, right or wrong, they are part of you. You also need to keep in mind the personal limits you've set for yourself.

If Sara decides to debate proper phone etiquette with her parents, she will be avoiding the real issue: as an adult, she is responsible for making her own choices about how she wants to be treated.

Sara says, "Dad, I appreciate the fact that you have different beliefs about me asking Mom to observe phone limits. I understand that the two of you might do things differently. But I am not you—I am me. And in order to respect myself and my own feelings, I need to limit phone calls to once a week and not stay on the phone and listen to criticism and blaming that makes me feel bad."

Reality statements help you and the BP find the grays in between the black and white of your "truth" and theirs. The two of you may negotiate. For example, Sara and her mother may ultimately agree on phone calls twice a week instead of once a week.

Once you've asserted your reality statement, you must shift responsibility for the BP's feelings and actions back to the BP. You can let them know that you support them, but they are ultimately the only person who can make themselves feel better.

Even if the BP acknowledges they have Borderline Personality Disorder, it is usually unwise to make this shift by bringing up the diagnosis. This may be viewed as dismissive and disrespectful. Here is a more positive way of shifting, using the example of Sara and her mother: "I understand, Mom, that you disagree with my phone limits. I can see that it is upsetting to you that I am asserting my own feelings about the negative things you say about me when we are talking on the phone. Perhaps you can think about this for a few days, and hopefully you will realize that I still do want to talk with you when you are not criticizing and blaming me. I care about you and I want to hear from you—I just want to be treated like the mature, responsible adult that I am."

If you've made a mistake and the BP is upset, you should share the responsibility. Let's say that your borderline daughter is upset with you because you forgot to pick up a book from the library for her as you promised. But her reaction is all out of proportion. She insists that you "always" forget these kinds of things, that you must have forgotten because you don't care about her, and that you wish she was dead.

In this instance, you might want to share the responsibility rather than just shift it. (As you read this, remember that you've already gone through the process of paying attention, understanding fully, and so on.) Here's what you might say: "I know you feel very hurt and angry that I forgot to pick up the book. And you've said you feel that I 'do this all the time' and that 'this means I don't love you.' I can try to make up for forgetting the book by saying I'm sorry and offering to pick it up tomorrow—which I've done. And I can point out the times I have remembered to do you favors. And I can tell you that I do love you—which I do, very much. That's all I can do. I can't change the past. I can't make you believe that I love you. I can't make you see the things I've done for you, if you choose not to look at them. I know it hurts and you're mad, and I wish I could make it all better for you. The way I see things, you need to step in here and help yourself. You can choose to keep thinking these things, or you can choose to try to calm down, accept my apology, and see where we can go from here. I can't do it for you. Perhaps with my support, you can do it for yourself."

Build Communication Skills

When the BP is not agitated, you can pursue the issues even further than Cynthia was able to do with Jessie and attempt to clarify and even resolve issues. When engaging in this type of discussion with the BP, it is essential that when it is your turn to listen, you really listen. Don't think about what you are going to say. Do not become defensive and tune the person out, even if they are accusing you of things you never did or said. You'll have the chance to address this later. Pay attention to the person's words, body language, expressions, and tone of voice. This will help you validate their feelings. People with BPD are not always in touch with their own emotions, and by listening closely you may be able to hear beyond the words and detect the feelings that lie beneath the surface.

It is also important that you understand fully what the BP is upset about. Sometimes the person with BPD will say something or accuse you of something that makes no sense to you. It's easy to get frustrated and angry, which simply escalates the situation if the BP feels invalidated and misunderstood. When this happens, remember that you and the BP may be speaking two different languages. Try to stay calm and gently ask the person to clarify what they mean.

Following is an example of how to go about better understanding the BP, in a conversation between Tara (BP) and Cory (non-BP). No matter how angry or upset Tara gets, Cory remains calm and composed.

Tara: I know you're having an affair.

Cory   What makes you think that?
(surprised):

Tara: Because you don't love me anymore, you never loved me, and you want to leave me.

Cory: Whoa, let's take those one at a time. Why do you doubt my love for you?

Tara: You don't spend enough time with me, for one thing.

Cory: You said I don't spend enough time with you. Can you tell me what you mean?

Tara: You know what I mean!

Cory: No, I'm not sure I do. But I want to understand. Can you help me?

Tara: Last Saturday, you went out with your friends to a movie without me.

In this situation, asking Tara to elaborate gave Cory some much needed information. If he had immediately responded by denying the affair, they probably would have fought at length without uncovering the real issue—Tara's fear of abandonment sparked by Cory going out with friends without her.

If you want the conversation to facilitate change, you must validate the BP's emotions. This combines the paraphrasing and reflective listening skills you learned in chapter 6.

Lynn (BP)

When I finally got counseling, it was like a miracle to be given permission to feel my feelings and to be told those were healthy, intelligent reactions to have, given the situation I had been in. My family had been telling me I shouldn't feel the way I did, which just made me angrier and more upset.

The feelings of the person with BPD may not make sense to you, but they do make sense to the BP. Don't judge the person's feelings, deny them, trivialize them, or discuss whether or not you think they are "justified." Restate them; dig a bit beneath the surface for feelings that may not be as obvious; ask the other person if your perceptions are correct; and show the borderline that you are hearing what they're saying. Avoid sounding patronizing or condescending, however, or the BP may get enraged because you don't sound like you are taking their concerns seriously.

This conversation demonstrating validation is a continuation of the one between Tara and Cory:

Tara: Last Saturday, you went out with your friends to a movie without me.

Cory: You sound really upset and angry—both about me going out to the movie and about thinking that I don't love you. I can see that from the tone of your voice and the expression on your face. Tara, I can understand that if you thought I didn't love you, that would be upsetting. If that were true, it would be more than upsetting—it would be devastating. Are you feeling hurt and sad right now?

Tara: Yes!

After you have validated the BP's feelings, assert yourself with "my reality" statements. In this example, Cory's reality is straightforward: he knows that he asked Tara if she wanted to go to the movie, and she refused. And he knows that indeed, he does love her. In this case, he could say, "Tara, it's true that I did go out with friends. You didn't want to go, so I went by myself. I had a good time—I enjoy being with my friends. But that doesn't mean I don't love you—I do, in fact, very much."

Some reality statements will be factual (e.g., "When I said that I smelled something burning, I wasn't commenting on your cooking. I was just noticing a burning odor."). Other reality statements will reflect your opinions (e.g., "I don't believe that wanting to see a movie with friends is selfish. I think that even when two people are married, it's good for them both to have other friends and pursue their own interests.").

Express your reality statement clearly. The BP may try to argue with you about who is "right" or who is to "blame." Some of these arguments may be illogical; for example, one BP insisted that she was justified in punching and kicking her husband because he had called her "violent." Resist the temptation to justify, overexplain, or debate. Simply stay focused on your message, for example, an appropriate response to an accusation would be: "I understand that you feel this way, but I see it differently." Repeat it as often as is necessary.

Ask for Change

Once you know what your personal limits are, it's time to communicate these to the BP. But before you do, be clear on what you can reasonably ask for—and what you can't.

It is reasonable to ask the BP to change their behavior. Chances are they act differently with you than they do in front of friends, when they're out in public, or when they're at work. If the BP can control their behavior under some circumstances, it's likely they can control it in others.

Of course, people with BPD may need help in order to change their actions. If the BP in your life seeks help, they may have a much easier time observing your limits. But as you know, this is a decision each person with BPD must make for themselves.

But while it's reasonable to ask someone to change their behavior, it isn't reasonable for you to tell someone how they should feel. In other words, you can ask the BP not to yell at you, but you can't tell them not to be angry. You can request that the BP not call you more than twice a day, but you can't tell them not to feel alone and panicky when you're not around. If people with BPD could change their feelings through sheer willpower, they would have done so already!

Harriet Goldhor Lerner (1985) writes:

> Most of us want the impossible. We want to control not only our own decisions and choices but also the other person's reactions to them. We not only want to make a change; we want the other person to like the change that we make. We want to move on to a higher level of assertiveness and clarity and then receive praise and reinforcement from those very people who have chosen us for our old familiar ways.

Communicate Your Limits

Pick a good time to talk—a time when the BP is feeling grounded and in good spirits. Many times, when things are going well, non-BPs don't bring up difficult issues because they do not want to spoil the mood. You will need to overcome the urge to leave well enough alone. Perhaps you and the BP can schedule a time to talk that is good for both of you.

BPD researcher Marsha M. Linehan (1993) has developed a communicating style known as DEAR, which stands for Describe, Express, Assert, and Reinforce. Following are each of the steps and how you can use them to explain your personal limits.

Describe

Describe the situation as you see it without exaggerating, making judgments, or explaining how you felt about it. Be as objective and as specific as you can. It may help to pretend you are a video camera capturing the action exactly as it happened. Do not use judgmental or loaded words or phrases. Do not claim that you are privy to the person's inner motivations or feelings, although you can say that it "appeared as if" they were upset, angry, etc.

For example: "Yesterday, we were driving home from our vacation. Around lunchtime, we began talking about when we were going to stop to eat when you began speaking to me in angry tones that got louder and louder. You seemed to be very upset about something that happened the day before. After about ten minutes, I asked if we could continue the conversation at another time. Then you continued to yell at me. After several more minutes, I asked again if we could talk about this after we got home. You refused and swore at me and called me names."

Express

Express your feelings or opinions about the situation clearly. Take responsibility for your own feelings; do not say, "You made me feel this way." Instead say, "I felt this way." You may need to do some thinking beforehand in order to determine your exact emotions.

For example: "When you were shouting at me, I felt very bad. I was afraid because I didn't know what you might do or say next. I felt helpless because there was no place for me to go because we were in the car. I felt sad because you were angry at me. And when I asked you to stop and you didn't stop, I became mad because you were not responding to me. I also felt concerned because our son was in the back seat, and I was worried about how the argument was affecting him."

Remember, it's very difficult for people with BPD to understand that you can be angry or upset with them and still love them. So you may wish to remind them that even though something is bothering you, you still care about them deeply.

Assert

Assert your limits, making them simple. Again, explain that you've decided on this limit *not* because it is right, expected, normal, or how the other person "should" act. Instead, you want this because it is *your* personal preference, it is how *you* would like to be treated, and it is behavior that makes *you* comfortable.

For example: "I do care about your feelings, and I do want to resolve our difficulties. When things get intense and we start yelling at each other, I may need to stop the conversation and return to it later when we have both calmed down. This is something I need to do to make myself feel better."

Again, the BP may try to engage you in a debate about what is right or wrong or who is at fault. Once more, resist the temptation to justify, overexplain, or debate. Listen carefully, then repeat your message: "I hear what you're saying, and understand that you think it's all my fault. However, I see things differently. My firm position is that this kind of behavior toward me is unacceptable, and I want it to stop."

Reinforce

Reinforce the benefits of your limits, if appropriate. Explain the positive effects of getting what you need. If appropriate, help the person with BPD see the negative effects of the status quo, too.

For example: "When we resume the conversation, I can be more in a position to hear your concerns because I feel calm and more centered. And we will not get bogged down in angry conversations that do not seem to resolve anything and leave us both upset."

Don't threaten your loved one in an attempt to control their behavior. For example, let's say that you and the BP are attending your grandma's eighty-fifth birthday party. The BP sees that everyone else is dressed very nicely and gets mad at you because you dressed informally in shorts and a faded T-shirt. The BP screams at you, calling you a slob in front of everyone. A natural—but unhelpful—response would be to say in an angry tone of voice, "If you don't stop it right now, I'm walking out the door!"

Instead, make it clear that you are not acting against the other person, you are acting for yourself. For example: "I am extremely uncomfortable when you yell at me—especially when other people can hear. It makes me feel angry and helpless. I am asking you to stop this right now, so we can keep on having a good time at the party." You may need to assert your wishes and reinforce the positive consequences (e.g., "we can keep on having a good time") more than once.

You may also wish to bring up the negative consequences: "If you don't stop this, I am going to have to go somewhere else and take a break." Then do it if the BP still doesn't respond.

Be Prepared for Countermoves

When people give up ineffective fighting and make clear statements about their own needs, desires, and beliefs, the other person usually shifts their behavior in response. This happens in all relationships. But when one of the people has BPD, it is crucial to anticipate the ways in which they might react to the changes you are making.

People with BPD try to manage their pain through their inter-actions with other people. As we have explained, projections, rages, criticism, blaming, and other defense mechanisms may be attempts to get you to feel their pain for them. When you assertively redirect the pain back to the BP so they can begin to deal with it, you are breaking a contract that you didn't know you signed. Naturally, the person with BPD will find this distressing. They will probably per-form a countermove. This is an action designed to restore things back to the way they were. Countermoves also help people justify their actions, both to themselves and to you. This element is crucial because it seems to make the blackmail acceptable—even noble. Your ability to withstand these countermoves will determine the future course of your relationship.

According to Lerner, people will react to limit setting in three predictable and successive steps: mild disagreement, intense dis-agreement, and threats. (Be aware that someone with BPD, however, may skip right to threats.) In our discussion of these steps, we will focus on mild and intense disagreement. In chapter 8, we'll discuss unsafe threats.

How to Respond to Mild Disagreement

Following are some countermove tactics discussed by Susan Forward (1997).

- **The Spin:** The blackmailer tells you that their motivations are pure and honorable, while yours are underhanded, unscrupulous, and self-serving. (It's common for non-BPs who set limits to be split into the "bad" person.)

- **Labeling:** The blackmailer calls you names that reinforce their "spun" viewpoint and undermine your sense of reality. Many of these are actually projections.

- **Pathologizing:** The blackmailer tries to convince you that you are not just acting bad—you are bad (or sick, messed up, damaged, etc.). The higher the stakes, the more likely it is that this will happen. Many non-BP's told us that the BPs in their lives accused them of having BPD.

- **Enlisting Allies:** The blackmailer asks other people to pressure you. This seems to be most common when the BP is a parent. In one case, a borderline mother showed up at her daughter's door with four relatives to back her up.

When responding, it's important to stay away from arguments about whether your limits are right or wrong. Here are some sample responses to some typical statements:

BP: You're a bad (selfish, etc.) person for making this request.

Non-BP: I understand you think that I'm a bad person, but I feel good about myself and I'm proud that I respect myself enough to set this limit.

BP: You must hate me.

Non-BP: No, I don't. In fact, I care about you so much that I want to work together to make our relationship better. I also care for and respect myself, which is why I'm bringing this up.

BP: You're manipulative and controlling.

Non-BP: I understand that you think I'm manipulative and controlling. I feel it's your job to make choices and decide how you want to act. And it's my job to think about the things I'm comfortable with and the things I'm not. I've thought about this a great deal, and this is very important to me and my own self-respect.

BP: You shouldn't feel that way.

Non-BP: Perhaps if you were in my position, you wouldn't feel this way. We're two different people, and we each have our own beliefs, feelings, and opinions.

I am asking you to respect my feelings, even if you don't share them.

BP: You're the child. I'm the parent.

Non-BP: I am your child. And I'm not a little girl (boy) anymore. I'm an adult, and it's time for me to make my own decisions based on my own feelings and beliefs. You may not agree with me, and that's your right. It's my right to act in ways that respect myself.

Other non-argumentative responses include:

- That's your choice.
- I would like to talk about this later when things have calmed down.
- I need to think about this more.
- There are no villains here. We just see things differently.
- I'm not willing to take more than 50 percent of the responsibility.
- I know you don't like this, but it's not negotiable.
- I know you want an answer right now, but I need time to think.
- I won't be put in the middle. You need to work that out with them.

How to Respond to Intense Disagreement

When the BP increases the intensity of their responses, the implicit message is: "You are taking away my method of coping and I cannot stand these feelings—so change back!" If they shouted before, now they will rage out of control. If they previously accused you of being selfish, now they will call you the most self-centered, egotistical, and controlling person in the world. If they coped by using violence (self-mutilation or battering), the violence may become more severe. Chapter 8 will address how to protect yourself from violence.

Remember Countermoves Are Normal

It is important to remember that countermoves are not a sign that what you did was wrong or did not work. It means that you have asked the BP to do something difficult. Nobody likes doing things that make them uncomfortable.

It is possible that over time, your limit setting will lead to the BP taking a hard look at themselves and deciding to seek help. Or they could devalue you, accuse you of abandoning them, and claim that they never want to see you again. Or they could do both. Whatever happens, it is possible that it would have happened eventually anyway. Your actions may have just accelerated the pace of things.

Persisting for Change

If Your Limits Aren't Observed

If you want the BP to change, you have to be willing to make some changes yourself if the person does not observe your limits. Think about the things you can do, not the things you feel you can't do. Be creative. For example:

- You can change the subject or refuse to discuss the matter.

- You can leave the room or hang up the phone.

- You can change your phone number, get Caller ID, or change the door locks.

- You can go in your room and shut the door.

- You can be with the person only when a third party is present.

- You can refuse to read the person's mail or E-mail. You can change your Internet address.

- You can stop the car or refuse to drive with the person.

- You can say no firmly without changing your mind.

- You can ask for help from therapists or friends, even if the BP doesn't want you to do so.

- You can call a crisis line or shelter.

- You can call the police and get a restraining order.

- You can stop seeing the person for awhile or break off the relationship altogether.

- You can find alternative places for a child to stay (e.g., a group home, a distant relative, etc.).

- You can take steps to protect children from abusive situations (e.g., taking the kids out when the BP is raging, reporting child abuse, and seeking sole custody).

Naturally, all of these things will be perceived as abandonment by the person with BPD. That's why you may need to gently point out that you are not acting against them, you are acting for yourself. Explain that your limits are essential to the health of the relationship and that you are asking the BP to observe them so you can be with them for a very long time.

Consistency Is the Key

Within reason, we suggest you observe your limits in a gentle way every time—even when you're tired or when you'd rather avoid a fight. You may not always be able to take immediate action, but you can't let unacceptable behavior go unnoticed, or you may actually reinforce it. Again, preparation is key. Think through the "what ifs" and decide ahead of time, if you can, what steps you will take in each case.

Use the Utmost Caution

BPD is a serious personality disorder. It is crucial that you seek outside help from a competent mental health professional if you have any reason to believe that the countermoves may be more severe than you can handle alone.

If children are involved, we strongly suggest that you consult with a qualified mental health professional about how to best protect children under difficult circumstances. It is essential that this person be knowledgeable about both BPD and issues involving children. If this person's recommendations go against your gut instincts, you may wish to get a second opinion. Remember, each person with BPD is different, and each child is different.

If you are a father who is worried about visitation, custody, or false accusations, we strongly recommend talking with an attorney who is familiar with father's rights issues before you make any sudden moves. It is crucial that anyone you consult with is familiar with these types of situations and has dealt with them successfully (see appendix D for references).

If the BP in your life is your parent and you were physically or emotionally abused as a child, we suggest that you work with a mental health professional to make sure that you are emotionally ready to ask your parent to observe your limits and that you are prepared for any response they might have.

Whatever your circumstances, you may need a great deal of love, support, and validation as you stand up for yourself. Some of the important people in your life may be able to support you; ask for their help. Other people may disagree with your actions because they feel it threatens their own relationship with the BP, or because it contradicts their own firmly held beliefs about how things should be. This is normal. Acknowledge their right to have their own opinions, and express your desire to keep your relationship with them separate from your relationship with the BP.

Measure Your Success by the Things You Can Control

The person with BPD in your life may or may not respond as you would like during any one particular conversation. This is beyond your control. So measure your success by the factors you can control. Ask yourself:

- Did you respond as an adult, not as a child?

- Did you act in a way that demonstrates your self-respect?

- Were you clear about your position?

- Did you remain focused, even if the BP tried to draw you off track?

- Did you remain calm and composed?

- Did you refuse to be baited and drawn into a losing argument?

- Were you considerate of the other person's feelings, even if they did not give you the same consideration?

- Did you maintain a firm grip on your own reality while maintaining an open mind toward the BP's concerns?

If you can answer yes to any of these questions, pat yourself on the back.

We've covered a great deal in this chapter. Don't try to absorb it all at once. It may seem overwhelming now—but you can change the way you interact with the BP in your life. Just remember these key points:

- Believe you're asserting your limits for the long-term health of the relationship—not just for yourself.

- Be a mirror, not a sponge.

- Stay on track. Don't let the BP distract you from your communication goals.

- Feel good about the steps you've taken. You've come a long way.

In the next chapter, we'll discuss what to do when the BP's behavior becomes unsafe for you or them.

8

Develop a Safety Plan

Yeah, make your arm bleed, bang your forehead on the headboard, harder, harder! Scream at those you love until they slink off terrified of you, the traitors! Burn your fingers on the stove, prick your hand with a pin over and over and over and over. Take those pills. Buy more, stock up. This might just be the big eclipse.

—Melissa Ford Thornton, *Eclipses: Behind the Borderline Personality Disorder*

Rages, physical abuse, self-mutilation, and suicide threats are the most isolating, frightening kinds of behaviors non-BPs must contend with from the BPs in their lives. Sometimes non-BPs also rage, become abusive, or consider suicide. In addition to the mirroring skills we discussed in chapter 7, the keys to managing these difficult situations are preplanning and obtaining outside help. Hopefully your behavior will encourage the BP to get the professional assistance they so desperately need.

Out-of-Control Rages

Borderline rages can be terrifying. The BP may seem to be completely out of control, acting on impulse, and heedless of the consequences of their behavior.

Karen Ann (BP)

When I am angry, I can't think rationally. I'm possessed by a whirlwind of emotions that cause me to act out viciously. The feelings overpower me and I have to lash out to let them escape. It's an attempt to protect myself, knowing full well that what I am doing will actually drive a person further away.

Dick (BP)

When I rage at someone, they are no longer a real person with real feelings. They become the object of my hatred and the cause of my distress. They are the enemy. I get paranoid and believe they want to hurt me, and I am determined to strike out to prove a state of control over them.

Laura (BP)

I think that borderlines are concerned about only one thing: losing love. When I am cornered, I get very scared, and I show that by getting angry. Anger is easier than fear and makes me feel less vulnerable. I strike before being struck.

Rage and Logic Don't Mix

In our interview with clinician Jane Dresser R.N., she said, "When someone with BPD is highly emotionally aroused, do not expect them to act in a logical way. It isn't going to happen. Not because they're not willing to, but because they cannot."

Dresser discussed information that seems to indicate that when people who have experienced trauma are emotionally aroused, the logical centers of their brain do not seem to function as well. This finding is not a surprise to most non-BPs, who find reasoning with an enraged BP pointless and frustrating. The time for rational discussion is later, when both you and the BP have calmed down.

Dresser also points out that because some people with BPD do not have the capacity to regulate their emotions, all their anger can have the same intensity. A mild irritation seems indistinguishable from an impassioned fury. Dresser suggests, "Sometimes it's important to ask the person with BPD, 'On a scale of one to ten, how mad are you?'"

What to Do

During a rage, the best thing to do is temporarily remove yourself and any children from the situation. In our interview with Margaret Pofahl, A.C.S.W., she suggested that non-BPs say calmly, "I will not discuss this further with you if you continue to yell and scream at me. I am willing to be supportive if you can calmly tell me what it is that you want or need." Note that you've given the BP a choice and made it clear that their actions will be responsible for your temporary withdrawal. If the raging continues, immediately retreat to safer ground. Some ways to do this are to:

- Retire to a room that is off-limits to everyone else.
- Call a friend and go to their house.
- Call a relative and have them come to your house.
- Take the kids and go to a movie.
- Put on some headphones and listen to music.
- Take a taxi home.
- Turn on the answering machine or disconnect the phone and take a hot bath.
- Refuse to read the BP's letters or E-mail.

If the BP in your life routinely loses control, think through your options now and make concrete plans for the next time they fly into a rage. Make arrangements to leave quickly if you need to: for example, know the location of your purse or wallet, or have the phone number of a friend written near the phone.

What Not to Do

It's important that you don't continue to ignore or accept rages. Realize that extreme rage directed at you or your children is verbal and emotional abuse. Even if you think you can handle it, over time it can erode your self-esteem and poison the relationship. Seek support immediately.

It is in your own best interest not to respond to borderline anger with rage of your own. Cory F. Newman, Ph.D., who treats many BPs and non-BPs, said during our interview, "This will escalate the pattern of hostility and coercive control. When you fight fire with fire, the problem gets worse and nothing is resolved." Remember that the BP may be trying to provoke you into anger, consciously or unconsciously. If you find yourself losing control, stop and leave the scene. If you do get angry, however, don't be too hard on yourself. It's human nature to want to fight back. Just tell yourself that you'll try to be calmer next time.

You probably know how to fight back and say things hurtful to the BP, and retaliation can be tempting in the face of a rage. However, try not to push the BP's shame or invalidation buttons if you can help it. Comments like, "Shush, people can hear," or "You have no right to be angry," can make things worse. You can't control the BP's actions, but with the knowledge that you handled their rage well, you can feel good about yourself.

Finally, don't take out your frustration on other people. This is another reason why enduring abusive behavior is a bad idea. When you try to swallow your feelings, they usually ending up surfacing elsewhere in a way you didn't expect. This can leave you even more isolated in the long run.

Set Personal Limits Around Rages

If possible, discuss your limits with the BP beforehand so the two of you have a shared understanding of what steps you're going to take the next time this happens. Set this limit when things are on an even keel, using the communication tools described in the last chapter. Assure the BP that if you leave, you will be back. Explain that they have some control in the matter: if they choose to calm down, you will stay. If they choose to rage at you, you may leave and return when things are calmer. The decision is theirs.

Before you implement the plan, review the information in chapter 7 about responding to countermoves. You must be prepared for any escalation. And remember the importance of consistency. In our interview with therapist Margaret Pofahl she said, "If you say today that you are not going to take angry blaming, then tomorrow you cannot take it, either." Otherwise, you may intermittently reinforce the behavior.

The BP may apologize very sincerely—and then repeat the behavior the next time they get angry. This may be because the BP doesn't have the tools they need to calm themselves down and choose another course of action. Certain types of cognitive-behavioral therapy can give people with BPD the skills they need to change their behavior. However, if the BP won't seek help or keeps repeating the behavior, you may need to decide what you will and will not accept in the relationship. It's up to you.

Suggestions from Borderlines

Many BPs have given us suggestions to pass on to non-BPs who must bear the brunt of borderline rages. Evaluate these recommendations in light of your own unique circumstances. Because each person and situation is different, these suggestions may or may not work for you. You may wish to discuss them with a therapist.

Chris (BP)

When people try to calm me down or soothe my anger, it only makes me feel more angry and invalidated—like they are telling me that I shouldn't feel the way I do. I feel this way even if I intellectually understand that they did not mean things the way I've interpreted them.

Laura (BP)

The only thing that helps me get less angry is when my husband says to me, "I know you are scared, not angry," and gives me a hug. At that moment, my anger melts away and I can feel my fear again. Reacting in anger only makes it worse, even though I can understand why people get angry when a borderline is attacking them.

Jean (BP)

If a borderline is being dangerous, others better stay away until things are safe. It can help to let the borderline know that anger is okay and normal, but that they need to express it in ways that do not attack another person's self-esteem.

Annie (BP)

When I am angry, the best thing someone else can do to make me feel better is to listen to me and believe what I am saying. I am afraid that a good deal of current literature on BPD encourages others to ignore what the borderline is saying because supposedly

they do not know what the truth is or they are "manipulative."
Most of my anger is caused by others not listening to me or believ-
ing me. This is very painful. It makes me feel as if I don't exist.

Physical Abuse

In our interview with Don Dutton, a psychologist and researcher
at the University of British Columbia, he estimated that about 30
percent of men who batter their partners or children have BPD.
The percentage of physically abusive women who have BPD is
probably much higher.

Take all forms and instances of physical violence very seriously—even if it never happened before and you doubt that it will
happen again. The potential is there for the violence to escalate.
Children who witness violence experience many of the same ill
effects as those who are directly abused. You must be prepared.

Space limitations prevent us from listing all of the steps that
victims of domestic violence should take to protect themselves and
their children. But the information is widely available from shelters
or crisis intervention programs. Look under "Domestic Abuse" or
"Crisis Intervention" in your yellow pages. Plan what you will do
if the situation arises again. Find out your legal options.

Male Victims

It's taken years and several high-profile domestic violence
cases to convince this society that family violence is a serious
problem for women. The subject of battered men, however,
remains a joke: a cartoon image of a heavyset woman in curlers
and a robe wielding a rolling pin while a tiny, undignified man
covers his head with his hands and runs away.

Male non-BPs have reported being slapped, scratched,
punched, clawed, and stabbed with small objects by the BPs in
their lives. One man was tripped and fell down a flight of stairs.

Mike (non-BP)

Sometimes when my ex-wife was in a towering rage, she would
claw me, smash me across the side of the head, and punch me in the
chest. I'm six feet three inches tall and weigh 215. Yet she could
knock the wind out of me. My father taught me not to hit a
woman—that was almost a religion in our house. So what was I
supposed to do?

Men who are physically attacked by women may not interpret themselves as having a problem. More often, they see the woman as the one with the problem. Many men also believe they should suffer in silence in order to "protect" the abuser or avoid being embarrassed.

When men do realize they need help, they are often unable to find it in a society that does not believe or understand their complaint as credible. This hurts the non-BP and denies the violent women the opportunity to get help of their own.

If you are a man who is being battered, we have some suggestions of how you can address and cope with the situation.

First, do not, under any circumstances, hurt the other person. This goes double if you are bigger or stronger than the BP. Maintain control of yourself and remain calm at all times—especially when talking to authorities.

Organizations involved with domestic violence vary tremendously as to their attitudes about the physical abuse of men by women. However, reports of battered men are not as uncommon as you might think. (Some come from men battered by other men, usually a gay partner or male relative.) If you're being battered, don't wait for an emergency to discover the attitudes of the police, justice system, and social service agencies in your town. Talk to someone now.

Consult with legal resources about documenting the abuse and protecting yourself and your children. Know your legal rights and responsibilities. Don't make assumptions or go on advice from a friend of a friend. Find out the facts and be assertive about using your resources to protect yourself. See appendix D for resources that may be of help.

Self-Mutilation

Non-BPs may feel frightened, angry, frustrated, disgusted, and helpless in the face of borderlines who mutilate themselves. Responding to such behavior requires a balancing act: you should be concerned and supportive without unintentionally rewarding the behavior or making the person feel even more ashamed.

What Not to Do

- Don't take responsibility for someone else's actions. You did not cause this to happen. If an event that involved you preceded the episode, recall the difference between causes and triggers (chapter 5).

- While you can do your best to provide a safe environment, realize that you can't remove every potentially sharp object in the house or watch the BP twenty-four hours a day. As the mother of a borderline teen says, "If my daughter is determined to hurt herself, she will."

- Don't try to be the person's therapist. Leave that to the professionals.

- Don't keep weapons such as guns in the house. (This also applies if the BP rages.)

- Don't define the person with BPD in terms of the self-mutilation. It is something they do, not something they are.

- Don't dwell on the details of self-injury when discussing it with the person. Self-harm can be addictive; you don't want to trigger the behavior. In our interview with Cory F. Newman, Ph.D., he said, "Addictive behaviors can be cued, such as when a cigarette smoker craves a smoke when he hears someone else talking about lighting up. However, this doesn't mean that it's your fault if the person with BPD engages in self-mutilating behavior after you confront them about it. I am merely stating that you have to handle dynamite with great care."

- Don't moralize, preach, or act disgusted. One woman who hurts herself says, "My friends lecture me about self-injury— as if I didn't know it was wrong. What if I were overweight? Would they follow me around and slap my hand every time I reached for a candy bar?"

- Don't say things designed to evoke shame or guilt, such as "How could you!" The BP already feels ashamed.

- Don't make threats in an angry or controlling way ("If you do this again I'm leaving you!"). This may come across as punishing. Even if you choose to set this limit, it should come across as something you are doing for yourself, not something against the other person (e.g., during times when you're both calm, you could explain which actions you can not tolerate and which of these will force you to leave the relationship).

What to Do

- If the BP threatens harm to themselves (or others) notify the person's therapist (if they have one) at the earliest possible time. You, the BP, and the therapist may all want to meet to discuss how you will handle self-harm in the future. If this is not possible, seek professional help on your own to discuss how to handle the situation. If you believe that the BP may be a danger to themselves or others, they may need to be evaluated for hospitalization.

- Remain calm and speak in a calm and matter-of-fact way. Richard Moskovitz (1996) says, "Since self-mutilation usually occurs when the borderline feels out of control, it is important that those around them do not add to the inner chaos with their own panic." Moskovitz points out that although the behavior may be shocking and new to you, it may have been going on for a long time.

- Seek appropriate medical treatment for the BP if warranted. You may wish to call medical professionals to obtain their advice. In our interview with Elyce M. Benham, M.S., she said, "This also needs to be handled in a supportive, yet composed and factual manner. What I usually say is, 'Let's take care of this,' or 'I'm going to take you to the doctor and have them check this out.'"

- Help the BP put together a support team so you don't feel overburdened and exhausted. The first person should be the BP's therapist, who can work with the BP to reduce self-harm.

- Empathize with the BP. Show that you are trying to understand how they feel. Really listen. Ask questions in a concerned way, such as "How are you feeling?" and "Is there anything I can do?" Don't underestimate the BP's fear, anguish, and inner turmoil. Imagine the worst you have ever felt, and then triple it.

- Emphasize messages of love and acceptance for the person, while making it clear that you wish they would find another way of handling their problems. One BP suggests saying, "I feel helpless and angry when you hurt yourself. I want to understand this, even though I don't fully. But I know I don't want you to do this anymore, and if you feel those urges again please talk to me or call your therapist."

- Stress the positive and offer encouragement (e.g., "Before you did this you went fourteen days without cutting yourself, and I know you can get back on track.").

- Suggest alternatives to self-harm such as squeezing ice, plunging their hands into very cold water, heavy exercise, biting into something strongly flavored (hot peppers or unpeeled lemon, lime or grapefruit), or other activities that produce an intense sensation that is not harmful. However, realize that using these alternatives—or not—is up to the BP.

- Refuse to be put in no-win situations—for example, promising not to seek outside help because the BP is embarrassed and ashamed. This is unfair to you both. If the BP insists that you keep the self-mutilation a secret from people who could help, point out that you are not qualified to handle this on your own. (See the upcoming section in chapter 8 for no-win situations involving suicide threats.)

- If you start to feel consumed by the BP's behaviors, step back. You may be exaggerating the influence you have on the person's self-mutilating behaviors. The best way to be there to support the BP in the long run is to make sure that, in the short run, you're taking care of yourself.

Set Personal Limits Around Self-Harm

As with rages, planning and setting limits beforehand is the key to reclaiming your own life when someone you care about hurts themselves. Make sure that you can follow through with the consequences that you set.

Penny (BP)

I have friends I usually lean on when I am drinking and cutting. My therapist taught me to tell these friends that if I contacted them before doing anything self-destructive, they could talk to me and reassure me if they wanted to do so. But if I contacted them during or after doing something like drinking or slashing, they were to simply say, "Penny, I love you, but I'm absolutely not going to deal with you when you're like this." Then they were to hang up and refuse to accept any contact with me while I was in that condition.

This gave them an escape route so that they wouldn't feel pressured to be my caretakers, and so our friendship would have a better chance of surviving because of less stress placed upon it. It also kept my self-destructive behavior from being reinforced, because drinking and cutting would no longer be rewarded with solicitude from my friends. There have been times when I came close to the old patterns, but a phone call before the fact has so far been sufficient to prevent relapses. I dread the dial tone and what it represents enough to find other ways of coping. Plus, my friends have said that this contingency plan relieved them considerably because they knew they wouldn't have to feel guilty about abandoning me.

Karen (non-BP)

In a way, my husband Eric's self-harm used to hurt me more than it hurt him. He sensed this and used it as a trump card—when nothing else worked and he felt awful and couldn't get what he wanted, he would self-harm. The guilt trips were powerful. Imprisoning. It was controlling my life.

But I had my own trump card—my refusal to keep being put in this position. I told him explicitly and clearly when he was calm that I was not taking responsibility for his actions. If I saw blood, I was calling an ambulance and leaving. If I stayed and soothed him, I would be enabling him. So he knows that if he doesn't want to be alone, he has to maintain that boundary. Also, in Eric's more cooperative moments, his therapist and I each made separate contracts with him not to self-harm. He values his honor and honesty, so this works.

Suicide Threats

According to the *DSM-IV*, 8 to 10 percent of all people with BPD commit suicide. Of the six million people in North America who have the disorder, 180,000 to 600,000 will die by their own hands. This number is equivalent to a *Titanic* sinking every day for four months to a year.

According to John Mann and Beth Brodsky (1997), when compared to people with depression or schizophrenia, borderlines are more likely to make nonlethal suicide attempts, constantly think of suicide, and make repeated suicide threats. The presence of other illnesses such as major depression, substance abuse, and eating disorders seems to magnify the likelihood of actual suicide.

If the BP in your life really wants to die, you need assistance beyond what we can provide in this book. Please seek immediate professional help. You may also wish to call a local crisis line or hospital emergency department and ask for guidance. Then, keep the phone numbers of these people and places right by the phone.

Feeling Manipulated by Suicide Threats

When the suicide threats appear to be an attempt to scare you or make you do something you don't want to do, your sympathy and concern may begin to dissolve into anger and resentment. For example, many non-BPs said that when their relationships with the BPs were over, the BPs implied that they would kill themselves if the non-BPs did not return. Non-BPs on the receiving end of these threats feel extremely guilty, confused, and worried.

Ellis and Newman (1996) explain,

> The sense of collaboration and togetherness you once had with the suicidal person diminishes, while the uncomfortable power struggle increases. Comments like, "If you really cared whether I lived or died you would come back to me," and "You make me want to die" have something in common: they make someone else's decision whether to live or die conditional on your response. This is unfair to both parties.

Sometimes the BPD sufferer will try to make you believe that you are responsible for their misery, and that you will be to blame if they kill themselves. Remind yourself that you are not threatening the other person with homicide—the other person is threatening suicide. You're dealing with someone who needs immediate professional attention much more than they need your capitulation.

What Not to Do

Newman and Ellis suggest avoiding the following actions with someone threatening suicide:

- Don't get into an argument with the BP about whether or not they are serious about wanting to die—even if you're angry and feel like venting. The person may attempt suicide simply to prove you wrong.

- Don't confront the BP and accuse them of manipulating you. Again, this may turn into a power struggle. If the BP is asking you to do something that is against your better judgment, follow your instincts. However, if the two of you are in a session with a mental health professional, it can be helpful to talk about how this behavior is making you feel.

- Be extremely cautious about relenting just to prove that you really care. Contrary to what an angry, distraught BP may be telling you, you don't have to prove anything. Say Newman and Ellis, "When you give in to the threats, you will still be angry, the BP will still be at risk for self-harm at any time, and the underlying issues will not have been addressed. Plus, it is likely that the same scenario will repeat itself again and again."

If you have a history of complying with demands because you believed that suicide was imminent, we suggest obtaining professional help for one or the both of you before the next crisis occurs.

What To Do

Suicide threats that feel manipulative are the ultimate in no-win situations. Whether you comply with the BP's wishes or not, the risks are unacceptable. So, Newman and Ellis say, the best thing to do is to simply refuse to be put in this position, despite the BP's attempts to make you feel responsible for their life and death. Just say no, following the guidelines that follow.

Express your support and concern for the BP while firmly maintaining your personal limits. You can do both, even if the BP thinks otherwise. You can accomplish this with mirroring responses that put the choice of life or death back where it belongs—with the BP—while stating as strongly as possible that you care about the BP and you want them to choose life and seek help. Newman and Ellis give these sample responses, which we have paraphrased:

In response to "I'll kill myself if you leave me":
"I'm not breaking up with you to be cruel. I'm very, very sorry that this hurts you. I want what's best for you in the future, but I just can't be part of it. And even if I were to stay with you, that wouldn't solve our problems. For one thing, your life's worth should be based on much more than just being in a relationship with me. Secondly,

I know that you know deep inside that our relationship shouldn't be based on me staying because I'm afraid of you dying and you staying because you think you can't live without me. That's not healthy. I care about you. And because I care about you, I want you to live. And I want you to find your own happiness, and your own life's worth, without me."

In response to "If you really cared whether I lived or died, you would come home every weekend":
"The fact that I love you and am concerned about you is already beyond doubt. I feel like I have proven my love time and time again, and I suspect that even if I did come home every weekend, that wouldn't be enough for you. I want to see you, and I do plan on coming up once a month or so. The fact is that I can't visit every weekend because I have my own family now and my own life to attend to. Perhaps the answer is that you need more things to do on your own, or more friends you can get together with on Saturday and Sunday. You used to talk about a lady you played cards with from your church; have you seen her lately?"

These statements should be accompanied by statements that show that you are taking the threats of suicide very seriously. Show warmth and concern in your voice and actions. For example, you might say, "We have to get you to the hospital. This is a matter of life and death." Show that a serious threat warrants a serious response. In this way, you give appropriate attention to the BP's cry for help while making it clear that you aren't qualified to give the professional help that is necessary in such extreme situations.

In certain circumstances, you may wish to enlist the support of other people in the BP's life: parents, relatives, friends, teachers, etc. Don't keep this kind of behavior a secret; find other people who are willing to support you and the BP.

If You Are Suicidal

Like everyone else, many (if not most) non-BPs have their own unresolved, painful issues that frequently stem from childhood. These issues, combined with the challenges of living with someone who has BPD, can trigger thoughts of suicide.

Loraine (non-BP)

For twenty years my husband has been telling me what an awful person I am, that I am stupid, severely deranged, and that I should be committed to a mental institution. He has blamed me for every fight and for forcing him to commit adultery with my sister. He told me that I had BPD, and I was severely ashamed and frightened that I had such a disorder. So I went to a therapist to get rid of the demons inside me. My therapist told me emphatically that I do not have the disorder, but that my husband may.

My problem is that I now feel depressed and humiliated— humiliated that I gave up my friends at his request, that I believed the lies, and that I put up with this for so long. I wasted twenty years of my life. What is the use of going on? What kind of person am I that I let this happen to me?

If you feel this way, you are not alone. There are others taking the same journey; they are on the path behind you, in front of you, and by your side. If you have access to the Internet or a local non-BP support group, you will find these friends ready to listen and help.

Don't condemn yourself. Even trained professionals have difficulty dealing with the emotions that borderline behavior can provoke. When you take into account that professionals are less emotionally involved than you are and they only see the BP once a week for fifty minutes, you can see how fruitless it is to beat yourself up. You have been doing the best you can with the resources available to you. And hopefully, this book has shown you that the BP has been doing the best they can with the resources available to them, as well.

Keep in mind that the BP's feelings can be contagious and that projection can make it hard to separate the BP's feelings from your own. Seek professional assistance now. Keep in mind that nearly all the non-BPs we interviewed told us that using the techniques in this book improved their lives significantly. Either their relationships with the BPs in their lives improved, or they were able to get their own lives back on track and regain their equilibrium and self-esteem.

When the BP Is Your Child

When a child or teenager becomes a danger to themselves or others, parents are often at a loss as to where to turn for help.

Believing the child's behavior is always their responsibility, they may tolerate behaviors they would never accept in anyone else. If your child is violent to themselves or others, it's all right to ask for help from therapists and other outside authorities, family and friends, crisis hot lines, treatment centers, and support groups.

Admission into a treatment facility is usually voluntary; the child must agree to treatment. However, if professionals believe that the child is a danger to themselves or others, they and the police can authorize a legal commitment that can last from twenty-four to seventy-two hours.

Sharon, who manages an Internet support group for parents of children with BPD, says that some parents in her group are concerned that their child may be discharged before the parent feels the situation is really safe. In one instance, a prematurely discharged child took an overdose of pills and ended up back in the hospital. As a last resort, Sharon advises simply refusing to take the child home—even if the hospital protests. This, she feels, gives the parents additional time to make other arrangements such as residential care. However, the laws about this vary from state to state, and even from county to county. In some areas, you might be charged with neglect. So seek legal advice from a qualified professional as soon as possible.

You can call the police to intervene if the child is becoming violent or threatening. As with most police and 911 calls, response time is based on the perception of immediate risk. If you explain that the threat of harm is clear and present, the response may be quicker.

Sharon suggests telling the police as soon as possible—beforehand, if possible—that the child has a mental disorder. "Otherwise they will assume this is just another rebellious teen getting out of hand," she says.

Christine Adamec (1996) suggests that you immediately give police a Crisis Information Form you have prepared ahead of time and kept in a safe place. This form consists of a brief medical history, the diagnosis and what that means, the names of the child's doctors, and the names of the medications the child is taking. You can find a copy of the form in her book.

When the police arrive, they will first contain the situation and then discuss alternatives. If the crisis has passed, no further intervention may be made. If parents choose to press charges, the police will explain the procedure. According to Sharon, parents in her group who were concerned that the child would become violent after the police departed insisted that the authorities take the child to a safer environment.

If the child's behavior continues to escalate and the child is not agreeable to treatment, they may be placed in juvenile detention overnight or be treated as "allegedly mentally ill" and placed under emergency psychiatric detention at the nearest county-operated hospital.

Unsafe behavior is probably the most difficult aspect of caring about someone with BPD. But by planning for it and asking for outside help, you can defuse its power and make it a lot less frightening.

9

Protecting Children from BPD Behavior

My father never noticed my BP mother's behavior, never spoke to me about it. He emotionally abandoned me when I was still in grade school. I wish he could have shown me unconditional love. I wish he had stayed around emotionally enough to love me and not leave us alone with her and her moods.

I am glad I was born. But sometimes I wish I wasn't. I am still on the emotional rollercoaster looking for a way out. I can't find the door to peace and happiness despite the fact that by all measures, I have a nice life. A house and a job.

I will live the rest of my life trying to overcome the damage. At the bottom of my heart, I am still that child looking for the unconditional love I never got. It is too late for me, but my hope is by writing this that it is not too late for the other kids of BPs out there.

—Joan (BP)

Many people with BPD never act out in front of their children. Others feel the urge, but consciously make an effort to shield their children from their BPD behavior. Indeed, borderlines who are aware of their issues and work to overcome them can be excellent parents—better parents, even, than those who don't have the disorder but aren't as introspective.

However, some people with BPD are unable or unwilling to adjust their behavior around their children. Perhaps they raise their voice more than they should. Or, they may experience states of depression that leave them unable to focus on their children as much as they would like to. At the other end of the spectrum, BPD can cause parents to be extremely abusive or neglectful.

As you read this chapter, keep in mind that not all people with BPD act out toward their children. In addition, borderline behaviors directed toward children can vary greatly in their intensity depending on the situation and the BP involved.

Typical Problems with BP Parents

As we said in chapter 3, in some ways people with BPD are emotionally and developmentally similar to children. Like children, they may find it difficult to set aside their own needs to focus on those of others. The BP may not be able to adequately consider the children's needs, feelings, and wishes. They may be so preoccupied with their own emotional difficulties that they overlook their children's emotional needs. They may also resent that the children's needs and feelings are different from their own, and may therefore ridicule, invalidate, or dismiss them. If the child is happy when the parent is sad, this may be taken as a sign of disloyalty and insensitivity.

Some BPs find it difficult to separate their relationships with their children from their problems with others. For example, they may have a hard time acknowledging that their children can have their own positive relationships with people the BP may not like. They may also try to get back at others through their children. Some BPs try to force a child to choose between a relationship with them and being true to themselves; for example, they may tell a child they are selfish for wanting to spend time with friends.

Other BP parents are inconsistent with their parenting. They may vacillate between overinvolvement and neglect, depending upon their mood and emotional needs at the moment. They may only pay attention to the children when the kids are doing something to meet the borderline's needs. Some BPs try to cope with their own feelings of inadequacy by demanding that their children be perfect. Children may then feel worthless when something goes wrong. They may also try to get their emotional needs met through the children in ways that are inappropriate (e.g., having a ten-year-old sleep in the same bed because the BP doesn't want to sleep alone).

Some BPs act toward children as if they are all good or all bad. This can hurt children's self-esteem and make it difficult for them to develop a consistent sense of self. BP parents may turn their love off and on; their children thus learn not to trust them (and sometimes, not to trust anyone else). The BP's behavior may be so unpredictable that the child's focus becomes stabilizing the parent, to the detriment of the child's normal development. Some BPs alternate between taking too little and too much responsibility. For example, the BP may ignore the negative effects of their actions on the children, but then feel guilty or depressed when a child gets a bad grade.

BP parents may feel threatened by children's normal behavior. As children grow and become more independent, the BP may feel abandoned and become depressed and may rage at the children. The BP may also unconsciously try to increase their children's dependence on them. Children thus may have a hard time separating from the parent or feeling competent at handling their own life. When children become angry themselves, the BP may take it personally and rage back, escalating the situation.

Some BPs may need children to be a certain way and may have a hard time loving them unconditionally. They may need the children to be perfect in order to make up for their own feelings of inadequacy. When children disobey, the BP may feel unloved, become angry or depressed, and withdraw their own love. Children then learn that their parent's love is conditional. They may need to believe that their child is stupid, a failure, or unattractive so they don't have to be alone with similar feelings about themselves. Also, this allows the BP to feel more competent than someone else in their life.

They may need their child to be just like them and may feel threatened when the child has different feelings and opinions. This parenting trait is common in people with another personality disorder: Narcissistic Personality Disorder. Elan Golomb (1992) writes:

> The pressure to conform to expectations is like the water in which a fish swims, so relentless and uniform that the

child is hardly aware of it. [These children] feel as if they do not have the right to exist. Their selves have been twist-ed out of their natural shape since any move-ment toward independence is treated as a betrayal that can cause the parent irreparable harm.

Though Golomb writes about another disorder, the effect on children is similar. Some BPs may be physically or emotionally abusive or neglectful. Their impulsive behavior may threaten the safety or well-being of their children, or they may hit or slap the children. The BP may also call the children damaging names or tell them outright that they are bad and unworthy. This sabotages the child's self-concept, self-esteem, and self-worth. In a less directly abusive but equally damaging way, the BP may be unable or unwilling to protect children from the abuse of others, either because they feel that doing so might threaten their relationship with their partner or because they are too consumed by their own problems. Children often interpret this as a reflection of their own lack of self-worth.

Potential Consequences of Uncontrolled BPD Behavior

In our interview with Andrew T. Pickens, M.D., he said, "Parents who verbally abuse their children will cause emotional damage. How much damage depends on many factors, such as the inher-ited temperament of the child, the amount of love and empathy given to the child by other adults, the age of the child (the youn-ger the child, the more vulnerable they are), the intensity of the abuse, and other factors."

Janet R. Johnston, Ph.D., the executive director of the Judith Wallerstein Center for the Family in Transition, believes that the impact of BPD behavior on children varies according to the behavior of the BPD parent and the temperament of the child. For example, if a BP parent who primarily acts in is matched with a child who has a "caregiver" personality, the child may feel responsible for keeping the parent alive and happy.

Sela (BP)

My three-year-old, Bess, watched when the ambulance took me away after I had taken too many pills. She plays quietly with her toys when I lie in bed, so depressed that I can barely get up to feed her. When I even pretend to cry, her eyes well up with tears. Her first full sentence was, "Is mommy okay?" When I am happy and beginning to pull out of the black pit, she grows and changes at lightning speed, as if to make up for the time she has lost trying to cope within my shadow. I am determined to get through this horror so I can be a real mommy, not a burden to her.

A primarily acting-out parent combined with a more assertive child could create a unique type of chaos. When one BP mother raged, her son would write phrases like "shut up!" and "I hate you!" on pieces of paper and throw them at his mother.

Many studies have shown that BPD tends to run in families. Children who do not develop BPD themselves may be at risk for developing BPD-related traits such as difficulties regulating their emotions; problems with eating disorders, addictions, and substance abuse; tendencies to overidealize or devalue people; and feelings of shame, emptiness, and inferiority. This tendency may result from biological factors as well as environmental ones.

According to MaryBelle Fisher, Ph.D., when a parent has BPD the normal formation of the child's identity may be derailed. In our interview with Fisher she said, "The child's 'self' becomes a mechanism to regulate the borderline parent rather than an internal, cohesive event."

Elan Golomb (1992) says:

> To grow up as a whole person, children in their formative stages need the experience of genuine acceptance; they have to know they are truly seen and yet are perfect in their parent's eyes; they need to stumble and sometimes fall, only to be greeted by a parent's commiserating smile. Through parental acceptance, children learn that their "is-ness," their essential selves, merit love.

Children with BPD parents may also receive a distorted view of how interpersonal relationships work. For example, one of Fisher's patients feels that he can't become emotionally involved with anyone because he's afraid the other person will take over his life. He stays on the edges of all his relationships and his emotional life is very sterile. Children whose borderline parents vacillated between extreme love and raging or abandoning behaviors often have particular difficulty developing trusting relationships with others. They may unconsciously set up tests designed to prove the other person's love, or they may feel abandoned because of small or imagined rejections.

Matthew McKay and his co-authors (1996) summarize studies showing that children of angry parents grow up to face more severe problems than those raised in less angry homes. In women, effects include depression, emotional numbness, painful yearnings for closeness and intimacy, a sense of powerlessness, and a limit of achievement in school and work. In men, the primary outcome seems to be difficulty sustaining emotional attachments.

Practical Suggestions for Protecting Children

Most BPD parents love their children very much and worry about the effects of their borderline behaviors. Many BPs told us that the knowledge that they could be harming their children gave them the courage and determination to recover from BPD. If the BP in your life has a similar attitude, then it will be easier to be supportive, set limits, and help the BP in their efforts to improve their parenting.

However, if the BP refuses to admit that their behavior is abusive and damaging to their children, or if they are unwilling to change, then you may wish to take a more assertive role. Keep in mind that while borderline behavior can be difficult for adults to cope with, it is much harder for children. They have no sense of perspective, little experience, and little or no intellectual understanding of BPD. Furthermore, they are dependent on their borderline parents to meet their most basic physical and emotional needs.

Your ability to shield children from these behaviors will depend on many factors, including your legal and emotional relationship to the child, the nature of your relationship with the BP in your life, the laws in your locality, and your willingness and ability to set limits. In general, however, the closer you are to the BP and the children, the greater an impact you can have—and the greater your responsibility. Following are some suggestions.

Determine Your Priorities

Some non-BPs don't take action because they fear harming their own relationship with the BP. They're afraid that if they set limits regarding children, the BP will rage at them, belittle them, or cut them out of their life.

Only you can decide what risks you can afford to take. Whatever you decide, you must be able to live with the long-term consequences. Be honest with yourself; don't downplay or explain away the negative effects of the BP's behavior toward the children. One non-BP justified his inaction by telling himself that his children would learn a valuable lesson from their stepmother's rages: that the world can be a bad place. These justifications may make things easier on the non-BP, but they do nothing to shield children.

Set a Good Example

Children mostly learn by observation. What you do is more important than what you say. Watching you put the steps discussed in this book into practice is a powerful way for them to learn the basics of detachment, self-care, limit setting, and so forth. Of course, the opposite is also true: if you model less healthy coping mechanisms, they may learn those as well.

Sam, for example, was embarrassed when his children witnessed fights between him and his borderline wife. He mistakenly believed that his wife's behaviors reflected negatively on him. So he did everything he could to keep the peace—including allowing her to be verbally abusive. If he protested, his wife would call him names and make angry accusations. When this happened in front of the children, he felt ashamed.

Sam's intent was to be kind and responsible. But his children learned that when their mom acted out, it was their job to absorb it. They began to believe that she must be right about what she was saying, because if she were wrong, they believed their dad would say so. If Sam had used limit setting and mirroring techniques and defused the situation, while simultaneously keeping his limits in place, the children could have learned that although their mom acted unlike other mothers sometimes, her behavior was her responsibility.

We have two additional ideas for demonstrating healthy behavior in front of children. First, make sure that you hold to your limits in front of the children. Explain, "Mommies sometimes get mad, and it's okay to be mad. But it wasn't okay for mommy to scream at daddy." Second, if the BP is often unpredictably moody, don't let their moods affect everyone else or spoil the children's plans. Show children that it's all right to be joyful and have fun even when a parent is feeling down. And try not to cancel fun activities with your kids when your BP partner is feeling upset.

Enlist the Support of the BP

Janet Johnston (1997) says that people with BPD want to feel support, caring, and acknowledgement that they try their best. But even if you couch your criticisms and suggestions in a supportive way, whatever you say may be interpreted as devastating criticism. Johnston has three suggestions for overcoming this:

- Appeal to the BP's natural inclination to want the very best for their children. In other words, don't imply that the BP's parenting may be poor. Simply point out that all parents want the very best for their kids and that certain actions are good for kids and some are potentially damaging.

- Emphasize that parenting is the toughest job there is, and that all parents need some help now and then.

- If the BP had an unhappy childhood, appeal to the BP's desire to give their children a better experience than they had themselves.

In our interview with MaryBelle Fisher, Ph.D., she said she advises approaching the BP when they are calm and starting out by acknowledging the BP's genuine love for and dedication to their children. "Build an alliance with the person by emphasizing the positives and the areas in which you agree. Appeal to their sense of fairness. Don't blame, shame, or attack, which simply makes people defensive." Two examples of shaming phrases are "What's the matter with you?" and "How could you do that?" Instead, you might say something like: "It's so hard to bring up kids these days, and I know you want the best for Tim. But we just can't ignore that you seem to be losing control with him sometimes. I can certainly understand what a handful he is after you've come home from a long day at work. And I know you've been under a lot of stress lately. But the other day it looked like you were about to hit him, and I'm very concerned about that. We need to figure out a strategy that allows you to do something differently when you're losing it—perhaps call someone or go somewhere. A lot of people find it helpful to get some outside advice from a counselor about how to make things work out better—even people without a lot of problems."

Assist the person with BPD in obtaining help and building a network of support. Offer positive feedback and constructive comments rather than criticism and blame. Fisher says, "Tactfully work with the BP parent so they don't become alienated. There's a tendency for people to close ranks and think, 'Mom's the problem,' and leave it at that. Instead, say, 'Mom's the problem, but how do we maintain respect for her and the integrity of the family?'"

Ask the BP how and when they would like feedback about their parenting. Above all, try to enlist their support in helping the children adapt to having a parent who loves them but sometimes can't regulate their own emotions.

Strengthen Your Own Relationship with the Children

Whether you're a parent, family member, or a friend of the family, you can make a big difference simply by increasing the amount of quality time you spend with the children. Ask the children questions about what's going on in their lives. Be involved. Give them lots of hugs—even the older ones, if they let you. Consistently show them love and affection.

If appropriate, try to subtly counteract the types of behaviors that concern you. For example, twenty-seven-year-old Lisa was concerned that her boyfriend's daughter didn't have enough privacy at home. At the time, the ten-year-old girl, Stephanie, was sleeping in the same bed as her mother, who had custody. Whenever Lisa was with her boyfriend and Stephanie was visiting, Lisa would take special care to respect Stephanie's boundaries and give her as much privacy as possible. She also spent time developing a trusting relationship with the girl. Eventually, Stephanie insisted on having her own space at home.

Listen to the children nonjudgmentally. Help them trust their own perceptions. Encourage them to talk about their feelings, which may range from grief to rage. They may even be angry at you—perhaps because it feels safer than being angry at the BP. Let them know that their feelings are normal. Be as consistent as you can. Keep your promises. Let the children know they can count on you. Encourage them to call you when they need to, and let them visit as often as feels comfortable for you.

At the same time, encourage other adult relatives to develop relationships with the children as well. Grandparents, aunts, uncles, in-laws, and friends of the family can all make a real difference in children's lives. Everyone involved should make it clear that they are not taking sides, but they are offering their love and support to both parent and child.

Encourage Independent Thinking and New Experiences

Children who feel dependent on the BP parent can benefit from interaction with other parents and children. Provide experiences without the BP parent and reward children's natural curiosity and sense of adventure. Encourage kids to follow their own dreams.

In our interview with Fisher she said, "Take care not to wrench the child from the BPD parent. If Janey doesn't want to go somewhere without Mommy for several hours, don't force it. But you might take Janey on a short walk and point out that Mommy's going to be there when she gets back."

If you are a non-BP parent, and the BP parent objects to the child's independence, you may need to set some limits: "Hanna really is old enough to go on a sleepover at her friend's house. I know that this upsets you, but I feel very strongly that we need to encourage her normal friendships with other children. I gave her permission, and she is going to go. Perhaps the two of us can go out to dinner and a movie that night."

Help Children Depersonalize the BP's Behavior

Most children believe that everything is their fault. So you'll need to help them depersonalize the BP's behavior—especially if the BP outwardly blames the children.

Peter (non-BP)

My borderline wife knew of and agreed with her BPD diagnosis. I would tell my two young children: "Mommy is sick. Not the kind of sick that makes your throat or tummy hurt, but the kind of sick that makes you very, very sad. Mommy was in the hospital because there was a special doctor to work with this kind of sickness, a doctor who would help Mommy get better and not cry so much or get so mad. Mommy didn't get so mad or cry because of anything you've done, kids, but because she is sick. As a matter of fact, Mommy loves you so much and you two make her so happy that you are one of the biggest reasons she can smile or laugh at all." My wife and I said this over and over again. And it really made a difference—you could see the relief in their eyes.

Jennifer (non-BP)

When my BP husband yelled at our children for ten minutes for disturbing him when he was reading the newspaper, I took the kids aside and told them: "I know that Dad is upset because of what you did. But it's important for you to understand that Dad is really upset about more than that. We can tell by the way he's reacting so strongly. He could have asked you quietly to talk to him later, but instead he got really excited and yelled. That's just way out of proportion to what you did. Even though Daddy is grown up, sometimes he loses control of himself. Remember when you got really upset yesterday when I said you couldn't have candy at the grocery store? You started to cry and you couldn't stop, and Mommy had to calm you down. Daddy's reaction is kind of like that. It has very little to do with you; you aren't responsible.

Older children, of course, may understand this intuitively. However, even if a child realizes intellectually that the BPD parent's behavior is not their fault, they may still feel responsible on some level. Your own close relationship with the child is your best guide to helping them understand the BP's behavior and handle their own feelings.

Set Limits with the BP Concerning Children

Linda (BP)

My husband, Kirk, set firm limits with me regarding the children. In the worst of times, there were plenty of out-of-control episodes of rage and hysterics. Kirk knew my actions scared the hell out of our kids—you could see it in their faces. So he'd pull me aside and let me know, quite firmly, that the kids were listening and the kids were scared by it. "You're not going to put the kids through this," he would say. "You're out of control. Why don't you just go upstairs?" Fortunately for the kids, I almost always did. And the very few times I didn't, he'd find a place to take them until things calmed down.

Like most borderlines, I had moments of control and moments of loss of control. My husband's firm reminders were not just limits, but reality checks, pulling me out of childish regression long enough to realize that I had adult responsibilities and that my behavior could have an impact on my kids. It might not have been enough to get me to snap to and think rationally, but it was enough to get me to take it elsewhere.

Some parents with BPD, however, will not be as agreeable. When one father came home and discovered that his wife had just hit their son on the head and called him an asshole, he soothed his sobbing son and took his wife out to their planned dinner. As they ate and drank, he gently suggested that hitting and name calling were not the best ways for her to express her frustration. The mother agreed, but excused her behavior by saying, "I had a headache." The father then felt frustrated that his wife didn't understand the seriousness of the problem.

There are times when making gentle suggestions to the BP is the best course of action. This was not one of them. Children are unable to set limits for themselves; therefore you will need to do it for them. In this case, the father could have postponed the dinner and addressed the problem on the spot, explaining the damage that her behavior could do to their son, insisting that this never happen again, and working with the mother to help her find other ways to cope with her frustrations.

Take all physical and emotional abuse of children very seriously the first time you see or hear of it. Ignoring it may give the BP permission to do it again. And once you set limits regarding the children, observe them consistently.

MaryBelle Fisher warns that some non-BP parents may find their relationships with the BPs so difficult that they begin staying away from home. This may leave the children in jeopardy. "You need to be there to protect the children and provide a stable presence," Fisher says. "Yes, non-BP parents have the right to a life of their own. But it must be balanced with the children's right to a safe environment."

Seek Therapy for the Children

Signs that children may benefit from therapy include the following:

- **Difficulty coping with painful feelings:** Intense or long-lasting feelings of sadness or other distressing emotions; recurring thoughts of harming themselves, others, or animals.

- **Self-defeating behaviors:** These include actions that lead to problems at home, school or with friendships (e.g., substance abuse, fighting, unusually poor grades, and other unmanageable behavior.) In younger children, signs may include frequent, unexplainable temper tantrums or persistent disobedience or aggression.

- **Unexplained physical problems:** Marked change in sleeping or eating habits; hyperactivity.

To find a child therapist, ask your pediatrician for a referral or call a local helpline or Alliance for the Mentally Ill. Interview clinicians by phone or in person to make sure you feel confident in them.

Remove the Children from Abusive Situations

Remember that you may need to take the children and withdraw when situations become unsafe. Before you retreat, ask the BP to speak with you out of earshot of the children. Like Kirk in the preceding example, point out that children should not be exposed to this behavior and offer to discuss the situation later, just the two of you. Or, offer to take the kids elsewhere to give the BP some time to calm down.

If the BP remains out of control, take the kids shopping, out for ice cream, over to a relative's house, to a park, to the movies, to a children's museum, to the playground, to the zoo, etc. If the BP frequently acts out in front of the kids, you may wish to prepare ahead of time by generating a list of things to do and places to go, keeping a few of the children's things packed and ready to go, and/or making arrangements with friends or relatives to be "on call" to help.

When children are older, help them become involved with rewarding after-school activities. This accomplishes four things: it minimizes the children's exposure to the behaviors; it boosts their confidence and self-esteem; it puts them in contact with other caring adults; and it takes some of the pressure off you. Boarding school may be another option.

If you have decided to seek a divorce from your BPD spouse, you may be worried that you won't be there to run interference if the BP becomes abusive. About 25 percent of the men we interviewed were so concerned about leaving their children alone with the BP that they decided to seek sole custody. They told us they faced three major obstacles:

- The court system is often biased in favor of mothers. This is changing but very slowly.

- The court system, by and large, is unconcerned with the type of emotional abuse we've been discussing in this chapter. Judges, lawyers, and activists tell us that while physical abuse can be verified and measured in court, emotional abuse cannot. Judges know that parents battling for custody often make false or exaggerated claims. So unless you have expert testimony (which can be expensive) or credible witnesses, judges may discount or ignore even what you believe to be extreme emotional abuse.

- Some borderline soon-to-be-ex-wives, frantic at the prospect of losing custody and furious at their husbands for abandoning them, engage in dishonest tactics to discredit their spouses. Their strategies included denying visitation, filing for restraining orders, and making false accusations of sexual abuse of the children. For the sake of your children and yourself, if you are a man seeking custody it is absolutely critical that you obtain legal help as soon as possible from an attorney who specializes in father's rights issues. Seek help before the wheels of divorce are in motion and before you move out of the home. Keep in mind that you can appeal bad decisions. Choosing the right divorce attorney may be one of the most important decisions you will ever make for yourself and your children. Resources that may help are listed in appendix D.

Divorce and Parental Alienation

Many men told us that their relationship with their children was suffering because their soon-to-be-ex told the children things like "Your father doesn't love you anymore" and "Daddy's new girlfriend is a whore." If this is happening to you, we have some suggestions that may help.

Janet Johnston (1997) says "Don't explode or the child will be frightened and may stop telling you what Mommy is saying. Maintain a loving connection with the child and let them tell you whatever they want without any cost involved." Johnston advises fathers of children age four to six to simply give the children good, positive messages like, "That's not true, Daddy loves you very much no matter what anybody says." She advises, "Don't worry about undoing what their mother is saying; they're too young to understand motivation and they can only hold one set of information in their mind at a time."

When the children are older—age eight to ten—they have the ability to sort out different perspectives. Your goal is not to put the children in the middle by telling them "your side of the story," but to give them factual information that will gently guide them to believe the truth. Remind them of all the loving things you've done together, using concrete examples from the recent past. Help them explore their feelings and assure them of your love. Whatever you say, do not denigrate the other parent.

Here is an example of what you might tell a young child. The central message to a teen will be the same, but the language you use will be different: "You know, divorce is a very hard on moms and dads. When people break up, everyone's feelings get hurt. And I think that right now Mommy is very mad at Daddy. And when your mom is mad, she tends to think very bad things about people. Remember the time that I came home late on your birthday? Your mommy told you that I was out with my friends, and when I came home you found out that a nail punctured my tire. That night, I gave you a basketball for a present and we went to the playground and played and had a lot of fun. I loved you back then, and I love you today, and I will always love you, no matter what anybody tells you. And if you feel scared and someone says something like that, call me up right away and I will give you a big hug over the phone, day or night."

Abe (non-BP)

A few weeks ago I was on vacation with my three kids (without my wife). I told them that they may have heard bad things about me from their mother. I told them that they didn't have to believe what she says—that they can believe what they feel or see is true. I also told them that I wouldn't force them to see things my wife's way or my way—that they get to decide on their own what is true. And if they decide to have an opinion that's different from mine, I will still love them and I won't get mad at them. I could tell that this really helped my kids a lot.

In this chapter, we've provided a variety of suggestions for protecting children from borderline behavior. We would like to close with this thought: if you don't have children with the BP in your life but are considering doing so, we suggest postponing having a family until the BP is well into their recovery.

Here's why: having their emotions invalidated is one of the biggest triggers for people with BPD (chapter 6). Yet children constantly invalidate their parents—it's what being a child is all about.

When parents set necessary rules and boundaries, children don't thank their parents for providing guidelines. They cry, scream, and may shout, "You're the worst parent in the world!" When parents feel hassled and ask their children to give them some peace and quiet, children may instead demand that the parent read them a book or take them to the mall.

Just when parents want closeness with their children, the children may decide to assert their independence. Parents may teach their children certain values that their children choose to reject. And children usually don't appreciate the sacrifices their parents make until they're grown and have children of their own.

Parenting is the toughest job in the world. Constant invalidation is part of it. Make sure that you do what's best in the long term for you, the BP, and any children you might bring into the world.

PART 3

RESOLVING SPECIAL ISSUES

10

Waiting for the Next Shoe to Drop: Your Borderline Child

Well I've got this feeling I've been trying to stop
I've been waiting for the next shoe to drop.
You say, "How can you say that?"
And, "Why do you think that?"
And, "How do you know that it's true?
Sometimes love can withstand every trial
And sometimes there's only one shoe."

—Carrie Newcomer, "Only One Shoe,"
from *An Angel At My Shoulder*

Sharon and Tom are the parents of two teenagers, Amy and Kim. Amy was diagnosed with BPD at age fourteen, a year after she had sex with several men at a party and tried to hire gang members to kill her parents. The day Sharon learned of the plot, she had Amy admitted to a psychiatric facility. Says Sharon, "Amy tells us that had we not hospitalized her, three days later we would have been dead."

In the hospital, psychiatrists diagnosed Amy with bipolar disorder. A year later, they changed the diagnosis to BPD when the medication proved ineffective and Amy began mutilating herself with a razor blade. At the time, Amy met each of the nine criteria for BPD.

During the years that followed, Sharon and Tom lived from crisis to crisis. When things seemed to be going well, Amy would do something to shatter the calm. "We were always waiting for the other shoe to drop," says Sharon. "At times, it would be a whole closet full of shoes. And sometimes, it was a big, heavy boot." Tom's hobby was listening to a police scanner; one evening he heard an ambulance being dispatched to his address. In her room upstairs, Amy had taken a handful of pills, panicked, and called a suicide hot line.

Aside from running their printing business and trying to pay more attention to their non-BP daughter, Kim, Tom and Sharon's main challenge was helping Amy cope with depression, overeating, and social problems while surviving the fallout from her lies and distortions. Once, Amy spread rumors about a popular girl at school being pregnant; another time she told an African-American printing customer that her family didn't like his kind. At one point, authorities were going to remove Amy and Kim from the household for supposed neglect; Kim finally convinced them that Amy's accusations were false.

Amy, now eighteen, is attending college and living on her own in a trailer park a few miles away from her family. She has a part-time job and receives financial assistance from her parents. She believes she has become more stable because of the support of her family, the proper medications, and successes at school and work, which boosted her self-esteem. "I wasn't ready to work at therapy until recently," Amy says. "I finally realized that seeing a therapist was nothing to be ashamed of, since people who don't have BPD see counselors, too."

Today, Sharon and Amy have a very close relationship. When we asked Sharon how she was able to put aside the past, she simply said, "That's why they call it unconditional love." She says, "The pain of this mental illness is the worst pain any of us have ever felt. We live with it twenty-four hours a day, seven days a week. There is no way to explain the hell it was for Kim growing up; how hard it was for my family to watch Amy hurt me to the core. But our determination to get through this with all the love and support we can muster is what will make it possible for Amy to find her little niche and happiness in the world."

As a result of her experiences, Sharon formed an Internet support group for parents of borderline children of any age. The group is called NUTS, an acronym for Nice, Understanding, Tense, Sensitive Parents.

Over the past fourteen months, about 180 sets of parents have participated in NUTS. Like Amy, the children of the NUTS parents show unmistakable signs of BPD. Yet most of the parents spent years playing diagnostic eeny meeny miney mo, seeing one specialist after another and getting one diagnosis after another.

Can Children Really Have BPD?

At the heart of the problem is this contentious question: Can children be diagnosed with BPD? Clinicians who say no believe that an individual's personality fluctuates during childhood and is not formed until late adolescence. Part of the definition of BPD, they point out, is that the behavior is pervasive, persistent, and unlikely to change. Since a child's personality is still developing, these professionals argue that children can't be borderline.

Other clinicians disagree. They believe that the emotional and behavioral problems associated with personality development are clearly present early in life and are often evident for one or two years before help is sought. This, they believe, demonstrates "persistence" and "pervasiveness."

To resolve this debate, the *DSM-IV* (1994) provided new guidelines for diagnosing BPD in people younger than eighteen. It states that children can be diagnosed with BPD as long as the borderline traits have persisted for at least one year, and the behavior is not better accounted for by either a normal developmental stage, the effects of substance abuse, or a more transient condition, such as depression or an eating disorder.

However, many professionals are still reluctant to diagnose a child or adolescent with BPD, because patients with the disorder are often labeled and stigmatized by the mental health system. On the other hand, an inaccurate diagnosis often serves to deprive the child of the appropriate therapy and medication.

If you believe your child meets the criteria for BPD as outlined in this book, make sure you use the guidelines in appendix A when selecting treatment.

Adoption and the Incidence of BPD

About 20 percent of the parents in NUTS adopted their children. Psychiatrist Richard Moskovitz (1996) has noticed from his own practice that adoptees make up a significant portion of adults with BPD and adolescents with borderline tendencies. He believes this may be so for the following reasons. (Keep in mind that these represent Dr. Moskovitz's professional opinions—not necessarily the results of research.)

Early Separation and Loss

Some states require a delay in the adoption process in order to protect the rights of the child's biological parents. During the waiting period, infants may be placed with foster parents for weeks, or even months, until the adoption is final. The experience of being torn from their very early caretakers could interfere with the infant's capacity to develop basic trust.

Identity Issues

Regardless of the circumstances that led to their adoption, many adoptees struggle at some point in their lives with concerns about rejection, which are in turn connected with feelings of defectiveness. These may occur despite the best efforts of many adoptive families to help their children feel chosen and cherished.

Inherited Temperament

While many scenarios may lead to adoption, a common one is accidental pregnancy. Moskovitz says, "We might expect this to occur most frequently among people who tend to be impulsive and take risks. If this were true, adoptees might be genetically predisposed, as a group, to impulsiveness." Impulsivity is an important criterion of BPD.

Temperament Mismatch

While children raised within their biological families may not always fit well with their parents' temperaments and values, with adoption the fit is possibly less likely. This may cause a child's behavior to be met more often with disapproval than praise, which could predispose the child to loss of self-confidence and self-esteem.

Experiences of Non-BP Parents

Sharon (non-BP and creator of NUTS)

Most NUTS parents realize something is wrong when their child is in grade school. The BPD child doesn't get along with other kids and punishments seem to be ineffective at reducing problem behaviors. Amy's grade school teachers, realizing there were major problems, called in the school psychologist. But the psychologist maintained that Amy was just spoiled and would grow out of it.

Most NUTS parents, like us, finally receive a diagnosis of BPD after a life-threatening event such as violence toward others or a suicide attempt. One NUTS parent who was threatened by his son put a lock on his bedroom door and slept in his clothes with the car keys under his pillow. No one can live like this. I tell parents that if they cannot control the abuse, they should call the authorities. You have the right to say no to abuse—even if it is from your own child.

If you have a child with BPD, expect your feelings to vary widely and change constantly. The unconditional love is always there, but it can be challenged beyond belief. Your heart is broken again and again because it hurts to see someone you love suffer so much. Destructive acts may cause you to actually feel hate toward your own child. And in between the love and hate come fear, confusion, resentment, wonder, happiness, and guilt.

Every parent wonders whether they did something to cause the BPD or whether they could have done something to prevent it. We fear for our children's future—will they ever be on their own? Will we spend the rest of our lives trying to help our children live a normal life? As much as we love them, we look forward to the empty nest.

It's important to share your feelings with your spouse. Having a BPD child can destroy your marriage. It can also make it stronger. It is crucial that parents approach their child as a team and understand and support each other. Don't let the BP child "split" the two of you, in either sense of the word. It's going to be a long roller-coaster ride, and it is much easier when the two of you are facing in the same direction.

Money is a big worry. Some parents have given up everything they have to pay for treatment. Residential facilities can be up to $1,500 per day; every trip to a therapist or psychiatrist is well over $50. Other children in the family may need to do without to help their brother or sister.

It would be nice if extended families were always supportive. But mental disorders are not well understood or accepted, and sometimes people deny that someone in their family could have a problem. Family members don't have to agree with the diagnosis. But they should respect that you believe the diagnosis and proceed from there.

On top of all this, people may believe terrible things about you. Amy tells stories and has convinced people that she is a prostitute and a drug addict. And of course, whenever a child has problems everyone figures that the parents are to blame—especially the mother. I just had to keep telling myself that we knew the truth, and that what other people thought did not affect who we really were.

Parents of borderline children try their best despite the void of information. There are no real-life support groups we know of. One common mistake is blaming the child for having BPD or expecting them to change too quickly. Unlike a child with a physical impairment, no physical cues remind you that your child has a disorder. It is important to keep in mind that there is a biological basis for BPD, and if the child could easily change and put a halt to their own suffering they would do so!

Another difficult area is knowing when to come to the rescue. Our children need extra care and nurturing, and we give it freely. But if we step in too much, we may teach our children that they cannot survive without us. We must walk a fine line between letting our children learn from their mistakes and protecting them when things go beyond their control and ability.

Effects on Siblings

According to Moskovitz, it's common for siblings of troubled children to starve for parental attention until they cry for help with disruptive behavior of their own. Parents should be aware of how the intrusive behavior of one child might threaten the security of another. "Just as borderlines have problems defining their own personal boundaries, they are often disrespectful of the boundaries of others," says Moskovitz. "Boundary violations may be subtle, or, at worst, may extend to physically or sexually abusing a sibling." You must be on the alert for this.

Sharon recommends trying to find a friend or family member to help out so you can give your other children the time and attention they need. Be very open with siblings. Talk to them about BPD and explain that the borderline child feels they have no control over their behavior. Siblings may be afraid to tell you their negative feelings. So explain that angry and even hateful feelings are normal. Make sure that your other children have a safe place to go that is all their own, a place they can retreat when things become overwhelming.

Kim, Sharon's daughter and Amy's older sister, describes what it's like growing up with a BP sibling.

Kim (non-BP)

I have a lot of guilt about my sister. At times, I wished her next suicide attempt would be successful. When I have cooled down, I feel sickeningly guilty. Sometimes I find it hard to find any love for her at all—even when I'm not mad at her. She can be so socially inappropriate, like the time my friend came over for dinner and Amy asked her if she was still a virgin.

I am worried about my future family. Even though I don't even have a boyfriend, I'm anxious about my wedding. I know I will feel obligated to make her a bridesmaid, even though I don't want her to be one. I am afraid of the temper tantrums she will throw—will it be about the dresses, who is the maid of honor, or something else? What will my future husband think of her? What kind of aunt will she be for my children? Can I trust her to baby-sit? Will my own children have this horrible disorder?

But right now, I have more immediate worries. My mother is supposed to visit me at college for parents' weekend. Will she have to call home to check on Amy every fifteen minutes? Will Amy throw a fit and ruin everything? Will I always have to fight for our mother's attention?

The Role of Non-BP Parents

Members of NUTS have found they can divide their responsibilities into four major tasks: keeping family members safe; taking care of themselves; taking charge of their child's medical care; and providing a structured, consistent, and loving environment that stresses self-responsibility.

Keep Family Members Safe

It can be very difficult to balance the needs of the borderline child with the needs of the rest of the family. But the safety of each family member is of paramount importance. Use the information in chapter 8 and ask for help when you need it.

Take Care of Yourself

The next time you're on an airplane, read the safety material. When oxygen is running low and the oxygen masks appear, the literature instructs parents to put on their own masks before putting masks on their children. This makes good sense—a parent who isn't breathing is of little help to a child.

In the same way, it's vital that you take care of yourself first. An emotionally exhausted and physically run-down parent can barely nurture an emotionally healthy child—let alone one who has Borderline Personality Disorder. Think of yourself as a whole person, not just your child's parent. It's common for one parent, usually the mother, to take on the lion's share of the burden of caring for a child with BPD, but we urge you to share the work more or less equally, so that one parent doesn't become burned-out or resentful.

Parents may also try switching roles (e.g., if one tends to provide the emotional nurturing and the other handles more practical matters, try reversing tasks for a while to give each person a break). Most importantly, don't become isolated. Sharon says, "You may lose friends because of this. Some won't be able to handle your child's behavior problems. Some will judge or blame you. Look for people whom you can count on to validate your feelings. They don't need to solve your problems; they only need to listen with a sympathetic ear."

Take Charge of Your Child's Medical Care

Over the years your child may see many different clinicians, receive numerous diagnoses, and encounter several agencies designed to stabilize them. Consider yourself the CEO of your child's care, directing the professionals, managing the budget, and making decisions based upon what's best for all concerned. Don't depend on anyone else to do this for you because they won't. Remember, you care the most about your child and are ultimately responsible for them.

One important duty is keeping a record of your child's behaviors, moods, and encounters with the legal and mental health system. Jot down your child's medications, dosages, and clinical appointments; note your conversations with school officials, specialists, and other involved parties. This journal may assist clinicians in making a diagnosis, and it could be vital if you ever need documentation for legal purposes. The journal doesn't have to be elaborate; a few brief words will do. See the following example:

Date	System	Note
11-2-98	Clinic	Appointment with Dr. Smith. Changed Prozac to 40mg.
11-5-98	School	Met with Mrs. Jones (math) who said Mari has missed six assignments, was tardy three times, and is "mouthy" at times.
11-15-98	Clinic	Family therapy today. Worked on "expectations."
12-4-98	Clinic	Appointment with Dr. Smith. No med changes.
12-5-98	Home	Big blow up tonight. Mari threatened suicide but cooled down after an hour. Stated we didn't "trust" her after she missed curfew by two hours.
12-6-98	Police	Mari picked up for underage drinking. She was with two older boys who she met tonight.
12-7-98	Home	We found cuts on Mari's left wrist. She had superficial bleeding. Mari cried a lot tonight, and said she feels "bad."
12-9-98	Clinic	Counseling appointment. Mari was very quiet afterwards.

Some parents are intimidated by mental health professionals. Keep in mind that they're working for you. Respect their position and expertise, but don't assume that they will always know best. Listen to clinicians with an open mind, even if it's something you don't want to hear or it seems to be critical of you. But pay attention to your inner voice and assert yourself when you feel it's necessary. The final decisions are always yours.

If the clinician mistakenly thinks that BPD is *always* the result of abuse, or if they implicitly or explicitly accuse you of mistreating your child despite lack of evidence, consider switching professionals.

Many NUTS parents find that dealing with health insurance providers, the schools, the legal system, and other bureaucrats can be

almost as challenging as coping with the behavior of their borderline child. Gail, a NUTS parent, says, "Do your best to ensure that
your child doesn't fall through the cracks. It may mean making
phone calls and personal visits; it may mean telling the powers
that be that you won't take 'no' for an answer. When you advocate for your child, you may find you possess an inner strength
you never knew you had."

The book *How to Find Help for a Troubled Kid: A Parent's Guide
to Programs and Services for Adolescents*, by John Reaves and James
B. Austin, Ph.D., is a sourcebook for parents who know their child
needs help but don't know how to find it. It may help guide you
through the maze of available programs and services.

Provide an Appropriate Environment

Borderline children and teens require structure and consistency in the same way that roadways require traffic lights and
stop signs. Without them, utter confusion reigns, and physical or
emotional injuries are more likely to result.

Structure refers to consistent routines. NUTS parents find
that their children do best with firm schedules that tell them when
to get up, when to go to school, what to do after school, when to
eat, and so forth. Sharon even wrote a morning routine for her
daughter to help her remember to brush her teeth and get
dressed. "When something unexpected happens—even a good
thing like a surprise birthday party—Amy doesn't know what to
feel or how to act," Sharon explained. "A rage often results. We
found that Amy needed to know in detail what was expected of
her and what she could expect from others at all times."

As part of creating this structure, try to help your child grasp
what will happen if they do not meet their responsibilities. Be as
specific as possible. For example, "If you are late for school they
will mark you tardy. If you are tardy three times without an
excuse, you will be suspended. If you are suspended again, we
may have to look at alternatives such as boarding school."

It is extremely important that you let your child learn from
their own mistakes at an appropriate level for their age. If you continually rescue your child from the results of their own actions,
they may never learn to function at a higher level without you. It
may be difficult to watch your child suffer the consequences of
their own impulsive behavior, but in the long run, your child may
suffer more if they never learn to control themselves.

Consistency means holding your child accountable for their actions every time. All parents have to fight the urge to let things slide sometimes. But with a borderline child, inconsistent enforcement of rules can be outright disastrous.

Brannon (non-BP)

I wanted my son, Michael, to be happy. So when he was ten, if I told him he couldn't watch TV for a week, by the third day I pretended to "forget" the punishment and ignored it when he turned the set on. But Michael was smart—he quickly realized that he had the run of the house.

Eventually, Michael learned not to take any punishment seriously. If I grounded him, he simply walked out the front door. As a teenager, Michael became involved with drugs and began skipping school and threatening violence. I placed him in one residential facility that allowed too much freedom; the drug use simply continued. Eventually, Michael settled into a very strict residential facility that meted out privileges for good behavior. There, he seems to be learning accountability for his actions.

Borderline children need love and affection as much as other kids. Says Sharon, "The key to loving your child is to remember that their behavior is caused by Borderline Personality Disorder. Love your child; hate the disorder. Having a BPD child can be tough. But there are wonderful moments as well. When your child learns how to cope with certain aspects of their illness, there is cause for celebration. When they finally make that most important step of realizing and accepting their love for their parents, it is so strong, so sweet, and so very precious."

For more information about raising a borderline child, see the book *Hope for Parents: Helping Your Borderline Son or Daughter Without Sacrificing Your Family Or Yourself,* by K. Winkler, which is listed in appendix D.

11

Lies, Rumors, and Accusations: Distortion Campaigns

Hell hath no rage like a borderline scorned.

—from the non-BP Internet
support group

Some non-BPs told us that they have been falsely accused of harassment and abuse by the BPs in their lives, been the subject of damaging rumors, and even faced legal action brought against them by borderlines without legitimate cause. We call these distortion campaigns.

Jerry (non-BP)

My soon-to-be-ex-wife got a protection order and had me evicted from my own home. She cut me off from our daughters and told all the neighbors that I am violent. They won't even look me in the eye. She systematically sought out the people in social and professional organizations I belong to and attempted to turn them *against me. She told my boss that I was impotent—and that I gave her herpes! Huh?? She told her lawyer that I raped her ten years ago because we had had sex when she didn't want to—and she hadn't even told me she wasn't in the mood! We'll be in court this week to see what the hell she's alleging next. I haven't seen the woman in months, nor have I called her. In the meantime, I am paying $3,500 a month for support. I am so desperate to rid myself of this torment. I can't sleep at night thinking of the injustice of it all. I am terrified of what she is going to allege next.*

Here are other examples of distortion campaigns:

- Valerie's borderline mother, Hannah, told family members that Valerie had stolen money from her and had been violent on several occasions. Family members refused to speak with Valerie, even to hear her side of the story. Hannah made the accusation after Valerie told her she couldn't visit her over Christmas.

- Judy was stalked by her former borderline friend, Elizabeth, who sent threatening letters to herself in Judy's name. Elizabeth would then call Judy's answering machine and beg her to "stop threatening her." The matter ended up in court, where Elizabeth broke down under questioning and insisted that Judy had "forced" her to write the threatening letters to herself.

- Majel's son, Rick, was engaged to a borderline woman named Jeri. Jeri began telling Rick that Majel had made some highly negative comments about him to her when no one else was around. Although these comments were pure fabrications on Jeri's part, Rick felt torn and didn't know whom to believe—his mother or his wife.

We must emphasize that we are not accusing all people with BPD of distorting the truth. Many borderlines would never do such a thing. We are not invalidating the experiences of people with BPD who have been victimized; we are merely validating the experiences of those non-BPs who have been falsely accused. In addition, we'd like to stress that all types of people, both those with and without mental disorders, may make false claims.

Motivations for Distortion Campaigns

Following are theories about what might motivate someone with BPD to engage in a distortion campaign.

Abandonment and Anger

We have explained that BPD does not cause fundamentally different behavior, but behavior that is very far to one side of the continuum. Or, as one BP put it, "Borderlines are just like everyone else—only more so."

We all experience feelings of loss and rejection when relationships end or are threatened. These emotions are especially intense when the other person decides to leave and we want the relationship to continue. Many distortion campaigns seem to revolve around either real or perceived abandonment, loss, and rejection—terrifying issues for people with BPD.

Divorce—the issue in Jerry's case—is an example. Hannah may have felt rejected when her daughter decided not to come home for Christmas. Elizabeth may have felt humiliated when her friend Judy terminated the friendship. But sometimes the perceived loss is not so apparent. Jeri, for example, may have felt that her own relationship with her husband Rick was threatened by his close relationship with his mother, though he had love enough for them both.

Johnston and Roseby (1997) explain how grief can manifest itself as anger:

> Loss—whether that of a loved one, the intact family, cherished hopes and dreams, or the threatened loss of one's own children—evokes powerful feelings of anxiety, sadness, and fear of being abandoned and alone. Some people have difficulty acknowledging these feelings. Instead, they seal over their grief with anger and try to prevent the inevitable separation by embroiling their spouse in unending disputes. Fighting and arguing are ways of maintaining contact (albeit of a negative kind). Even throughout the fighting these same individuals harbor reconciliation fantasies. People who have suffered a dramatic loss in the past (e.g., parental death or divorce) may be also reacting to these earlier, unresolved traumas.

Identity and Aggression

A woman whose husband divorces her loses her identity as wife; a woman whose children are grown may feel as if she's lost her identity as mother. In the face of these real or perceived losses, people with BPD may feel empty, insignificant, helpless, and unable to survive. Johnston and Roseby believe this may lead people to adopt a false front of being fiercely independent, refusing to negotiate lest they lose part of themselves. (They call this, "I fight, therefore I am.") People may also become overly dependent and clingy—or alternate between aggression and clinginess. BPs who see themselves as victims may thus feel that distortion campaigns help give them an identity.

Shame and Blame

Divorce and relationship problems can also spark feelings of rejection, which in turn evoke feelings of inadequacy, failure, shame, and humiliation. As you know, people with BPD often feel awash in shame and have low self-esteem. They may then try to cover up with a mask of absolute competency. Johnston and Roseby say that this exaggerated sense of failure may lead people to try to rid themselves of all blame by proving that the other person is totally inadequate or irresponsible. They write, "The fragile self-esteem of these people depends on keeping all sense of failure outside the self. So they present themselves with a self-righteous air of angry superiority and entitlement and accuse the ex-spouse of being psychologically and morally inferior."

When a psychologically vulnerable BP views the spouse's desertion as a total, devastating attack, they may develop paranoid ideas of betrayal, exploitation, and conspiracy. Johnston and Roseby write, "As the spouse surveys the rubble of their marriage, they begin to rewrite history and perceive their partner as having intentionally plotted and planned from the outset to exploit and cast them off."

At that point, they say, the "betrayed" spouse may respond aggressively with a counterattack that becomes the central obsession in their lives. "The spouse, along with any allies, is viewed as dangerous and aggressive. Having been wronged, these people feel justified in seeking retaliation. Or, more urgently, they believe in launching a preemptive strike. Their motto is 'attack before being attacked.'"

Assessing Your Risk

In analyzing dozens of distortion campaigns, we noticed several similarities:

First, BPs who set up distortion campaigns often claimed to have had a history of being victimized by others. Sometimes, they even described how they sought revenge against people who they said had victimized them in the past.

Second, the borderlines often possessed the ability to appear calm, logical, and persuasive under certain circumstances. However, when under emotional distress or alone with the non-BP, they appeared to lose contact with reality or become paranoid.

Third, non-BPs victimized by distortion campaigns often viewed themselves as protectors and caretakers. As a result, they had great difficulty looking out for their own best interests. Many overlooked warning signs, disregarded admonitions from friends, denied what was happening, and refused to take precautions or defend themselves.

It is hard for most people to accept that someone they love could do something to hurt them. If love for the BP in your life, or happy memories of the good times you shared, are preventing you from protecting yourself, it's essential that you understand that the BP may not feel the same way. Splitting may render the BP unable to remember the good feelings they had for you or to see you as a whole person with both good and bad qualities. As a result, they may view you as an evil monster who deserves to be punished. The sooner you realize this, the better chance you have of emerging from a distortion campaign with your dignity and rights intact.

Finally, most complaints of distortion campaigns came from men who had recently asked for a divorce from the BP or who had broken up with a borderline girlfriend. Parents of borderline children were the second most frequent source of complaints, followed by children of borderline parents.

Combating Distortion Campaigns

First, an important disclaimer: each person's situation is different, and each person with BPD is unique. The right approach for one person could be totally wrong for another—even if the situations seem similar. The following guidelines may help. But before you take action, we strongly urge you to consult with a qualified mental health professional who is familiar with your unique situation. If the allegations involve the law, it's vital that you discuss the situation with a qualified attorney as soon as possible.

Secondly, recognize that BPD is a mental disorder. People who have it deserve to be treated with sensitivity, respect, and dignity. Protect yourself, but don't try to hurt the other person out of spite or revenge. For example, it might be prudent to remove your clothing and personal belongings from the house before asking for a divorce. However, hiring a moving company and taking half of everything the two of you own is probably going too far. (In fact, it might understandably trigger a hostile response.)

Reduce Your Vulnerability

The best way to handle a distortion campaign is to prevent it from happening. If you can't do this, be proactive and protect yourself as much as you can—legally, financially, and emotionally.

Some distortion campaigns seem to occur for no discernible reason. But others seem to be triggered by actions the BP perceives as hostile. Start by considering any major actions you may be taking that involve the BP—anything from setting limits to seeking a divorce. What kind of reaction might you anticipate from the BP?

Next, consider yourself: what are your vulnerable areas, and what could you do ahead of time to guard against any actions the BP may take? Hope for the best; prepare for the worst. Non-BPs have found that typical areas of concern include their finances, children, property, job, reputation, and friendships. Formulate a plan and implement it before you take any action that could trigger the BP.

Consider the example of Lyndia and Elicia. Lyndia needed to tell her borderline daughter, Elicia, that Elicia can't come home from the residential facility for the upcoming weekend. (The last time Elicia came home for a visit, she threatened to burn down the house if Lyndia wouldn't let her spend the night with her drug-abusing boyfriend.)

Lyndia knows from experience that after Elicia hears the news, she will immediately go to her counselors, grandparents, and anyone else who will listen and possibly believe Elicia's story, and tell them that Lyndia hates her (and always has) and that her behavior is spotless and that Lyndia is a bad parent.

So before Lyndia told Elicia the news, she communicates the reasoning for her decision to anyone who might become involved. By the time Elicia speaks with them, they will already know what is going on.

Consider Not Responding

There may be times when responding in any way at all simply prolongs the BP's abusive actions. That is because this entire matter may be an effort on their part to keep you engaged in the relationship. Any response—particularly an emotional one—may reward their behavior.

Think through the short-term and long-term ramifications of the other person's actions. If the consequences are insignificant or simply embarrassing—or if you believe the BP is trying to goad you into more contact with them—it may be best to simply let the matter go.

Answer Questions Without Being Defensive

Alison was alternately suicidal and incensed when Luke broke up with her. She called Luke at work several times a day, screaming at him and begging him to take her back. When Luke had his work number changed, Alison retaliated by calling Luke's boss, David, and informing him that Luke often snorted cocaine while at work. "Luke's a crack head," she insisted. "Don't trust him."

Naturally, David confronted Luke with Alison's accusation. The truth was that several years earlier, David had tried cocaine at work when it was offered to him by one of the stagehands. But it happened just that once. Other than that, Luke was a responsible employee and did not drink or use drugs on the job.

Public relations firms that advise major corporations have a saying for clients in crises: "Tell the truth, tell it all, and tell it fast." Luke owned up to what he had done, but emphasized that it had happened just once. Luke also explained what was going on without intruding upon Alison's privacy any more than was necessary. Luckily, David understood and did not fire Luke for violating the company's drug policy.

A BP may also tell family, friends, and acquaintances things about you that have no basis in fact whatsoever. Before you decide whether or not to respond, ask yourself what you hope to achieve. Do you want to clear your name? Or is there something tangible at stake, such as the loss of friendship of people who are important to you?

When consequences of the BP's actions are relatively minor, it may be best to act in a way that reveals the lie for what it is. For example, if the BP in your life tells the neighbors that your new wife is a shrew, it may be best to simply let them meet her and make their own decisions. However, if the BP in your life tells the neighbors you've been arrested for battering her and their opinion matters a great deal to you, you may wish to try to set the record straight.

When talking with people about false accusations, keep the following guidelines in mind:

- Act calm, composed, and in control—no matter how upset you feel.

- Validate the other person's concerns before explaining the facts. Say that if the rumors had been true, it would be a very serious matter.

- Do not disparage the BP—no matter how much you think they deserve it. Instead, sincerely express your concern for the BP, or acknowledge your own confusion about why the BP would say such things. Be cautious about discussing BPD or any other psychological problem—people may misunderstand and think you are trying to belittle the BP.

- Realize that you cannot control what other people think about you. Say what you need to say and then let it go.

Benjamin (non-BP)

Here's what I said to a neighbor who wrongly believed I'd been violent toward my former wife:

"I'd like to clear the air about something. It may make you a bit uncomfortable, and I understand that because it makes me uncomfortable too. But it's important, so I'm willing to stick my neck out. I heard that my former wife, Kassidy, told you that I was arrested for battering her. Someone told me that she had some cuts on her arm and she was showing them to people and saying that I attacked her. Well, I wouldn't blame you if you felt horrified and didn't want to talk to me. If I thought that someone I knew had done such a thing, I would probably avoid them too. But I want to be very frank with you and let you know that it never happened. The divorce hasn't been easy, it's true. But I never did anything remotely like that. And I'm very concerned for Kassidy's sake—both that she would tell this to people and that somehow her arm is being cut. I'll understand if you feel confused and wonder about what really happened. But we've known each other for awhile, and I did want to set the record straight with you. I appreciate your listening."

Talk to an Attorney

Obstetricians, psychiatrists, and allergists are all physicians. Yet you wouldn't want any of them to operate on your heart. That's a job for a cardiac surgeon. In the same way, if there is any possibility that the BP you are divorcing or leaving might initiate a distortion campaign, it is imperative that you hire an attorney who specializes in cases such as yours. James Novak (1996) says, "Choosing a divorce attorney may be one of the most important decisions you make in your lifetime." Especially if you are a man who is the victim of a distortion campaign, it may make the difference between gaining custody of your children and going to prison. You can find guidelines for choosing an attorney in the resources listed in appendix D.

Jeffrey M. Leving (1997), a leading father's rights attorney, suggests that men divorcing a potentially hostile ex-spouse protect themselves with several actions. First, if the possibility exists that you might be falsely accused of battery or abuse of your wife or children, always have a third person present. You may even want to videotape your visits with your child. Also, be prepared to document all of your claims. In court, it's so common for couples to make accusations against each other that judges often disregard statements that are not backed up by credible witnesses or a paper trail. Preparation and documentation is crucial. After you hire an attorney, keep a diary of all interactions with the BP and anything else that might be relevant in court. Note witnesses, addresses, phone numbers, dates, times, and other information. This may be crucial to your credibility and your ability to remember key details. Discuss with your attorney the possibility of tape recording conversations between you and the BP.

If you have children, do not move out of your home until the court has determined temporary custody and visitation issues. If you leave prematurely, you may lose access to your children. In addition, the BP may claim that you "abandoned" the family. (Exception: If you are in physical danger, do not remain in the house.)

Several months before you initiate a divorce, seek counseling with a therapist to help keep things calm, defuse volatile situations, and potentially testify in court regarding false allegations. Make sure this therapist is not biased for or against women. If you are being harassed or physically abused, consider filing a restraining order or an order of protection. Do not suffer in silence.

It is not uncommon for BPs to make clear, specific arrangements and then deny those arrangements exist. For example, a
non-BP returned his children to their mother at an agreed-upon
time and location, and discovered that the children had been
reported abducted. Another non-BP arrived at his former home to
pick up his belongings at an agreed-upon time, and the BP then
called police and accused him of stalking her. For this reason,
Novak also recommends that you consider communicating with
the BP only through a third party, speaking to the BP only in the
presence of a third party who can back you up, or making sure
that all arrangements are in writing.

Dean Tong (1996) wrote a road map for men falsely accused
of child abuse, and he recommends the following actions for men
in this situation:

- Treat the accusation very seriously. It will affect every area
  of your life.

- Find the money to defend yourself properly. Protect yourself financially, as Tong says it will take "every cent you
  have" to fight the allegations.

- Hire a competent and qualified lawyer who specializes in
  cases like yours. Not all father's rights attorneys are
  equipped to handle false accusations. Obtain multiple
  opinions on your case by objective, competent individuals.

- Steadfastly maintain your innocence; go on the offensive
  and demand accountability. Consider retaining a civil
  rights attorney to sue for damages.

- Do everything possible to halt further psychological interviewing or treatment of any children unless you feel
  confident that the individuals involved will avoid teaching
  the child that they have been abused.

- Keep a daily journal of events that pinpoint where you
  were and what you were doing at all times. Document
  visits with your children (including conversations, comments, and actions, or reasons your visits were canceled).

Prepare for False Accusations of Abuse from BP Children

Children who falsely accuse parents of abuse is a growing
phenomenon. Reasons for doing this include revenge for

perceived abuse, retaliation for being treated "unfairly," and an attempt to split their parent's loyalty to one another.

As you may suspect, an angry child's phone call to 911 or to the local child protection agency can have devastating effects on the family. Typical investigations can often take more than a month to complete. In the meantime, the accused parent is often ordered by the court to stay away from the child and temporarily live outside the family home. The child is often required to remain with the other parent, who experiences the conflict of trying to be supportive and loyal to both the child and their spouse or partner. The family's friends, relatives, and employers may be caught in the same trap of feeling they must either demonstrate support for the child or loyalty toward the accused parent.

In our interview with attorney Charles Jamieson, he advised that parents whose child makes false accusations do the following:

- Keep detailed records documenting the child's diagnosis or BPD behaviors. Examples include letters from school authorities, medical records, court papers, and reports that unsubstantiate prior allegations. This will enhance your credibility.

- Keep a diary of your activities, including where you were, who you were with, and what you did. If allegations come weeks or months after the supposed event, this may provide you with an alibi.

- Ask your other children if they would be willing to help explain your innocence to the authorities.

- If necessary, make sure that a third party is present when you are with the child.

- Take all accusations seriously. They may quickly snowball out of control. If you need to, hire an attorney who specializes in false allegations.

From an emotional perspective, there are some things to keep in mind that can help you cope with the situation. Usually, false accusations center around abuse or neglect. Therefore, they are followed up with investigations by your county's social service department or child protection unit. While the investigation will seem to be accusatory, remember that the investigation is merely a fact-finding process. Only hard evidence can be used to render charges.

Remember that being defensive and uncooperative can hurt your case. Do not take questions personally; keep telling yourself that the process is necessary to ferret out real cases of abuse. In some cases, parents may be separated from their children while the investigation is going on. Siblings of the borderline child need to know that the separation is temporary and that they may be asked questions during the investigation. Stress your love for them and the need to answer the legal authorities' questions honestly.

Finally, remind yourself that BPD is a mental illness. Anger toward your borderline child is normal; however, remember that the illness is really to blame—not the child.

If the BP is trying to hurt you by mounting a distortion campaign, you might consider the BP to be your enemy. In reality, your enemies are:

- **Denial:** Doing nothing about the problem in hopes that it will go away.

- **Wishful thinking:** Doing nothing because you're sure that a miracle will occur and the BP will have a change of heart.

- **Emotionality:** Reacting emotionally rather than remaining calm and thinking through logical solutions to your problem.

- **Martyrdom:** Doing nothing because you can't bear to hurt the BP's feelings, which you may think are more important than your own.

- **Isolation:** Trying to handle the problem by yourself instead of asking for help.

- **Legal delays:** Not hiring the right attorney before you lose legal rights and the situation becomes critical.

Most non-BPs find that if they react quickly and logically and obtain the right legal help when needed, distortion campaigns sputter and fail. The truth has a way of revealing itself, and lies are eventually exposed for what they are. By acting appropriately, you can help that occur sooner rather than later.

12

What Now? Making Decisions about the Relationship

Sometimes I'm scared and I back away
I just can't go but I just can't stay.
Half my life it seems to me
I've been running around with
Bruised knees.
Cause I have to stumble in the dark sometimes
Reaching my hands out to see what I find
When I touch some light it feels so sweet
and kind.

—Carrie Newcomer, "Piece of The
Truth," from *October Nights*

People who care about someone with BPD are usually in a great deal of pain. Staying in the relationship as it is seems unbearable. But leaving seems unthinkable or impossible. If you feel this way, you are not alone. Nearly every non-BP we spoke with echoed the same sentiments. But you do have options, even if you can't see them right now. This chapter will help you think through your choices and come to a personal decision that feels right for you.

Predictable Stages

People who love someone with BPD seem to go through similar stages. The longer the relationship has lasted, the longer each stage seems to take. Although these are listed in the general order in which people go through them, most people move back and forth among different stages.

Confusion Stage

This generally occurs before a diagnosis of BPD is known. Non-BPs struggle to understand why borderlines sometimes behave in ways that seem to make no sense. They look for solutions that seem elusive, blame themselves, or resign themselves to living in chaos.

Even after learning about BPD, it can take non-BPs weeks or months to really comprehend on an intellectual level how the BP is personally affected by this complex disorder. It can take even longer to absorb the information on an emotional level.

Outer-Directed Stage

In this stage, non-borderlines turn their attention toward the person with the disorder, urging them to seek professional help, attempting to get them to change, and trying their best not to trigger problematic behavior. People at this stage usually learn all they can about BPD in an effort to understand and empathize with the person they care about.

It can take non-BPs a long time to acknowledge feelings of anger and grief—especially when the BP is a parent or child. Anger is an extremely common reaction, even though most non-BPs understand on an intellectual level that BPD is not the borderline's fault. Yet because anger seems to be an inappropriate response to a situation that may be beyond the borderline's control, non-BPs often suppress their anger and instead experience depression, hopelessness, and guilt.

The chief tasks for non-BPs in this stage include acknowledging and dealing with their own emotions, letting BPs take responsibility for their own actions, and giving up the fantasy that the BP will behave as the non-BP would like them to.

Inner-Directed Stage

Eventually, non-BPs look inward and conduct an honest appraisal of themselves. It takes two people to have a relationship, and the goal for non-BPs in this stage is to better understand their role in making the relationship what it now is. The objective here is not self-recrimination, but insight and self-discovery.

Decision-Making Stage

Armed with knowledge and insight, non-BPs struggle to make decisions about the relationship. This stage can often take months or years. Non-BPs in this stage need to clearly understand their own values, beliefs, expectations, and assumptions. For example, one man with a physically violent borderline wife came from a conservative family that strongly disapproved of divorce. His friends counseled him to separate from her, but he felt unable to do so because of his concern about how his family would react.

You may find that your beliefs and values have served you well throughout your life. Or you may find that you inherited them from your family without determining whether or not they truly reflect who you are. Either way, it is important to be guided by your own values—not someone else's.

Resolution Phase

In this final stage, non-BPs implement their decisions and live with them. Depending upon the type of relationship, some non-BPs may, over time, change their minds many times and try different alternatives.

Beyond Black and White

It is easy to adopt the BP's black-and-white way of thinking and believe you only have two choices—stay or go. But many other options also exist. For example:

- Leaving the situation temporarily whenever the BP violates your limits.
- Taking a temporary break (days, weeks, or months) from the relationship.
- Learning to depersonalize the BP's actions.
- Remaining in the relationship but living apart.

- Making the relationship less close.

- Spending less time with the BP.

- Achieving more of a balance in your life by cultivating your own interests, friends, and meaningful activities.

- Telling the BP that you will remain in the relationship only if they are willing to work hard with a therapist or make certain specific changes. This means holding them to any promise they make, and it may mean leaving if they violate such a promise.

- Putting off making a decision until you feel comfortable making one.

- Putting off making a decision until you see a therapist and work on some of your own issues.

Questions to Ask Yourself

These are questions you should ask yourself about your current relationship with your BP partner. Most of these questions address important needs that should be met in relationships. The answers to these questions can provide you with some direction on how to proceed in the relationship. Generally, the more needs and wants that go unfilled and the more "unbalanced" with respect to who in the relationship receives more of the attention and energy, the more likely it is that the relationship is unhealthy.

- What do I want from this relationship? What do I need from this relationship?

- How open can I be with my feelings with this person?

- Am I in physical danger by staying in this relationship?

- How will this decision affect any children?

- How does this relationship affect my self-esteem?

- Do I love myself as much as I love the borderline?

- Have I accepted the fact that the BP will change only if and when they are ready to do so? Am I able to wait until that happens or live with things the way they are if it never happens?

- What practical considerations do I need to consider, particularly financial ones?

- Do I believe that I have the right to be happy?
- Do I believe that I am only worthwhile when I am sacrificing myself for others?
- When am I currently the most content: when I am with this person, when I am alone, or when I am with others?
- Do I have the energy and fortitude to go against my family or other people who might be upset with my decision?
- Am I truly making my own decision, or am I doing what other people want me to do?
- What are the legal ramifications of my decision?
- If a friend was in my place and told me the story of this relationship, what advice would I give them?

When Children Are Involved

One non-BP says, "I am not one who believes that unhappy people should stay together for the sake of the children. I think they would be far better off living with one happy parent than one miserably unhappy parent and one who is completely delusional."

While many parents worry about the effect of divorce on children, Janet R. Johnston, Ph.D., executive director of the Judith Wallerstein Center for the Family in Transition, said in our interview that studies consistently find that children's exposure to unresolved conflict and verbal and physical abuse is a better predictor of children's adjustment than the marital status of their parents. According to Johnston, children do the best in a happy, intact marriage with both parents present; next best is a divorce in which the parents protect the children from conflict. Third best is an unhappy, intact marriage in which children are exposed to unresolved conflict and verbal abuse. Worst of all is a conflict-ridden divorce where the children are put in the middle.

Chosen Relationships

When it comes to chosen relationships, we found that the BP's willingness to admit they had a problem and seek help was by far the determining factor as to whether the couple stayed together or not.

Of the hundreds of people we spoke with, when the BPs were truly committed to recovery, non-BPs were almost always willing to stand by them and help them through it. But when BPs refused to take any responsibility for the couple's problems, no matter how hard non-BPs tried to rescue the relationship, the relationship usually ended.

Richard (non-BP)

I stayed with my wife for the same reasons I fell in love with her. She is bright, beautiful, witty, passionate, and fun to be around. When we got married, I didn't know she had Borderline Personality Disorder. In fact, I didn't know what BPD was until it was clinically diagnosed.

I knew early on that there were problems, sometimes they were frustrating, sometimes they made me angry. Sometimes they scared the hell out of me. No matter what, however, she was still the person I loved who just happened to have a mental illness. Even during the worst of it, I never considered leaving. I wasn't about to throw away a relationship so easily, especially one where so much of it was good. She was sick—very sick—but I could always see the good in her.

After her four years of therapy and hospitalizations, our marriage is very close. The reward for loyalty has been great, the same passion, the same beauty, the same wit that attracted me to her in the first place are all there. But the fear and confusion of BPD are gone. She wasn't the only one to grow through this experience. I did, too.

Rhoda (non-BP)

I have broken up with my BPD boyfriend many times. When he is able to see what he is doing, apologize for it, and tell me how he is going to change, I go back.

To me, he is worth it. He is a kind, beautiful, passionate, generous man. I have never met anyone in my life who has made me feel more loved. And he can't destroy me because he does not define me. I do. And I am very fortunate to have a "moderate" BP—he is not prone to rages or violent outbursts, doesn't cheat on me (he's terrified of AIDS), and makes a sincere effort to modify his behavior to make me happy.

This relationship suits me because I sometimes have a strong need for privacy and solitude. When I'm in the old "devalued" status, I take the time to be alone and enjoy other things without him.

Maybe he's coasting right now and something in his life could trigger a suicidal depression or a relapse into alcoholism—who knows? I am aware of the risks. But I love him and I plan to enjoy his presence in my life as long as I can.

Marie (non-BP)

My soon-to-be-ex-husband gave me a surprise visit this afternoon. The conversation started out all business and finances. No problem there. As he stood outside talking to me, our children went in and out right past him. He never spoke to them; barely looked at them. So very strange.

Then the conversation changed. He said I hadn't given him a chance (twenty years of chances are obviously not enough). I hadn't told him that I would leave if he didn't seek counseling (his indication that, as usual, I should have done more). I guess he forgot he threatened to kill me in no uncertain terms. Again, silly me—can't I just get over the death threat?

I could go on and on with the twisted logic, the convenient amnesia, and the transparent manipulation. But I will get to the point. Which is: there is no point. He just doesn't get it. It was my job to seek the proper ways to communicate with him. My job to set boundaries. My job to understand the illness. What was his part?

What kind of relationship can you have when one person must do all of the work? What kind of relationship is it when one person must have all of the understanding, have all of the forgiveness, and do all of the giving to the needy other?

Finally, he called me a few hours later and began sighing on the phone that he might as well quit his job. He told me he was eyeballing a handgun in the house where he now lives. My twelve-year-old kept motioning to me to hang up. It took every fiber of me to do so—the good old rescue syndrome was rearing its ugly head.

But I did hang up. I released him to his own pitiful misery. I did it. I did it. I didn't even know the power still existed within me. But it does. And it's perfectly okay for me to own my own feelings again.

As I'm writing this, I'm watching my eight-year-old fill a decorative birdcage full of oatmeal cookies. It's his science project. Why is this relevant? Because he's free and safe to be himself, without risk of raging or verbal abuse from someone he should have been able to trust. Because his mother is free and safe to just let him be an eight-year-old. Because all of us non-BPs have this option, and there should be no apologies forthcoming for an illness we did not cause.

Fill the birdcages with cookies, pour milk all over them, eat them with your fingers and make a big mess. Laugh until your sides ache, cry when something is wrong, spend some time doing absolutely nothing, say what you mean, and mean what you say. Invest in your own sanity for once.

Unchosen Relationships

With unchosen relationships, the choice is not stay or go as much as it is to set and observe your limits and not let the BP's problems overwhelm your own life. Unchosen relationships are ones you did not personally "choose" or select. But that doesn't mean you need to feel helpless and hopeless. While you may not be able to end the relationship or "break up," you can set limits on how much contact you have with that person and how much of your energy you are going to invest in maintaining the relationship. With unchosen relationships, you need to be the one in charge. Identify your emotional and physical boundaries. Reinforce the limits you set in the relationship with your BP by consistent modeling and consistent responding to the disturbing behavior of the BP.

Sylvia (non-BP)

I love my borderline son, John, very much. For many years, I lived or died depending upon how well he was doing. Was he drinking again? Getting involved with self-destructive women? Spending all of his money on things he didn't need? I continually gave him cash and provided him with a place to stay when yet another one of his roommates threw him out. I listened to him as he ranted and raved and blamed me and his father for everything that had ever gone wrong in his entire life.

Things changed after my husband had a heart attack. Paul is doing well now, but for a while, we weren't sure if he was going to pull through. This crisis helped me realize that I was concentrating on my son so much I was losing myself, my husband, and my relationship with my daughter.

I had to back away from my son's chaos. I set some personal limits around bailing him out and listening to his tirades. John wasn't happy about our new limits—he cut us off totally for three years. That was very painful. But eventually, John decided that having a relationship with us with limits was better than no relationship at all. We see him about once a month. There are phone calls, too. It's strained, but I can live with that.

I feel like a human being again, with goals, dreams, and happiness. Everyone benefited from the limits—even John, I think. He learned that he can manage to run his life without us.

I still wish that I could have a closer relationship with my son. I wish that he would take care of himself more and get help. But

I've learned to accept that I can't change John. I can only love him and be the best mother I know how to be while still loving myself and caring for the rest of my family.

Healing and Hope

Whatever you decide, there can be healing and hope: healing when a relationship ends and hope for your loved one's recovery from BPD.

Many people from the non-BP Internet support group resolved their relationship with the BPs in their lives years ago. But they stay on the list to provide support to others, and to assure them that life does, indeed, get better after a relationship with a borderline.

Marilyn (non-BP)

It has been ten years since my divorce from my borderline ex-husband, and I am still dealing with the aftereffects. I spent so much time trying to hide his behavior from others that it left its mark upon me. Trust in others, faith in the world . . . these were the things that were destroyed in me.

Yet now, in most ways life couldn't be better! I am a happy and confident person. The experience taught me many things about myself—things that I had avoided or would not admit to myself before that time. Now I use my energy to correct those things that I find negative or unhealthy. I live a more conscious life.

As far as not becoming bitter—I was angry for a long time, until I finally realized that my ex-husband had not deliberately set out to make my life miserable. It would have happened, to one degree or another, no matter whom he had married. Blaming him for who he is is futile and does not help the situation in any way.

A few months after the divorce I was having dinner with my parents. My father began to denigrate my ex-husband. I looked at my father and said, "Why would you say such things? Why would you hate someone like him? Don't you understand he has harmed himself more than he has me?" Bitterness and anger are emotions that tie one to the past. Besides, had I held on to negative emotions, I would never have been able to start my life again or ever be happy again.

The last thing my former husband ever said to me was, "I've never been happy, never in my life!" I'll never forget the tears that were streaming down his face. And I will never forget the pain and anguish in his voice. The isolation he felt and most probably still feels—his fear of being alone and isolated in the world—stills any feelings of anger against him on my part. I had been happy in the past. I knew I would be happy again someday. Yet for someone like him, who had never known happiness—what of him? I abandoned him, just as he felt everyone else had done in his life.

I felt a sense of terrible guilt for a long time. But if I was to survive, I had to let go of it. I could not help this man, and I could not destroy myself.

And finally, Diane, a woman who considers herself recovered from Borderline Personality Disorder, posted this note to the non-BP list to show that recovery is indeed possible.

Diane (BP)

There were plenty of times I felt far worse than when I started it all, and I wondered if I would have been better off never having known about my illness and never having entered therapy. My entire way of thinking had to be disassembled and rebuilt. And for someone inherently struggling with uncertainty about identity, there were dauntingly frightening times when I had disassembled the old ways of thinking but had not yet adopted new ones. During that time, I looked into a dark hole of nothingness and wondered if I had any identity at all.

Luckily, with the help of an excellent therapist and the support of my husband and children, I recovered from BPD. Yet, I know enough to realize that what happened to me doesn't always happen in the case of all borderlines. Some BPs are unwilling to take the journey. Other borderlines are outright incapable of it, for whatever reason. And thus I would never expect that everyone close to a borderline stay in the relationship. In some cases—perhaps many cases—it is necessary and wise to protect oneself and move on with life. Yet, at other times, if you hang around, you will be rewarded in the end with a relationship that is closer and better than you had dreamed possible.

One of the most profound lessons I learned in my journey was the incredible capacity that people have for goodness. That this world, despite its trials, pains, and injustices, is indeed a miraculous place. It is filled with as much love and kindness as it is with hatred. I have emerged from all of this with a view of life that will never, ever be the same as it was. And that has made all of the pain and struggle eminently worth it.

This book has taken you on a journey through a land that, until recently, you may not have known even existed. You've learned what BPD is, why people with BPD act the way they do, the part that you play in the dynamic, and how to take back control of your life.

But the trip is not over yet. As complex as BPD behavior can be, obtaining knowledge is the easy part. Now comes the wisdom: taking what you've learned and applying it to your own life.

This may involve questioning long-standing beliefs and values. It may mean facing issues that you've been avoiding for years. It may mean revisiting the unspoken "bargain" you've struck with the BP in your life: that their needs and views are always, always more important and more "right" than yours. No one can hold up this kind of bargain very long without seriously compromising their own mental health.

We can't promise that it will be easy. But we can promise that it will be worthwhile. In the process, you will find out what you really value and who you really are. You will discover strengths you didn't know you had. Few things in life are more important than this. As William Shakespeare said four hundred years ago, (*Hamlet*, Act I, Scene iii, Lines 78–80).

This above all, to thine own self be true,
And it must follow as the night the day
Thou canst not then be false to any man.

We hope that the knowledge and tools you've gained from this book serve you well on the rest of your journey.

APPENDICES

A

Causes and Treatment of BPD

According to John M. Oldham (1997), BPD, like many mental disorders, is caused by a combination of genetic influences and environmental circumstances. Yet many clinicians, and many of their patients, believe that BPD almost always stems from a childhood of physical or sexual abuse. So pervasive is this myth that one BPD treatment program diagnoses patients with BPD only if they come from abusive backgrounds.

Trying to diagnose BPD by the presence of childhood trauma flies in the face of current research. John D. Preston (1997) notes that 20–25 percent of borderline patients come from intact families without evidence of severe early stress or trauma. And, according to prominent BPD psychiatrist Kenneth R. Silk (1997), preliminary research suggests that BPD behavior may be influenced by neurotransmitter disturbances.

Neurotransmitters

Neurotransmitters carry the signals between all the nerve cells in the brain. According to Madeleine Nash (1997), they are "the most mind-bending chemicals nature has ever concocted." They underlie every thought and emotion, as well as memory and learning. About fifty different neurotransmitters have been discovered thus far.

The neurotransmitter dopamine involves thinking. Impulsivity and aggression are associated with serotonin, mood stability with acetylcholine, and sensitivity to the environment with norepine-phrine. People with BPD may have difficulties in all of these areas.

However, physicians cannot at this point simply prescribe medications to "correct" each of these neurotransmitters. Silk writes, "Neurotransmitters work in subtle ways and the level of one may directly or indirectly effect the level of another, and thus what is true in the lab does not translate directly into what is true, wise, or useful in a person."

Medication

Medications are often successfully used to help people with BPD by reducing depression, dampening their emotional ups and downs, and putting the brakes on excessive impulsivity. According to Larry J. Siever (1997) antidepressants can help with depression, while mood stabilizers such as Depakote, Tegretol, or Lithium can help with mood swings. Selective Serotonin Re-uptake Inhibitors (SSRIs) such as Prozac, Zoloft, and Paxil may help control impulsivity, as may Effexor, a related antidepressant. Tegretol may be helpful for controlling excessive anger and irritability. These medications must be carefully titrated; that is, the right dose must be found for each person so that it helps relieve distressing symptoms without causing troubling side effects.

When choosing a psychiatrist, we strongly suggest asking if the person has experience in treating people with BPD. Make sure that the person keeps abreast of the latest advances in research in this area. For example, ask if they've read articles showing that SSRIs may help with impulsivity.

Therapy

It is important to realize that medication alone is not enough. Therapy is also needed to help the person with BPD. Nevertheless, finding a mental health professional who is experienced in effectively treating BPD clients can be very challenging. Common problems reported to us by BPs and non-BPs include:

- Clinicians who are not educated about BPD and fail to appropriately diagnose it.

- Clinicians who diagnose BPD but are not experienced in treating it, and who do not know how to effectively work with borderline clients. They may give clients incorrect information such as, "there is no way to treat BPD" or "people with BPD never get better."

- Clinicians who bring negative expectations and attitudes about BPs into treatment, and thus unconsciously pass along this stigmatizing attitude to their clients.

- Clinicians whose beliefs about BPD are so rigid that when clients present information that conflicts with their theories, they tell the client that they must be mistaken. For example, some clinicians believe that all people who cut themselves or who have BPD were sexually abused. This is untrue.

If you are a parent seeking treatment for your borderline child and the therapist continually treats you with suspicion instead of respect, we suggest switching therapists.

It is also common for people with BPD to enter treatment, but then consciously or unconsciously sabotage the process. For example, the BP may:

- Enter treatment to please a family member (or because of an ultimatum or court order) but not really work at it. This can be a significant waste of time and money.

- Discontinue therapy when faced with issues that make them uncomfortable, accusing the therapist of incompetence. These BPs may see clinician after clinician until they find one who will validate their belief that all their problems are someone else's fault.

- Continually test the clinician and push against their limits until the clinician discontinues treatment. This is usually devastating for the client. Effective BPD clinicians anticipate this possibility and set firm but caring limits when therapy begins. This is one reason why it's crucial that therapists be experienced in treating borderline patients.

- Put up a false front to the clinician, who then refuses to believe that this model patient would ever go into uncontrollable rages. In our experience, this happens most frequently in couples therapy.

The book *How to Live with a Mentally Ill Person* by Christine Adamec (1996) is a good resource for choosing a qualified clinician. Her topics include getting referrals, understanding different types of therapies, conducting an interview, dealing with insurance matters, switching professionals, and overseeing the case of a child.

It's also crucial that you ask the clinician questions designed to evaluate the person's competence at treating patients with BPD or patients who are greatly affected by someone with BPD. These questions include:

1. **Do you treat people with BPD? If so, how many have you treated?** Watch the therapist's body language and tone of voice to determine their attitude about BPD clients. We suggest you avoid therapists who do not have a lot of experience with borderline problems.

2. **How do you define BPD?** If the therapist knows less than you do, keep looking. If the therapist believes that BPD is part of another disorder that you (or the BP in your life) do not have, move on. (For example, they may believe that BPD is really a form of Post-Traumatic Stress Disorder, yet you have no history of trauma.)

3. **What do you believe causes BPD?** If you are the non-abusive parent of a BP and the therapist believes that all BPD is caused by parental abuse, we urge you to find a more compatible therapist. Also, if the clinician does not mention possible biological causes, they are probably not up to date on the latest research.

4. **What is your treatment plan for clients with BPD?** Look for someone who can give you a clear general overview of the treatment they provide, but who also says that treatment is modified for each individual. Therapists who do not have a treatment plan tend to be diverted by

BPs' crises and never seem to get around to addressing long-standing issues.

5. **Do you provide specific treatment for self-injury? Substance abuse? Eating disorders? Loved ones of those with BPD?** Substitute or add your own concerns here.

6. **Do you believe that borderlines can get better? If so, have you personally treated BPs who improved?** According to Santoro and Cohen (1997), "What you want to hear is reasonable optimism. No one can give you a guarantee (if they do, skip them). If they hedge their bets too much, it is probably better to move onto someone else." Make sure that you and the therapist share the same goals.

7. **What are your views on medications?** If the therapist is not a psychiatrist, ask who would prescribe them, if any are needed.

Researcher Marsha Linehan's cognitive-behavioral method of treatment, called Dialectical Behavior Therapy (DBT), has been shown in empirical research to help BPD patients experience less anger, less self-mutilation, and fewer inpatient psychiatric stays than patients who received other forms of treatment.

Many BPs we met were very enthusiastic about this treatment and recommended it wholeheartedly. Melissa Ford Thornton (1998) says, "DBT gave me a set of tools to take with me and use forever when I am feeling hopeless." To locate a clinician who specializes in DBT, try contacting Linehan's office:

Marsha Linehan, Ph.D.
Dept. of Psychology
University of Washington
Seattle, WA 98195
206-543-9886

Outcomes

A fair amount of research has been conducted to answer the question, "Do people with BPD get better?" Here is a short summary:

- The McGlashan Chestnut Lodge study (1986) showed that 53 percent of patients with BPD were considered "recovered" and that patients seemed to do better once they reached their forties.

- A New York State Psychiatric Institute study (Stone 1990) showed that two-thirds of patients in their thirties and forties were rated as either "good" or "recovered" on the global assessment scale. (This scale is a standard tool used by clinicians to measure functioning.)

- In two studies (Stone 1990; McGlashan 1986), factors associated with positive outcomes were likableness, candor, perseverance, talent, superior intelligence, the lessening or elimination of obsessive traits, attractiveness (whether as a child or adult), and lessened or eliminated depression. Poor outcomes were associated with substance abuse (especially continued alcohol abuse.)

In our three years of interviewing BPs who greatly improved, we noticed several common threads. First and foremost, they accepted responsibility for their behavior and for their recovery. They also:

- Were willing to work through their inner pain instead of deflecting it onto other people or dealing with it through other means (e.g., drugs, self-mutilation, etc.). Frequently, they lapsed back into old patterns, but they got back on track.

- Had faith in themselves and believed that other people (or a supreme being) had faith in their inner worthiness—the "real them" behind the borderline symptoms. However, it was difficult for non-BPs to be supportive when the BP continued blaming all their problems on others.

- Had access to continued therapy with a competent clinician who did not take their actions personally, believed that recovery was possible, genuinely cared about them, were willing to stick with them in the long term, and who observed appropriate limits.

- Received the appropriate medication.

For more information about the causes and treatment of BPD, see the BPD books in appendix D. Keep in mind that the newest information will appear in medical and psychological journals long before it hits the popular press. If you are working with a clinician, you might wish to ask them to do a medical literature search and print out the most recent studies that interest you. The clinician may also be able to help you interpret these studies.

B

Tips for Non-BPs Who Have BPD

In the first chapter of this book, we explained that the term "non-BP" was shorthand for "relative, partner, friend, or other individual who is affected by the behavior of someone with BPD." It does not mean "person who doesn't have BPD." People with BPD are also considered non-BPs if they are coping with someone in their life who also has BPD. Mother-daughter pairings seem to be the most common, followed by two borderline individuals who are romantically involved.

If Your Parent Has BPD

If you have BPD and are coping with the behavior of a borderline parent, you may feel deeply hurt and frustrated by their behavior. Much of your life may have been spent in a seemingly fruitless effort to win their love and approval. Even if you're an adult, you may feel unable to set personal limits with your BPD parent or respond assertively to their criticism.

If you and your parent both have BPD, you may wish to help yourself in two ways: protecting yourself in current interactions with your parent and healing the wounds from your childhood. Chapters 5–8 will give you the skills you need to stand up for yourself. Practicing these skills with a trusted friend will be helpful. You may also do some additional reading about boundaries and verbal abuse.

When it comes to healing, we suggest that you work with a clinician who is experienced in treating people with BPD who had a BPD parent. Many people have found the book *Toxic Parents: Overcoming Their Hurtful Legacy and Reclaiming Your Life* by Susan Forward and Craig Buck helpful in helping them recover from the scars of emotional, verbal, and even physical and sexual abuse.

If Your Partner Has BPD

If you have BPD and you are in a romantic relationship with someone else who has BPD, openness and good communication are essential. Additionally, the relationship is most likely to be happy and fulfilling if both of you are willing to make changes to accommodate the other person.

Joseph Santoro, Ph.D., author of *The Angry Heart: Overcoming Borderline and Addictive Disorders*, contributed some of these relationship suggestions for people with BPD:

- Develop a nonverbal coding system to let your partner know how you feel at any given moment. This way, you can each be more sensitive to your partner's needs. One borderline woman says, "I wear a red scarf to let my boyfriend know when I'm in the throes of jealousy and rage. When I'm happy, the blue scarf comes out. Of course, there is green and orange in the middle, as well. On my red days, my boyfriend takes an extra work shift, goes fishing, or works in the garden. On my blue days, I allow him much more room for screwing up and I try to be there for him. It's important that our life not revolve completely around the disorder."

- Within reason, provide yourself with tangible reminders of your partner's love for you. This can help reassure you when they are absent or when you're feeling distant. Examples include an unwashed shirt, a letter, a stuffed animal they gave you, or photos of the two of you. Keep a journal of the good, close times and refer to it when you or your partner feel tempted to view each other or the relationship as all bad.

- Give other people room to make mistakes. At times, your partner will seem insensitive, hurtful, and unloving. Remember, they have BPD, too. Don't let resentments build. Explain to them in a calm manner why what they said or did bothered you. Then listen to what they say. They may have meant something entirely different than what you heard. If you can give your partner the space, time, and forgiveness they need, they may be more likely to do the same for you.

- When appropriate, apologize without being defensive. Sometimes, when you reflect on things you said and did when you were upset, you may realize that you reacted more intensely than was warranted by the situation. Many people with BPD have found that by apologizing and validating the other person's feelings, they help the relationship immeasurably. You might say something like, "I'm sorry for yelling at you and hurting your feelings," or "When I said that, I was upset because I though you didn't care about me. I realize now that this is not true. I'm sorry for hurting your feelings by accusing you of not loving me." Do not add a phrase to justify your actions, such as, "But I couldn't help it because you made me so upset." This takes away from the apology and invalidates the other person's feelings.

- The next time you feel that someone is making you angry or upset, ask yourself, "What is this person not doing for me that I want them to do?" Once you know this, ask yourself how you can explain your needs to them in a way that they will be comfortable with. (For example, write them a letter.)

- Avoid testing. Don't push your partner emotionally to see how much they can take. This is not the way to see if someone loves you. Instead, ask for what you want in a non-threatening but assertive way.

- Don't assume that the way you feel about yourself is the way your partner feels about you. Don't try to read your partner's mind.

Whether the BP in your life is your partner, parent, friend, or other relative, make sure that the relationship is meeting your needs and is positive for both of you. If being around the other person consistently triggers shame, suicidal thoughts, depression, or other emotional problems, it's possible that the relationship is unhealthy for you and is just contributing to your disorder. We suggest working with a therapist to help you evaluate your options.

C

Coping Suggestions for Clinicians

One borderline client calls their therapist at home, leaves hostile messages, and makes vague threats against the therapist's husband and son. Another reports feeling desperately suicidal at each session and taunts the therapist with, "I know my rights, you can't hospitalize me. I have an attorney." A third criticizes the therapist's abilities to do their job, threatens to expose the therapist's "incompetence," and insists that they meet more frequently for sessions. A fourth demands a hug from the therapist; when offered a handshake instead, the client collapses and swears they will not leave until the therapist finds them "human enough to be hugged."

Most clinicians who treat borderline patients have undergone an experience similar to those just described. Cory F. Newman, Ph.D., clinical director for the Center for Cognitive Therapy at the University of Pennsylvania, defines an emotionally abusive client as one who "demonstrates a pattern of hostile, undercontrolled, or otherwise emotionally provocative verbal behavior and boundary infringements that are directed at the therapist and are not diminished by the therapist's appropriate reactions."

Therapists who treat emotionally abusive borderline patients often experience the same emotional reactions and problems we described in chapter 4. Like other non-BPs, they may begin to doubt themselves and may have difficulty observing their personal limits. The client-therapist relationship may rupture and treatment may become ineffective or impossible. In desperation, the therapist may even discontinue treatment, which can be devastating to the client.

Newman (1997) recommends that therapists use the following self-help strategies to maintain their professionalism, their well-being, and the well-being of the client:

- Do not break long-standing clinic policies to mollify a client. While this may seem easier in the short run, it can be damaging in the long run. Instead, explain the policy to the client and document the interaction in your notes.

- Seek consultation from other clinicians. Even Marsha M. Linehan, Ph.D., author of several BPD-related books, articles, and research studies, discusses her own patients with a consultant or therapist at least twice a month. (In fact, supervision and consultation with other therapists is an integral part of Linehan's Dialectical Behavior Therapy.) Other therapists can help point out a client's progress, offer solutions to problems, validate feelings, and offer ideas from their own experiences.

- Rehearse troublesome interactions before the session. Anticipate hostile or confrontational statements and practice responses that convey confidence, decisiveness, nondefen- siveness, and empathy.

- Wait before responding to angry phone calls. Newman says, "I have been tempted to pick up the phone and fire back a terse reply. To feel this way is understandable. However, to act on this impulse is to risk feeding into a vicious cycle of hostility, control, and countercontrol."

- Take thorough notes, but compose them in a nonjudgmental way, as if the client, the client's future therapist, and the client's attorney will read them. Fully explain how you had to perform your duties under duress, quoting the client verbatim when appropriate. Newman says, "Document any client statement that indicates blatant defiance of the therapist's treatment methods. This helps therapists remain steadfast and confident in their positions without undue fear that they will be held accountable for the client's lack of progress or self-harm."

D

Reading List and Resources

Materials from Eggshells Press

Eggshells Press, based in Milwaukee, Wisconsin, specializes in publishing materials about borderline personality disorder that are easy to understand, empathetic, and offer practical suggestions to use right away. They are available only by calling 1-888-35-SHELL (357-4355).

The ABCs of BPD (2007) by R. Kreger and E. Gunn
An easy-as-pie, brief introduction to BPD suitable for anyone looking to understand the basics of BPD. The booklet describes the disorder, its causes and treatment, and steps you can take to improve the family environment.

Hope for Parents: Helping Your Borderline Son or Daughter Without Sacrificing Your Family or Yourself (2000) by K. Winkler and R. Kreger
An invaluable guide for parents with a child who has

BPD. It offers understanding, guidance, and hope for people who go through daily struggles with their children. Topics include using validation, raising a borderline child, protecting siblings, letting go of guilt, and handling the relationship after your child turns eighteen.

Love and Loathing: Protecting Your Mental Health and Legal Rights When Your Partner Has Borderline Personality Disorder (2000) by K. Williams-Justesen and R. Kreger

This publication shows partners how to deal with the unique challenges they face for themselves and their children, such as becoming isolated, coping with abusive behaviors, making decisions, protecting children, facing false accusations, dealing with relationship addiction, and seeking legal advice.

Splitting: Protecting Yourself While Divorcing a Borderline or Narcissist (2003) by W. A. Eddy

The author specializes in representing clients divorcing someone with a high-conflict personality. This booklet offers the best advice and emotional support anywhere for those facing an emotionally wrenching, legally convoluted divorce. Eddy is also the author of High Conflict Personalities: Understanding and Resolving Their Costly Disputes (see mainstream book section).

The Splitting Companion CD (2007) by W. A. Eddy

A lively discussion on two CDs with the author of Splitting, William A. Eddy (see previous book). He answers questions frequently asked by readers of his booklet and explains how a technique called the "assertive, balanced approach" can make divorcing a person with BPD a less harrowing experience for all and save thousands of dollars.

You're My World: A Non-BP's Guide to Custody (2001) by K. Lewis and P. Shirley

A set of three CDs featuring a therapist and a nationally known child advocate and custody expert who help listeners understand the legal system and explain how they can provide a stable, safe, loving home for their children after divorce.

Border-Lines Newsletter

Contains the latest news about borderline topics, articles, and new resources. Subscribe to this free newsletter by sending a blank e-mail to Border-Lines-subscribe@Yahoogroups.com.

Internet Family Support Groups

The Welcome to Oz Online Community for Family Members with a Borderline Loved One

The WTO Online Community for Family Members with a Border-line Loved One is a lifeline to individuals whose lives are affected by someone with BPD. It's a place where family members come for support, information, and understanding with others in their situation all over the world. Since Randi Kreger founded it in 1995, sixty thousand people have revolved through the community.

The WTO community is divided into "neighborhoods" reflecting the type of relationship with the family member and the person's situation.

To join, see the instructions at www.bpdcentral.com/.

Or, send a blank e-mail in this format:

[name of list]-subscribe@yahoogroups.com (for example, WelcomeToOz2-subscribe@yahoogroups.com.)

Notice the hyphen right before the word "subscribe."

- WelcomeToOz2 (combined group)

- WelcomeToOz (combined group)

- WTOAdultChildren1

- WTOStaying (for partners)

- WTOTransition (partners; for those contemplating their choices)

- WTODivorcing (partners)

- WTOCoParenting (coparenting with a borderline ex)

- WTOParentsOfBPs

- WTOGrandparents

- WTOSiblings

- WTOChristian

- WTOGLBT

- WTOMenOnly

- WTOWomenOnly

- WTOProfessionals (restricted to clinicians only; approval needed to join)

Books About BPD from the Mainstream Press

Stop Walking on Eggshells: Taking Your Life Back When Someone You Care About Has Borderline Personality Disorder (1998) by R. Kreger and P. Mason, New Harbinger Publications, Oakland, CA

A self-help guide for family members and friends of individuals with borderline personality disorder. It helps them understand this self-destructive disorder and learn what they can do to help their borderline family member and themselves. It is considered the "bible" for family members and has sold more than a quarter million copies.

Stop Walking on Eggshells Workbook: Practical Strategies for Living with Someone Who Has Borderline Personality Disorder (2002) by R. Kreger and P. Shirley, New Harbinger Publications, Oakland, CA

This book helps family members gain insight on their own role in the relationship. It also shows them how to navigate life with a person with BPD. It contains step-by-step suggestions for setting personal limits, communicating clearly, coping with put-downs and rage, developing a safety plan, and making realistic decisions. The book contains worksheets, checklists, and exercises that build on one another and enable readers to apply the suggestions to their lives.

Back from the Edge DVD (2007) published by the BPD Resource Center, White Plains, NY

This 48-minute-long video features compelling interviews with people recovering from the disorder and their family members. It also features interviews with renowned experts in the field, such as Dr. Otto Kernberg, Dr. Marsha Linehan, Dr. Perry Hoffman, Dr. John Gunderson, and Dr. Wayne Fenton. For ordering information, go to www.bpdresource center.org/.

Borderline Personality Disorder Demystified: An Essential Guide for Understanding and Living with BPD (2004) by R. O. Friedel, MD, Marlowe & Company, New York

Dr. Friedel, a distinguished clinical professor of psychiatry at Virginia Commonwealth University, offers information and hope, thanks to our emerging understanding of the biology of the brain disorder. The publication discusses effective ways to treat BPD using both therapy and medication. Friedel does an excellent job of explaining recent studies in a consumer-friendly way.

Get Me Out of Here: My Recovery from Borderline Personality Disorder (2004) by R. Reiland, Hazelden Publishing, Minneapolis

An accountant and mother of three, Reiland (not her real name) tells the poignant story of her life, which included all-too-familiar episodes of anorexia, promiscuity, impulsiveness, suicide attempts, institutionalization in a mental hospital, and behavior that was often unrelenting, anger intensive, violent, and unpredictable. With astonishing honesty, Reiland reveals what having BPD feels like from the inside and how healing is possible through intensive therapy and the support of loved ones. Very hard to put down.

High Conflict Personalities: Understanding and Resolving Their Costly Disputes (2003) by W. A. Eddy, published by the author, San Diego

This publication is a guide for courtroom professionals and laypeople about better managing legal disputes when one of the participants has a personality disorder. Eddy uses a four-step method and draws on his experience as a therapist and his thirty-year career in dispute resolution.

Sometimes I Act Crazy: Living with Borderline Personality Disorder (2004) by J. Kreisman and H. Straus, John Wiley & Sons,

Hoboken, NJ

This book delivers the latest information on borderline personality disorder. Rich with dramatic case studies of Kreisman's patients, the book describes and offers advice on today's most promising treatments, along with practical coping strategies for the loved ones of BPD sufferers. The book contains more recent medical information than I Hate You, Don't Leave Me, also by Kreisman.

I Hate You, Don't Leave Me: Understanding the Borderline Personality (1991) by J. Kreisman and H. Straus, Avon, New York

This was the first book published for laypeople about borderline personality disorder. It offers professional advice, helping victims and their families to understand and cope with BPD. The book has a unique and very interesting sociological section. The medical information in the authors' other book, above, is much more up-to-date.

Lost in the Mirror: An Inside Look at Borderline Personality Disorder (2001) by R. Moskovitz, Taylor Publications, Dallas

This book is for individuals diagnosed with BPD. Lost in the Mirror explores the origins of borderline personality disorder and offers sufferers a framework for beginning to heal. It elaborates on the kinds of psychotherapy that are practiced today. It describes mainstream approaches, such as psychoanalytic psychotherapy, cognitive therapy, and behavior therapy, as well as innovative treatments such as eye movement desensitization and reprocessing (EMDR) and dialectical behavior therapy.

Skills Training Manual for Treating Borderline Personality Disorder (1993) by M. M. Linehan, Ph.D., Guilford Press, New York

This workbook is intended for clinicians leading their patients in dialectical behavior therapy. However, laypeople can benefit from reading the book because it includes a large section of handouts and worksheets used in the skills training portion of the therapy. These training sheets, designed to teach concrete skills, revolve around mindfulness, interpersonal effectiveness, emotional regulation, and distress tolerance.

Surviving a Borderline Parent: How to Heal Your Childhood Wounds and Build Trust, Boundaries, and Self-Esteem (2003) by K. Roth and F. Friedman, New Harbinger Publications, Oakland, CA

This book, the first written specifically for children of borderline parents, offers step-by-step guidance in understanding and overcoming the lasting effects of being raised by a person suffering from this disorder. Learn what psychological criteria are necessary for a BPD diagnosis, and identify the specific characteristics your parent presents. Discover specific coping strategies for dealing with issues common to children of borderline parents: low self-esteem, lack of trust, guilt, and hypersensitivity. Make the major decision whether to confront your parent about his or her condition.

Understanding and Treating Borderline Personality Disorder: A Guide for Professionals and Families (2005) edited by J. G. Gunderson, MD, and P. D. Hoffman, Ph.D., American Psychiatric Association Publishing, Arlington, VA

This publication is a series of nine articles about various aspects of BPD. They are written in the language of professional research papers. However, the editors include a good dictionary for laypeople at the end of chapters. The book includes three articles for family members, "Family Perspectives," "From Family Trauma to Family Support System," and "Family Involvement in Treatment."

Other Helpful Books

The books most popular with Welcome to Oz community members are starred.

* *And I Don't Want to Live this Life* (1996) by D. Spungen, Ballantine Books, New York

* *Better Boundaries: Owning and Treasuring Your Own Life* (1997) by J. Black and G. Enns, New Harbinger Publications, Oakland, CA

Boundaries: Where You End and I Begin (1998) by A. Katherine, MJF Books, New York

Changing for Good (1994) by J. Prochaska, J. Norcross, and C. DiClemente, HarperCollins, New York

Children of the Self-Absorbed: A Grownup's Guide to Getting Over Narcissistic Parents (2001) by N. Brown, New Harbinger Publications, Oakland, CA

Choosing to Live: How to Defeat Suicide Through Cognitive Therapy (1996) by T. Ellis and C. Newman, New Harbinger Publications, Oakland, CA

Codependent No More: How to Stop Controlling Others and Start Caring for Yourself (1996) by M. Beattie, Harper and Row, New York

Controlling People: How to Recognize, Understand, and Deal with People Who Try to Control You (2002) by P. Evans, Adams Media Corporation, Avon, MA

Courtney Love, Queen of Noise (1996) by M. Rossi, Pocket Books, New York

Cutting: Understanding and Overcoming Self-Mutilation (1998) by S. Levenkron, W.W. Norton and Company, New York

* *The Dance of Anger, A Woman's Guide to Changing the Patterns of Relationships* (1997) by H. Lerner, Harper and Row, New York (also invaluable for men)

Diana in Search of Herself: Portrait of a Troubled Princess (2000) by B. Smith, Signet reissue, Essex

Divorcing a Parent (1990) by B. Engel, Fawcett Columbine, New York

Don't Let Your Kids Kill You: A Guide for Parents of Drug and Alcohol Addicted Children (2005) by C. Rubin, New Century Publishers, Petaluma, CA

Don't Shoot the Dog (1999) by K. Pryor, Bantam Books, New York

* *Emotional Blackmail* (1998) by S. Forward, Harper Paperbacks, New York

The Emotionally Abused Woman (1990) by B. Engel, Fawcett Columbine, New York

The Emotionally Abusive Relationship (2002) by B. Engel, John Wiley & Sons, Hoboken, NJ

Enough About You, Let's Talk About Me: How to Recognize and Manage the Narcissists in Your Life (2005) by L. Carter, Jossey-Bass, San Francisco

* *The Explosive Child* (2002) by R. W. Greene, HarperCollins, New York

Feel the Fear and Do It Anyway (1987) by M. Rossi, Pocket Books, New York

Get Fit in Bed (2006) by G. Tartell and T. Kavanau, New Harbinger Publications, Oakland, CA

How I Stayed Alive When My Brain Was Trying to Kill Me (2005) by S. Rose Blauner, HarperCollins Publishers, New York

How to Change Anybody (2005) by D. J. Lieberman, St. Martin's Press, New York

* *How to Escape the No-Win Trap* (2004) by B. Cowan Berg, McGraw-Hill, New York

How to Stop Worrying and Start Living (1944) by D. Carnegie, Pocket Books, New York

I Don't Have to Make Everything All Better (1995) by G. Lundberg and J. Lundberg, Penguin Putnam, New York

If You Had Controlling Parents (1998) by D. Neuharth, Cliff Street Books, Lewiston, NY

Is He Depressed or What? (2005) by D. B. Wexler, New Harbinger Publications, Oakland, CA

The Journey from Abandonment to Healing (2000) by S. Anderson, Berkley Publishing Group, New York

Loving Him Without Losing You (2000) by B. Engel, John Wiley & Sons, New York (appropriate for men, too)

Loving the Self-Absorbed (2003) by N. Brown, New Harbinger Publications, Oakland, CA

Neural Path Therapy: How to Change Your Brain's Response to Anger, Fear, Pain, and Desire (2005) by M. McKay and D. Harper, New Harbinger Publications, Oakland, CA

Perilous Rivalry: When Siblings Become Abusive (1991) by V. Wiehe and T. Herring, Lexington Books, Lanham, MD

Reinventing Your Life (1994) by J. Young and J. Klosko, Penguin Group, New York

Serenity to Go: Calming Techniques for Your Hectic Life (2001) by M. Hamilton, New Harbinger Publications, Oakland, CA

Stop Controlling Me! What to Do When Someone You Love Has Too Much Power over You (2001) by R. Stenack, New Harbinger Publications, Oakland, CA

Teach Yourself Body Language (2003) by G. Wainwright, Hodder Education, London

Through the Eyes of Children: Healing Stories for Children of Divorce (1997) by J. Johnston, The Free Press, New York

* *Toxic Parents: Overcoming Their Hurtful Legacy and Reclaiming Your Life* (2002) by S. Forward and C. Buck, Bantam, New York

When Anger Hurts Your Kids: A Parent's Guide (1996) by P. Fanning, K. Paleg, D. Landis, and M. McKay, New Harbinger Publications, Oakland, CA

When Anger Hurts Your Relationship (2001) by K. Paleg and M. McKay, New Harbinger Publications, Oakland, CA

When Your Child Is Cutting (2006) by M. McVey-Noble, New Harbinger Publications, Oakland, CA

Other Internet Resources

www.borderlinepersonality.ca
Borderline Personality Disorder (BPD) From The Inside Out features the writing of A. J. Mahari, a woman who has recovered from BPD. It contains more than a hundred articles that provide much insight about BPD thinking, feelings, and actions.

www.bpd.about.com/
This site offers a great deal of accurate information about BPD from therapist Erin Johnston, LCSW, who takes a particular interest in the topic.

www.bpdcentral.com/

Randi Kreger, coauthor of *Stop Walking on Eggshells* and Stop *Walking on Eggshells Workbook*, maintains this site. BPDCentral is one of the oldest, largest, and most popular sites about BPD on the web. In addition to offering an abundance of information about BPD for family members, it is the home of the Welcome to Oz Online Community for Family Members with a Borderline Loved One.

www.bpdrecovery.com/

BPD Recovery is for individuals with the disorder. It is a safe arena for those with BPD to share concerns, voice opinions, and seek like-minded people. It contains much information, a discussion board, and more.

www.bpdresourcecenter.org/

The BPD Resource Center is a nonprofit organization that provides reliable information on BPD and its treatment. It is associated with the New York Presbyterian Hospital, Westchester Division, in White Plains, New York. The toll-free phone number is 1-888-694-2273.

www.bpdresources.com/

Also called Helen's World of BPD Resources, this site is a compilation of hundreds of books, links, articles, studies, websites, and other materials for anyone interested in BPD. Its strength is the size and diversity of its collection; however, some of the links may not be up-to-date.

www.ContinuingEdCourses.net

An online course for mental health professionals titled "It's All Your Fault! Working With High Conflict Personalities." The presenter is William A. Eddy, a nationally known attorney, therapist, and mediator. It is approved for six continuing education credit hours.

www.mhsanctuary.com/borderline/

BPDSanctuary aims to "help stop the pain for those who suffer so incredibly due to mental health disorders." It has a large collection of BPD-related information, including an "Ask the Therapist" section, a chat room, bulletin boards, and book reviews.

www.nami.org

In 2006, the National Alliance for the Mentally Ill expanded its mission to include BPD. Once you get to the site, enter "borderline personality disorder" in the internal search engine.

www.toddlertime.com/

Information on borderline personality disorder, narcissistic personality disorder, and other conditions. The section on BPD has information for borderlines and family members, personal reflections, and articles for helping professionals.

video.google.com/videosearch

The site contains an excellent video titled "Recognizing BPD in Children." Once you get to the site, enter "borderline personality disorder" in the internal search engine.

Organizations

National Education Alliance for Borderline Personality Disorder
www.neabpd.org/

This organization, composed of some of the top clinicians in the United States, raises public awareness, provides education, promotes research on borderline personality disorder, and enhances the quality of life of individuals affected by BPD. It supports family education programs, hosts conferences, conducts family research, and publishes educational materials.

Personality Disorders Awareness Network
www.pdan.org/

PDAN is a nonprofit organization devoted to assisting family members of those with BPD, especially minor children affected by a parent's disorder. The address is 490 Sun Valley Drive, Suite 205, Roswell, GA 30076.

References

Adamec, C. 1996. *How to Live with a Mentally Ill Person*. New York: John Wiley & Sons, Inc.

Al-Anon Family Group Headquarters. 1981. *Detachment*. Virginia Beach, Va.

Beattie, M. 1987. *Codependent No More*. Center City, Minn: Hazelden.

Bradshaw, J. 1988. *Healing the Shame That Binds You*. Deerfield Beach, Fla.: Health Communications.

Brodsky, B., and J. Mann. 1997. "The Biology of the Disorder." *California Alliance for the Mentally Ill Journal* 8:1.

Cauwels, J. 1992. *Imbroglio: Rising to the Challenges of Borderline Personality Disorder*. New York: W. W. Norton.

DSM-IV. 1994. *Diagnostic and Statistical Manual of Mental Disorders*. Washington, D.C.: American Psychiatric Asociation.

Ellis, T. E., and C. F. Newman. 1996. *Choosing to Live: How to Defeat Suicide Through Cognitive Therapy*. Oakland, Calif.: New Harbinger Publications.

Engel, B. 1990. *The Emotionally Abused Woman: Overcoming Destructive Patterns and Reclaiming Yourself*. New York: Fawcett Columbine.

Evans, P. 1992 and 1996. *The Verbally Abusive Relationship: How To Recognize It and How To Respond*. Holbrook, Mass.: Adams Media Corporation.

Forward, S., and D. Frazier. 1997. *Emotional Blackmail: When the People in Your Life Use Fear, Obligation, and Guilt to Manipulate You*. New York: HarperCollins.

Gibran, K. 1976. *The Prophet*. New York: Alfred A. Knopf.

Golomb E. 1992. *Trapped in the Mirror: Adult Children of Narcissists in the Struggle for Self*. New York: William Morrow.

Gunderson, J. G. 1984. *Borderline Personality Disorder*. Washington D.C.: American Psychiatric Press, Inc.

Heldmann, M. L. 1990. *When Words Hurt: How to Keep Criticism from Undermining Your Self-Esteem*. New York: Ballentine.

Johnston, J. A., and V. Roseby. 1997. *In the Name of the Child: A Developmental Approach to Understanding and Helping Children of Conflicted and Violent Divorce*. New York: The Free Press.

Katherine, A. 1993. *Boundaries: Where You End and I Begin*. Park Ridge, Ill: Fireside/Parkside.

Kreisman, J. 1989. *I Hate You—Don't Leave Me*. New York: Avon Books.

Kübler-Ross, E. 1975. *Death: The Final Stage of Growth*. Englewood Cliffs, N.J.: Prentice Hall.

Lerner, H. G. 1985. *The Dance of Anger*. New York: Harper Perennial.

Leving, J. M., and K. A. Dachman. 1997. *Fathers' Rights*. New York: BasicBooks.

Linehan, M. 1993. *Cognitive-Behavioral Treatment of Borderline Personality Disorder*. New York: Guilford Press.

Linehan, M. 1993. *Skills Training Manual for Treating Borderline Personality Disorder*. New York: The Guilford Press.

Links, P. S., R. J. Heslegrave, J. E. Milton, R. van Reekum, and J. Patrick. 1995. "Borderline Personality Disorder and Substance Abuse: Consequences of Comorbidity." *Canadian Journal of Psychiatry*, 40:9–14.

Links, P. S., M. Steiner, and D. R. Offord. 1988. "Characteristics of Borderline Personality Disorder: A Canadian Study." *Canadian Journal of Psychiatry*, 33:336–340.

McGlashan, T. H. 1986. "Long-term Outcome of Borderline Personalities." The Chestnut Lodge Follow-up Study. III. *Archives of General Psychiatry*. 43:20–30.

McKay, M., P. Fanning, K. Paleg, and D. Landis. 1996. *When Anger Hurts Your Kids: A Parent's Guide*. Oakland, Calif.: New Harbinger Publications.

Moskovitz, R. A. 1996. *Lost in the Mirror: An Inside Look at Borderline Personality Disorder*. Dallas, Tex.: Taylor Publishing Company.

Nace, E.P., J. J. Saxon, and N. Shore. 1983. "A Comparison of Borderline and Nonborderline Alcoholic Patients." *Archives of General Psychiatry*, 40:54–56.

Nash, M. 1997. "The Chemistry of Addiction." *Time*. 149,18:69–76.

Newman, C. F. 1997. "Maintaining Professionalism in the Face of Emotional Abuse from Clients." *Cognitive and Behavioral Practice*. 4, 1–29.

Novak, J. 1996. *Wisconsin Father's Guide to Divorce and Custody*. Madison, Wisc.: Prairie Oak Press.

Oldham, J. M. 1997. "Borderline Personality Disorder: The Treatment Dilemma." *The Journal of the California Alliance for the Mentally Ill*. 8, 1:13–17.

Oldham, J. M., A. E. Skodol, H. D. Kellman, S. E. Hyler, N. Doidge, L. Rosnick, and P. Gallaher. 1995. "Comorbidity of Axis I and Axis II Disorders." *American Journal of Psychiatry*, 152:571–578.

Preston, J. 1997. *Shorter Term Treatments for Borderline Personality Disorder*. Oakland, Calif.: New Harbinger Publications.

Reaves, J., and J. B. Austin. 1990. *How to Find Help for a Troubled Kid: A Parent's Guide for Programs and Services for Adolescents*. New York: Henry Holt.

Santoro, J., and R. Cohen. 1997. *The Angry Heart: A Self-Help Guide for Borderline and Addictive Personality Disorder*. Oakland, Calif.: New Harbinger Publications.

Siever, J., and W. Frucht. 1997. *The New View of Self: How Genes and Neurotransmitters Shape Your Mind, Your Personality, and Your Mental Health*. New York: Macmillan.

Silk, K. R. 1997. "Notes on the Biology of Borderline Personality Disorder." *California Alliance for the Mentally Ill Journal.* 8:15–17.

Stone, M. H. 1990. *The Fate of Borderline Patients.* New York: The Guilford Press.

Thornton, M. F. 1998. *Eclipses: Behind the Borderline Personality Disorder.* Madison, Ala.: Monte Sano Publishing.

Tong, D. 1996. *Ashes to Ashes . . . Families to Dust: False Accusation of Child Abuse: A Roadmap for Survivors.* Tampa, Fla.: FamRights Press.

Waldinger, R. J. 1993. "The Role of Psychodynamic Concepts in the Diagnosis of Borderline Personality Disorder." *Harvard Review of Psychiatry* 1:158–167.